BIG ALMA
SAN FRANCISCO'S ALMA SPRECKELS

Portrait of Alma de Bretteville Spreckels painted by Sir John Lavery, London, 1932. (Courtesy California Palace of the Legion of Honor)

BIG ALMA

SAN FRANCISCO'S ALMA SPRECKELS

Bernice Scharlach

Scottwall Associates
San Francisco
1999

Cover: Portrait of Alma de Bretteville Spreckels by Sir John Lavery, 1932. Courtesy California Palace of the Legion of Honor

Book design: James Heig, Scottwall Associates
Typography: Melinda Breitmeyer

Scottwall Associates, Publishers
95 Scott Street
San Francisco, CA 94117

Printed in the U.S.A.

ISBN 0-942087-11-9

*This book is dedicated to
Julia, Leah, Benjamin, and Samantha*

Acknowledgments

SINCE I DIDN'T HAVE the privilege of knowing Alma de Bretteville Spreckels, I have had to rely on those who did. Therefore I am deeply indebted to her family, her friends, countless newspaper reporters who, over more than six decades, found her a never-ending source of news, and to others whose lives she touched.

I am particularly grateful to Alma's daughter Dorothy Munn for her candor, her willingness to share family secrets no matter how painful, and for her unflagging support and encouragement. To Alma's grandson John Rosekrans and his wife Dodie I offer my thanks for their foresight in having taped the reminiscences of Alma's contemporaries soon after Alma's death, and for allowing me the use of that material. It had long been their hope that some day a writer would undertake a book on John's grandmother, a fact made known to me by a mutual acquaintance, Norman Coliver. Florence Rosekrans, Elmer Awl, Jean Frickelton, Lloyd Howard and Walter Piezzi were all gone when I began this project, and their observations added greatly not only to my understanding of Alma, but — I hope — to the reader's as well.

The rest of Alma's family were equally generous with their time and with the letters from her they shared with me. My thanks to her grandsons Charles and Adolph Rosekrans, her granddaughter Lois Register, her nephews Kjeld Storm and Charles de Bretteville, her nieces Ulla de Bretteville Awl and Edith de Bretteville Walsh, and her cousin Alice de Bretteville.

To Thomas Carr Howe, who was the director of Alma's Palace of the Legion of Honor over three decades, and to Anona Dukelow, who was her nurse and her companion for more than ten years, I owe a great debt of gratitude for giving so unstintingly of their time and for patiently recalling incident after incident in their long relationship with Alma so that I would come to know her almost as well as they did.

My thanks also must go to those others whose lives she touched: Karl Kortum, David Nelson, Dr. Albert Shumate, Jay McEvoy, Millie Robbins, George Livermore, David Pleydell-Bouverie and Ellen Magnin Newman. I am also grateful to three people who contributed to this story but are no longer around to receive my thanks: Dr. William Lister Rogers, Edward Kallgren and Ina Claire Wallace.

To Margaret Haile Harris, whose book on the life of Loie Fuller will soon be published, I am extremely grateful for her insistence that I go to the New York Public Library's Lincoln Center Library of the Dance to read the correspondence there between Loie and Alma. But for Ms. Harris, I would never have known of its existence.

I offer thanks to Linda Brady Mountain, director of the Maryhill Museum, for her help and for her insistence that a book on Alma and her contribution to that museum was long overdue. I am grateful to Cecelia Bartholomew, a gifted writer and teacher, for her wise suggestions.

I am indebted also to two others who offered creative encouragement throughout this project: my son Gary Scharlach and my friends Ernie Weiner and Alma Moser.

I am extremely grateful to James Heig, my editor and publisher, for his faith in this project and for bringing his great skill and sensitivity to all phases of the editing and production.

Many people gave us invaluable help in locating and copying pictures for the book: Colleen Schafroth and the staff of Maryhill Museum; Philip Molten of the Tiburon Landmarks Society; Charles Long and Marty Leland of the Fine Arts Museums of San Francisco; Pat Akre and Gladys Hansen of the History Room of the San Francisco Public Library; Lawrence Dinnean of the Bancroft Library; and Sally Kibbee and Jody Carpenter of the *San Francisco Chronicle.*

Saving the best for last, I owe as always the biggest debt of gratitude to my husband, Arthur Scharlach, who made my research so enjoyable by traveling the Pacific Coast with me from Goldendale, Washington, to San Diego, California, across the continent from San Francisco to New York, and over Europe from Paris to Copenhagen, so that all our jaunts since I undertook this project have been in the footsteps of Alma Spreckels.

— *Bernice Scharlach*
Danville, California
July 1990

TABLE OF CONTENTS

LIST OF ILLUSTRATIONS

Alma de Bretteville at age 15, in a miniature by Myra Edgerly,
Alma's art teacher. The original of this beautiful portrait is lost;
only a photograph of it survives to show why Alma was famous
as a model for artists and photographers even as a teenager.
(Courtesy Dorothy Spreckels Munn)

CHAPTER ONE

Alma's Budding Beauty

 ALMA SPRECKELS WAS CLOSE to eighty years old, recently recovered from a brink-of-death illness, when she sailed into Copenhagen aboard the *Gripsholm* in 1959. Nevertheless she was able to dazzle the press and get the kind of publicity she adored.

"The most impressive great-grandmother we have ever met," wrote one awestruck Danish reporter. "Smoking cigarettes, scintillating with platinum jewelry and with quite a garden represented in the flowers of her hat, Great-grandmother Spreckels took most of the attention at the arrival of the Swedish-American flagship *Gripsholm* late this evening at the Free Harbour. Followed by her lady-in-waiting and a chambermaid, she arrived here to see fashionable acquaintances in the Danish nobility and science. She is the richest lady of the Western America."[1]

Not exactly true, but Alma liked to paint broad pictures and let the press come to its own conclusions.

Alma allowed it to be known that "her millions are connected with the Spreckels Sugar Manufacturing Company in California and numerous other dominating companies of the American world of industry, where she in her widowhood keeps up a considerable influence. The creator of the millions, Mr. Adolph B. Spreckels, is now long gone, but the memory of his enterprise lives in the dazzling Mrs. Alma le Normand de Bretteville Spreckels."

With a diamond-sparkling gesture, she declared, "The French originates from my great-great-great-grandfather, who fled to Denmark during the French Revolution. But I am more Danish than French." That's not, of course, what she told the French press.

From Alma the reporter learned about her love of art, "the fact that she donated to San Francisco a whole museum, that among her

1

sparkling jewelry sits the rosette proving her position as a Knight of the Legion of Honor. "Add to this," rhapsodized the newsman, "the surprising information that every day during her voyage from New York to Copenhagen she took two swims in the elegant swimming pool of the *Gripsholm*."

Perhaps because he didn't want to tarnish the image of the dazzling great-grandmother, the reporter discreetly omitted the fact, which also came from Alma's mouth, that she took those two daily swims with her heavy, six-foot frame free of the constraints of a bathing suit.[2]

Alma loved to shock people. It was part of her nature, just as it was her nature to undertake gigantic projects. "I have a great destiny to fulfill," she said many times.

Right now she was interested in only one thing: food. When the reporter suggested that the Palace Hotel, where she would be staying, would probably cancel some of its Danish cuisine in favor of American in deference to its distinguished guest, Alma gushed, "Oh, no! I love *øllebrød* and *rødgrød* — God bless you for these dishes!"

Then, in a cloud of cigarette smoke, she marched her entourage to the hotel, eager to attack the bowls of herring and the other delicacies that awaited her at the hotel's smorgasbord. Now that her health had returned, and with it her amazing energy, so had her tremendous appetite. She forgot — for the moment — all the work she intended to do on this trip.

All her life Alma labored unceasingly to leave her mark. Leave it she did, in the museums she founded, in the gigantic fund drives she spearheaded in the wake of two world wars, and in her countless contributions of art to so many communities. Yet all her achievements are overshadowed by her reputation as an outrageous eccentric. She infuriated and delighted people on two continents. She incurred both the thanks and the wrath of kings, queens, presidents, and governors. She was exalted by multitudes of strangers whom she had helped, yet she was bitterly resented by her own children, whom she often ignored.

"She wanted to do good, but she overdid everything," said her second husband, Elmer Awl.

Poor Alma! In her battle to prove her worth and in her hurry to get things done, she made up her own rules. She had to. What education did she have? "I've been a working girl since I was fourteen," she loved to remind people. It took a lot of guts and determination to become "the most impressive great-grandmother." She wasn't born rich.

◆   ◆   ◆   ◆   ◆

Alma de Bretteville was born on a blustery March day in 1881, on a farm on the outskirts of San Francisco. Outside, the howling winds rearranged the sand mounds on the soil her father made a futile attempt to cultivate. She was a big baby, and her lusty cry rang out stronger than the sound of the wind and the roar of the ocean nearby. From the very beginning, Alma made her presence known.

She was christened Alma Emma Charlotte Corday le Normand de Bretteville, the fifth child of Viggo and Mathilde de Bretteville. In spite of the elegant names, the family was dirt poor. Her sister, Anna, preceded her by ten years; in between were three brothers, Oscar, Walter and Alexander. A fourth brother, Gus, would soon follow her. Although both her parents were natives of Denmark, she had the blood of a noble French family in her veins. Her father, obsessed with family pride, would remind her of that often enough.[3]

The "Emma" in her name was for the French noblewoman, wife of the marquis, General Louis Claude de Bretteville, who had fled to Denmark with his family during the French Revolution. They left in the middle of the night, and Emma, in nothing but her nightgown, died of exposure before she reached safety.

"Charlotte Corday" honored the memory of the impetuous girl who stabbed Marat in his bathtub in a vain attempt to stop the killing of aristocrats. Alma actually was not related to Charlotte Corday, according to Kjeld Storm, Alma's grandnephew, who researched the family history. Corday was related to another de Bretteville, a not uncommon name in Normandy. But who cared about accuracy? More important to Alma was an opportunity to shock people. She loved to use the Corday relationship later by dropping it into a conversation and bellowing, "You got anyone you want murdered, Pet?"

Alma's formal education came to an abrupt end as she entered her teens. Her father thought it was time for her to go to work. He himself felt a great distaste for earning money. An educated man who could speak several languages, he came to California in 1866, at the age of twenty-two, expecting to make a fortune. He bitterly resented the fact that saloonkeepers and laborers who struck it rich in the gold fields formed the aristocracy here, while he, eminently qualified to lead a life of leisure, had to live like a lowly peasant. He made no effort to earn a living; he preferred to complain about his poor luck. His most strenuous activity was taking daily strolls down the street, using his cane as a weapon to clear the path of bicyclists, children and toys. Until his children were old enough to help out, he left the wage-earning role to his wife.[4]

Mathilde de Bretteville, a worn-out woman with a beautiful face,

Viggo and Mathilde de Bretteville (Courtesy Kjeld Storm)

was the sole support of the family. When she realized they couldn't survive on the farm, she persuaded Viggo to move to the inner city. There she found a small flat on Francisco Street. She turned the front room into a bakery. The children were tantalized by the delicious odor of Danish pastries loaded with almond paste and nuts and raisins wafting through the tiny house. All they could do was smell it, because Mathilde could not afford such luxuries for her own table. With fierce energy, she managed the shop, ran her household and even gave massages in a rear room that doubled as the boys' bedroom.[5]

She also took in laundry. When business in the store was slow, Mathilde would gather the bundles of dirty linens in a wheelbarrow, pack a lunch for the children, and haul them all to Washerwoman's Lagoon. The lagoon was out in Cow Hollow, down the hill a few miles from where they lived. After scrubbing and rinsing the clothes with rocks near the shore, Mathilde would hang them out on the chaparral to dry while the children picnicked. Then she'd take the laundry home to iron.

When Alma was old enough to deliver the clean clothes through the back doors of the elegant houses on Nob Hill, Van Ness Avenue and Pacific Heights, she had a glimpse of the life her father had taught her was hers by right of birth. She made up her mind there would be no back doors for her. Someday she was going to walk through the front door of the grandest house in San Francisco. Meanwhile, she wasn't going to sit idly like her sister, Anna, who shared her father's suffocating pride and his distaste for work, waiting for a miracle to happen. She would go out and make it happen. One day she would be rich and she would make the de Bretteville name stand for something again. Papa said she had a destiny to fulfill.

San Francisco in the 1880s was a city just beginning to reach out for a more genteel way of life. Thirty years before, it had been a rough, brawling outpost on the way to the gold mines. Although it was no longer a frontier town, visitors to the city had no trouble distinguishing it from the more refined and polished capitals of the East Coast. True, the old clapboard boardinghouses of those early days were gone. Now the city could point with pride to the Palace Hotel, renowned throughout the country for the opulence of its white marble court, its seven stories of magnificently furnished rooms and its glittering ballrooms. But in every one of those rooms there was at least one glaring reminder of the frontier days — the brass spittoons. And they were all used. Men in their formal attire — frock coats and top hats — they all spat.[6]

Children of the men who had made their fortunes with a pick and shovel were being raised in mansions on Nob Hill, like the castle built by former saloonkeeper James Flood. The Flood house boasted a two-block-long bronze fence costing $30,000, with a full-time employee to keep it polished.

The future heirs of Claus Spreckels, who made his gold in sugar, were raised in one of the grand houses along a wide, tree-lined boulevard called Van Ness Avenue in the newly-built Western Addition. The boulevard was named in honor of the mayor who successfully replaced the Vigilante Committee with more conventional law enforcement. Spreckels's four-story, sixty-room mansion contained doorknobs and bathroom fixtures of solid silver.

The artwork in most of the city's mansions came from Gump's, the city's finest art goods store, which had only recently switched from supplying heavily gilded frames for barrooms to importing art for genteel families. The first requirement was that paintings be massive, covering lots of wall space. And they had to have strong, masculine themes. *The Return of General Ambrioco to Genoa After the First Crusade,* which covered an entire hallway in the Spreckels house, was typical of the paintings that Gump's sold to Claus and the other new millionaires.[7]

While San Franciscans were learning how to spend money for better living, they were still a long way from attaining refinement. They lived in a city where grand pianos were in great demand while horses sometimes lay unburied where they dropped on the cobblestone streets. Despite its rawness, there was in the beautiful, lusty city a huge appetite for culture. No one could predict that Alma de Bretteville, a girl with the same characteristics, who would fill that culture gap a few decades later.

Alma had no clear idea of how she would become rich and famous and fulfill her destiny. All she had was her mother's boundless energy, along with a fierce determination to succeed. After all, she came from nobility. And she had her looks.

At fourteen, Alma was already taller than her father, and inching up to the full six-foot height she would ultimately attain. She was developing a generous bosom, well-rounded hips and a slender waist. Her face, with its finely chiseled features, creamy complexion and clear blue eyes, suggested a patrician beauty, handsome rather than merely pretty. She was fully aware of her beauty. She was eager to make it work for her.

Although Alma was a good student and loved school, she was not unhappy when her father told her it was time to quit and get a job. Despite a lack of skills, she had no difficulty getting employment. It is not hard to understand why. She was bright and she was industrious. One look at the tall, strikingly attractive young girl with her splendid figure, and men were more than happy to train her. Her first job was as a stenographer.

She continued to educate herself by reading. Her favorite books were biographies. She was fascinated and inspired by the lives of people who accomplished great things. But she learned much more from her favorite magazines, *The Argonaut* and *The Wave,* with their weekly news about what was going on in San Francisco society. She read about the luncheons given by Mrs. Eleanor Martin and her twin sister, Mrs. Peter Donahue, better known as "the Heavenly Twins." Often included in those affairs was the Princess Poniatowski, née Sperry, of the flour family. Alma fully understood why the Sperrys, like other newly rich families, thought it important to take their daughter to Europe to buy her a husband with a title.

She also was familiar with the names of the Misses Grace and Lillie Spreckels, girls about her own age, whose father, John D. Spreckels, honored them with a dinner dance at their new residence on Pacific Avenue, right around the corner from Grandpa Claus Spreckels's mansion.

She dreamed of dancing at the Greenway invitational cotillions. Percy Greenway was San Francisco's equivalent of New York's social arbiter, Ward McAllister. Greenway had sterling credentials. Not only did he come from a distinguished Baltimore family, but he was also the Pacific Coast distributor for Mumm's champagne, an essential in the bubbly life of the city.

The only dances Alma attended in those days were the students' annual costume balls at the Mark Hopkins Art Institute, the mansion at California and Taylor streets designed for the railroad magnate who died before it was completed. Alma was a night student, studying miniature painting. In order to save the nickel carfare, she walked all the way up Nob Hill after work each day.

To pay for her art lessons, Alma found work as an artist's model. Her statuesque proportions caught the eye of Edgar Walter, a painter of note, who was a member of one of the city's prominent German Jewish families. His cousin, Alice Gerstle Levison, recalled the day Alma posed at the family's summer home in San Rafael, where Walter painted the lovely young girl leaning against a tree. "She was a rather poor girl who had very little money," said Mrs. Levison, whose husband was president of the Fireman's Fund Insurance Company. "My sister and I gave her some things at the time."[8]

Some artists concentrated only on Alma's face. Myra Edgerly, Alma's miniature-painting instructor, used the girl's patrician fea-

*Alma looks very demure and proper in this portrait, made when she
was about seventeen. (Courtesy Dorothy Spreckels Munn)*

tures to do cameo portraits. Arnold Genthe posed her before his camera while he experimented with chiffon draped over his lenses to create the glamorous portraits for which he would later become so famous.[9]

Then Alma found that she could earn much more by posing in the nude. She needed the money. Most of her salary went to her mother for room and board, so there was little left for other things, like clothes. She wasn't going to be dependent forever on other people's castoffs.

The idea of standing naked before a roomful of staring men must have been intimidating, even to a girl as outwardly brazen as Alma. She never felt awkward about being six feet tall. With her head full of Papa's stories about royalty, she carried herself like a queen. But when it came time to mount the platform and drop her clothes, we can visualize her clutching her robe tightly. The self-consciousness couldn't have lasted long. From later examples of her uninhibited behavior, we can imagine that when she realized the painters were staring not at her but at their palettes, Alma's nervousness quickly turned to annoyance. We can see her coughing loudly to get their attention, and then, with the agility of a toreador swinging his cape to taunt the bulls, removing her robe and standing defiantly before them.

What the artists saw was a buxom, Rubenesque figure with full, rosy-tipped breasts suspended over a narrow waist. Well-curved hips supported legs that were long and tapered, and slender arms extended down to hands that were graceful and delicate. They saw the deep blue of her eyes looking coolly, almost mockingly, at them. They saw her classic features and the flawless complexion that matched the creamy texture of the skin on her body. They began to sketch furiously.

There was a ready market for sketches of nudes along San Francisco's famed Cocktail Route. The Route stretched down Montgomery and Kearny to Market Street, and then up Powell. For the price of a drink, bon vivants could feast not only on sumptuous lunches, but also on the decor, which whetted their other primal appetites. Ceilings were invariably strewn with plaster nymphs and satyrs in bas-relief. On the walls were oil paintings of plump nudes. In the heyday of the hourglass figure, personified in the 1890s by actress Lillian Russell, Alma was a model whose time had come. Sketches of what was purported to be the de Bretteville girl were springing up all over the Cocktail Route.

Posing in the nude must have stirred Alma's own feelings of sexuality. She wanted more than just to be stared at. She wanted to be touched. She was eager to find a release from all the wild, undefinable desires she was feeling.

Alma's first sexual encounter that we know of was with Ashton Potter, whom she met while doing walk-on parts at the Grand Opera House. Ashton later became a famous theater critic, but in those days he did whatever work he could get as long as it was connected to the theater.

Unable to afford the luxury of a hotel, the young man bedded Alma down on a secluded knoll in the Presidio. Years later, in Chicago, when Potter was reviewing a play in which comedienne Ina Claire was starring, he gave the actress, who was on her way to San Francisco, a message to deliver for him: "Tell Alma that I'll never forget our romps going from hill to hill."[10]

Neither would Alma. There is nothing to indicate that she didn't thoroughly enjoy the experience...the groping, the pleasurable sensations that she wanted to go on indefinitely, then the urgency, the rush of joy and, finally, the sweet letdown. But why couldn't it have happened in a proper bed?

It could have been this encounter that prompted Alma's desire— one she often repeated — that someday she was going to have a bedroom with the biggest, fanciest goddamn bed in all the world.

For the next couple of years, until about 1902, she continued to work by day and pose by night, but she wasn't getting any closer to the fine house and the elegant lifestyle her father taught her was her due. What she needed was a rich husband. She began her search for an older man. With characteristic bluntness, she let it be known that "I'd rather be an old man's darling than a young man's slave."[11] She thought she'd found him when she met Charlie Anderson, when she was nineteen.

Charlie was a miner, not much over five feet tall, who had struck it rich in the Alaskan gold mines. He married a dance hall performer who soon divorced him, taking with her a considerable chunk of Charlie's gold. Undaunted, Charlie returned to the Klondike, swung his pickax once again and came back with a fresh fortune. Then he met Alma. He wooed the beauteous young lady persistently for five weeks.

During that five-week courtship, Alma knew exactly where and how to take Charlie. They dined in the city's finest French restaurants such as the Maison Riche, on Dupont near Market; they ate caviar sur canard, and washed it down with the best French wines. She took him to the elegant Diamond Palace, in the Russ House, the most expensive jewelry store in town. There, in the shop's mirrored splendor, she allowed Colonel Andrews, the courtly owner, to select not one but two diamond rings for her. She smiled demurely while the colonel presented the bill to her startled suitor.

When Alma dropped her garter on their first buggy ride in Golden Gate Park, she made such a fuss about its "real ruby clasp" that Charlie said, "Never mind, I'll buy you another pair if you'll just keep quiet." She took him to Shreve's to pick out a replacement.

She showed him how important the finer things in life were to her when she got him to open his poke and give her twenty-dollar gold pieces for her art lessons and her piano lessons. She was able to take the first step in restoring the luster of the de Bretteville name when she induced him to buy her family a box at the Grand Opera House and to pay for their buggy rides and railroad tickets for outings. While Charlie was not exactly the man of her dreams, Alma was willing to accept him as a husband. Charlie had other ideas. That's when he found himself back in court. Alma sued him for $50,000 for breach of promise.[12]

For two weeks in February 1902, San Franciscans followed each detail of the sensational trial. The news accounts were enlivened with sketches, such as the one of the little miner climbing up a ladder to kiss the girl towering above him.[13]

Alma testified that Anderson was a whirlwind wooer. The whole affair lasted little more than a month, and in that time he gave her the diamond rings, pearls, furs and the pair of jeweled garters. The only gift she refused to accept from Charlie was a horse.

"My sister had a premonition I would be thrown from the horse. She had a premonition once before that my brother would be hurt and it came true," Alma told the court.

"You had no premonition about the diamond rings?" inquired Charlie's lawyer.

"I didn't think the rings would throw me," Alma shot back.

Charlie demonstrated his affection for the beautiful plaintiff in full view of her family. Alma's sister, Anna, told about a touching little speech Charlie had made. "He said that the de Brettevilles were one of the finest families in San Francisco and he was proud to enter into it. Then he said, 'Alma, give me a kiss,' and he reached up and put his arm around her neck."

Next her father took the stand.

"When that man broke off relations with my daughter," he said, pointing his cane in Charlie's direction, "I did what any father in my position would do. I challenged him to a duel if he refused to marry Alma. But he had no sense of honor. He just laughed it off."

Then it was Charlie's turn to present his case. Sure he gave her the presents, he admitted. But only because she asked for them.

*Alma has become more worldly by about 1900, when she posed for San
Francisco's most famous photographers, including Arnold Genthe.
This unsigned portrait may or may not be Genthe's, but it
suggests his style. (Courtesy Dorothy Spreckels Munn)*

That was his way, to be generous. But marriage?

"I wouldn't marry the best woman in the world. I got one dose of medicine. That's enough."

He told of taking Miss Alma to the Trocadero, a nightclub where "we all drank cocktails."

"Did Miss Alma have a cocktail?"

"Oh, yes. I never saw her refuse."

"When did you first kiss her?"

"She leaned over in the buggy and kissed me."

"Did you kiss her back?"

"No," said Charlie, "I couldn't reach up to her."

Whether or not Alma was as generous with Charlie as she had been with Ashton did not come out in the trial. The testimony never got beyond the kissing stage. But it is entirely likely that Charlie got a great deal farther than that in view of Alma's later remarks. She would refer to the episode as "the time I sued for personal de-floweration, and by God, I won."[14]

The jury found her innocent — in the eyes of the law. But instead of the $50,000 judgment she had sought, they awarded her $1,250.

When Charlie heard the verdict, he laughed and said he didn't care about a mere bagatelle like that. "The fun was worth it."

"Personally," Alma told the press, "I don't want a cent of Anderson's money. I shall use it to pay the costs of my trial and send the rest to Sweden to get Anderson's father out of the poorhouse. I have positive proof he is there; his sister told me."[15]

She was never able to get Charlie's father out of the poorhouse because Charlie never paid up. The next year, he was back in court again. On reflection, he decided he had been an easy mark, and he asked the court for a new trial. He confessed he couldn't pay for his fun after all, because he was broke. The motion for a new trial was denied, and that was the end of Charlie, who was last seen heading north once more.

But it was only the beginning for Miss Alma.

The trial had left her a celebrity — the kind San Francisco relished: a beautiful girl from a poor but noble family, with a questionable reputation in keeping with the spirit of the wide open city.

Shortly after Alma's victory, sculptor Robert Aitken, an instructor at the Art Institute for whom Alma had previously posed, asked her to model for a monument he was planning in memory of President William McKinley. The president had been the victim of an assassination attempt in Buffalo a few months previously. He lingered a week, but on September 14, 1901, McKinley died. San Francisco, like

Sculptor Robert Aitken stands by as his statue, for which Alma was the model, is ready for hoisting to the top of the Dewey Monument in Union Square in 1902. (Courtesy Adolph Rosekrans)

*Adolph Spreckels was a dashing young man who owned a
string of racehorses and wore a self-confident expression.
(Courtesy Archives, San Francisco Public Library)*

the rest of the country, mourned his tragic end. They remembered his visit in May, when he had christened the new battleship *Ohio,* and broke ground in Union Square for a monument to Admiral Dewey, the hero of the naval engagement in Manila.

The day following the president's death, a campaign was begun to erect a monument to him, also to be placed in Union Square. The fund was started by a concerned citizen who sent a letter to the *San Francisco Chronicle,* together with a $50 donation. The paper, receptive to the idea, reported that "a magnificent bronze statue of heroic proportions could be built for $20,000."

Daily, money poured into the newspaper, and the fund grew. While most of it came in the form of small contributions, a lot of them from schoolchildren, there was one check in the amount of $10,000 from sugar baron Claus Spreckels. The donation undoubtedly came at the suggestion of Spreckels's son Adolph, president of the San Francisco Park Commission, who had previously persuaded his father to donate the money for the bandstand shell in Golden Gate Park.

When all the necessary funds were in, it was announced that a contest would be held to select the design for a statue for President McKinley. While most sculptors struggled to get the best likeness of the president, Aitken had other ideas. Where was it written that a memorial, to be fitting, had to be a portrait statue? A great man, the sculptor reasoned, was not honored because of his height, or the shape of his nose or his head. He was honored for the mental and spiritual attainments that made him a leader of men.[16]

To exemplify those attainments, Aitken used Alma, fresh from her legal triumph, to pose. His concept was simple: a bronze figure of a woman, typifying the Republic, dignified and graceful, on a pedestal of granite. In her outstretched hand he placed a palm, denoting work well done, a tribute to the memory of the beloved president. In her other hand he gave her a trident, the three-pronged fork which was the scepter of King Neptune, king of the sea.

Thus, Aitken created one statue that performed double duty: it acknowledged both the martyred president, and the admiral whose victory at Manila Bay earned him the right to be called King of the Sea. The Citizens Committee chosen to judge the contest picked the sculpture of the voluptuous Alma, her body covered only by a diaphanous drape, as the winner from a field of six entries.

Alma's statue in Union Square would come to stand for more than a memorial to the two men whose names are carved on the granite pedestal. It became symbolic of the woman who was the incarnation of San Francisco. Like the city itself, she sprang from humble beginnings; like it, she was beautiful and uninhibited and aspired to noble things. The girl who had her first romantic encounter on the grounds of her beloved city would rise to become its queen of culture.

The man who would make all this possible for her was waiting in the wings. Adolph Bernard Spreckels, chairman of the Citizens Committee that chose the winning statue, was about to enter her life.

Chapter Notes:

1. Translated from the Danish newspaper by Alice de Bretteville, Charlottenlund, Denmark, from a clipping in her possession.
2. Interview with Anona Dukelow, who accompanied Alma on the trip.
3. Jean Frickelton papers.
4. Ulla de Bretteville Awl interview.
5. *Langley's City Directory,* 1881-1890.
6. Rudyard Kipling, Letters to the Civil and Military Gazette in Lahore, Sept. 1889, contained in *Letters From San Francisco,* Colt Press, 1949.
7. Carol Green Wilson, *Gumps' Treasure Trade,* New York, Thomas Crowell Co., 1949, 1965, p. 31.
8. Alice G. Levison, "Family Reminiscences," U.C. Bancroft Library, Berkeley Regional Oral History Office, 1967, p. 81.
9. Beverly Denenberg, California Historical Society Courier, April 1984, p. 5.
10. Ashton Potter to Ina Claire, from interview with Ina Claire.
11. Ulla de Bretteville Awl interview.
12. *San Francisco Examiner,* February 20, 1902, p. 2.
13. Ibid., February 25, 1902, p. 3.
14. Thomas Carr Howe interview.
15. *San Francisco Examiner,* February 27, 1902, p. 6.
16. *San Francisco Chronicle,.* December 18, 1902, p. 1.

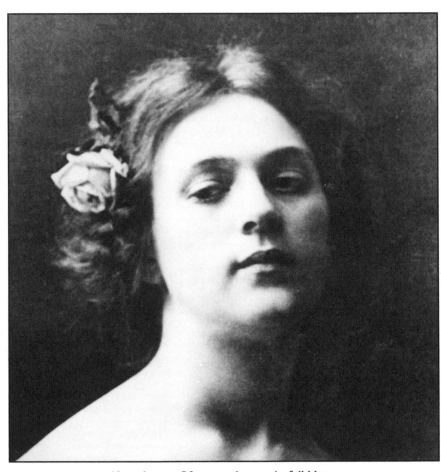

Alma, by age 20, was a beauty in full bloom.
(Courtesy Dorothy Spreckels Munn)

CHAPTER TWO

Miss Republic to Mrs. Spreckels

IT TOOK FIVE YEARS for Alma to overcome Adolph Spreckels's resistance to marrying her. The man who was more than twice her age—she was twenty-two, he was forty-six when he asked to be introduced to "Miss Republic"—was a confirmed bachelor. He had his own reason for remaining single.

Like everyone else in the West, Alma had known for years who A.B. was. The Spreckels name, like the sugar that was the source of his wealth, was a household word. The Spreckels family was in the news constantly, from the columns of *The Argonaut* and *The Wave,* which chronicled their social activities, to the front pages of the *Examiner,* the *Chronicle* and their own newspaper, the *Bulletin,* which reported every legal battle over their sugar monopoly.

She knew the family's enormous wealth started with Claus, who came as a poor young man from Germany. When he saved up enough money, he bought a grocery store, then sold it for a saloon. Then he bought a sugar refinery and worked his way up to become the sugar king of California. For his cane sugar, he was completely dependent on that grown in Hawaii. When the United States passed a treaty making Hawaiian sugar duty-free, which gave the growers a two-cents-a-pound advantage, Claus fought against the bill. He sailed immediately to Hawaii to buy all the crop available before the new treaty could go into effect. Once in the islands, he switched sides on the bill. Why couldn't he grow his own sugar in Hawaii and enjoy the duty-free benefits?

Shrewdly, Claus ingratiated himself with King Kalakaua, using his own money to support the king's projects. Claus soon wound up owning forty thousand acres of Maui land. In developing his Spreckelsville Plantation, he was hailed as a savior, revolutionizing the

19

planting, harvesting, marketing, shipping (for which he organized his own steamship company) and refining of Hawaiian sugarcane. He also added considerably to his already enormous fortune.

There was also a negative side to what Claus had done for Hawaii. He lent so many people money — at one point he held about half the national debt — that his influence on Hawaiian finance and politics soon lost him favor in the Islands.

The climax came during a poker game in Kalakaua's boathouse at which Claus, the monarch and a British admiral were present. The stakes were high. The admiral was about to take the pot with his three aces. Spreckels laid down his cards. "I win. I have four kings," he announced. The admiral, noting only three kings, said, "But where is the fourth?" "I am the fourth king," Spreckels replied. Kalakaua was not amused. He turned to the British for financial aid, and by 1898 Claus lost his Spreckelsville Plantation and his Hawaiian Commercial and Sugar Company. But by then he had turned to beet sugar and held a monopoly in refining it, so his enormous fortune never dwindled.

Alma also knew the gossip about Claus's son Adolph, whose first legal skirmish had taken place back in 1884. The story of the gun-toting young man who shot from the hip to avenge the family honor was a San Francisco legend. Adolph was regarded by many — especially the family-proud Alma — as a hero.

Adolph had cause to be angry. The editor of the *Chronicle*, Michael de Young, had been publishing defamatory, utterly unsubstantiated articles about Adolph's father all during Claus's Hawaiian years. One article accused Claus of using slave labor on his Maui plantation; another article, of using lepers to work the fields. He was even accused of being a pimp. The paper reported that in exchange for the Hawaiian sugar plantation, Spreckels agreed to provide the king with women from the mainland.

When a story charging Spreckels with stock swindling appeared on the eve of a stockholders' meeting, Adolph had had enough. He stormed into de Young's office, threw his hat on the desk of the editor's secretary and shouted, "Mr. Spreckels is here to shoot Mr. de Young." Then he proceeded with the task. Fortunately, his aim was not good, and de Young survived with only a minor wound. Adolph was accused of attempted murder, but the jury found him innocent after he pleaded insanity and self-defense.

Although A.B. was a model citizen henceforth, de Young continued his vendetta in the *Chronicle.* Many times, in later years, Alma would startle people with her retort to the snubs she always received whenever she was in the presence of de Young's daughters, the four pillars of San Francisco society. Alma would bellow after them as they passed by her like a cold wind, "We haven't been friends since my husband shot their father."

At the time Adolph walked into Alma's life, late in 1902, he was successful in his own right. He and his brother John, known as J.D., were owners of their own sugar refineries and a steamship company, and were partners in developing the sleepy little port of San Diego. A.B. was a renowned sportsman who bred prizewinning racehorses at his stock farm in Napa. He was also an accomplished yachtsman with shelves full of trophies won by racing his boats from a former yacht club in Sausalito, which he converted into another of his residences. Besides beautiful boats and beautiful racehorses, A.B. was attracted to beautiful women. While J.D. was welcoming grandchildren, A.B. was still squiring around town San Francisco's most attractive young ladies. With great anticipation, he added to his list the curvaceous model who had posed for the Union Square monument.

It is more than likely that on their first date A.B. took Alma to the Poodle Dog on Post Street for dinner. The restaurant's name was a distortion of the French *poulet d'or,* or golden chicken. It had a reputation for fine food — and discretion. There was a public dining room on the first floor for families, and more private dining rooms on the second floor for husbands and wives, but the third floor was something never mentioned by ladies. It had a special elevator in the rear which whisked couples up into private suites. Each suite had a dining table, a couch and a door that could be locked from the inside. In the basement of the restaurant was a secret passageway that led to a hotel next door. The same elevator that took couples up could speed them down to finish in a hotel bedroom what they had started over their cafe diablo. Men like A.B. appreciated not only the good food but the convenience of it all.

Adolph, a man of wide experience, was a spirited conversationalist. In Alma he had a fascinated listener. Educated abroad, he captivated her with talk of his travels in Europe, and amused her with stories about politics and how the Palace Hotel in San Francisco was the real capitol of the state. He spoke in a deep, richly timbred voice that acted like an aphrodisiac on her.

Given Alma's uninhibited personality and her determination to be a rich man's darling, we can imagine what happened next. As he talked, she moved closer. Their knees touched. When he put his hand over hers, her fork clattered to her plate. Alma, who usually had a ravenous appetite, suddenly wasn't hungry for food. The secret romance that was to last for the next five years had begun.

*In 1904 Adolph Spreckels sent Alma and her parents to Denmark,
where Alma had this striking portrait made. (Author's collection)*

It wasn't only A.B.'s wealth that appealed to Alma. In addition to the money, in addition to his being an expert lover far removed from the awkwardness of Ashton Potter or the crudeness of Charlie Anderson, A.B. had something just as important to her as money and sex. He had knowledge. To the girl who had to leave school at fourteen, who longed to do great things, she saw this man twenty-four years her senior as the means of fulfilling her lofty ambitions. Big Alma had big dreams, and A.B. was the man big enough to help her achieve them.

At first, Alma was willing to go along with their secret relationship. She became his mistress, confident that eventually she could get him to marry her. She lived at home with her parents, meeting him during the week at places like the Poodle Dog and spending weekends at his Napa ranch.

If A.B. had health problems, he kept them secret from Alma. She knew he was under the care of his friend Dr. John Gallwey, and that he walked with a funny, halting gait, but she also knew he had the enthusiasm and the desires of a much younger man.

Papa de Bretteville surely wasn't blind to what was going on between his daughter and A.B., but he did not press the matter of family honor. Spreckels was too good to the family. His daughter was now wearing the lovely clothes he felt she was born to wear. She no longer had to worry about paying her tuition at art school. A.B., although he never went with them, provided the family with tickets to the best performances in town. The noble de Brettevilles were now appearing *en famille* in box seats at the opera and at concerts; they dined at all the finest restaurants and went to opening nights of all the shows. Even Alma's haughty sister, Anna, was impressed.

While Viggo harbored no resentment for the man his own age who was his daughter's paramour, Alma certainly did. She seethed inwardly because her patience was not paying off. She was still a working girl; she hadn't moved an inch closer to her dreams of doing great things. She hadn't even taken a trip, except to Napa. Ever since that first night at the Poodle Dog when A.B. told her of his travels to Europe, she dreamed of the day he would take her traveling. "The Viking in me longs to explore the world," she hinted continuously.

Adolph offered one excuse after another for why he couldn't take her. First it was urgent business matters that kept him at home. Then it was an important horse race in which one of his quarter horses was entered. Then it was his brother, J.D., who wanted him to visit San Diego to see some more property he thought they ought to buy.

When it became evident that Adolph would not travel with her,

Alma decided to ask him for the money to go by herself. Well, not exactly by herself, because how could an unmarried lady — especially one from a noble family — travel alone? She would ask him to send her with her family. Soon after Alma made this resolve, Viggo received a letter from his nephew, Louis Claude de Bretteville, who wrote that his wife was expecting a baby. That was all the excuse Alma needed.

That weekend in Napa, she continually beseeched Adolph to book passage to Denmark for her and her parents. She told him she had received a great honor — she was to be named the baby's godmother, a fact that may have come as a surprise to its parents. She pleaded that her father and mother hadn't been back to their homeland since they left nearly fifty years ago. She reminded him that she had never gotten farther than across the bay.

A.B., perhaps propelled by guilt about his secret, acquiesced. He made all the arrangements for them: first-class compartments on the train to Chicago and then on a train for New York. There, he booked them in the Ritz Carlton Hotel until they boarded a German steamer for Copenhagen.[1]

The North Atlantic passage took nearly two weeks. Alma loved every minute. She didn't even mind the German food. Someday, she vowed, she would get Adolph to take her around the world. On her honeymoon. It would have to be on their honeymoon, because she learned that a man and woman must be married before they could share a stateroom aboard a ship. She discovered this when the purser interrogated Viggo, making sure Mathilde was his wife. A vague plan to entrap Adolph began taking shape in her head.

In Copenhagen they stayed with Kaj and Anna de Bretteville, the cousins who had financed Viggo's trip to America years before.

"I'm engaged to marry a very wealthy man," Alma explained to her bewildered cousins when they wondered how lazy Uncle Viggo had suddenly acquired money to travel. "We'll be married when I return."[2]

She showed considerable interest in the old family pictures and was very annoyed when her relatives refused to sell her the painting of Louis Claude, the *Emigre,* as the family called him. The *Emigre* was their French great-grandfather, the general who fought with Napoleon.

Alma wanted to know all about the history of the Danish de Brettevilles. She found that though they were "entitled nobility" — that is, the Danish government was perfectly willing to recognize their French titles — they never picked them up. They didn't have the money to live a noble lifestyle. They were even poorer than her own family. But they were well educated and had many titled friends.

Among the titled friends were the Baron and Baroness Bertouch Lehn. Having dinner in their palace, Alma stared at the liveried servants who moved silently among the guests in the banquet hall. The servants' attention was riveted on the baroness, who issued her orders by discreetly clapping her hands.

Alma had to remember to tell Adolph about that. Clap your hands and the platters of spicy herring are removed. Clap again and the trays of succulent Danish hams appear. All so quietly. So elegantly. Someday she would preside over a table like that. In an American castle. With liveried servants.

Knowing she loved art, Alma's relatives took her to visit the Ny Carlsberg Glyptothek, the museum that had opened in 1897, seven years before. The museum was a gift of Carl and Ottilia Jacobsen, the wealthy makers of Carlsberg beer. All of Denmark was talking about the generosity of the Jacobsens, who had been collecting the works of French masters such as Degas, Gauguin and Rodin for their private collection. The Jacobsens decided their treasures should be shared with the public. For this they needed a museum. They got support from the municipality of Copenhagen and the Danish government, and the beautiful Glyptothek, with its conservatory filled with green plants, was opened to the public. What the Jacobsens had done and the honor it brought to their name made a lasting impression on Alma.

◆　　◆　　◆　　◆　　◆

Alma's remarks to her Danish relatives that she would be married when she returned were not prophetic. Once home, her relationship with A.B. fell into the same pattern as before. Although her lover was overjoyed to have her back, he still would not commit himself to marriage.

She knew nothing of the doubts that were plaguing A.B. His greatest fear was that she would run from him when she found out his secret. Was she only interested in his money? He loved her. Doing things for her brought him as much pleasure as it did her. He loved her exuberance, her thirst for knowledge. He had grown to depend on her to brighten his life. His brother J.D. and his doctor, the only ones who knew of his attachment to Alma, strongly advised him against marriage. Leave things as they are, they told him. Sadly, he was inclined to agree.[3]

Alma's mood swung from gaiety one moment to deep despair the next. "I'm not good enough for him," she told her friend from art school days, May Slessinger. It was her lack of education. How

Claus Spreckels's magnificent house on Van Ness Avenue was gutted by fire after the 1906 earthquake; it was later restored and used as a school until its demolition in 1928. (Courtesy Dorothy Spreckels Munn)

could a girl who quit school at fourteen ever hope to marry a man like A.B.? How foolish of her to imagine she was ever destined to accomplish great things! What a joke that was! In her despair, she would scream at her brother Alex, whom she adored, and she would lash out at her youngest brother, Gus, who was always her willing lackey. She hated her life. She was nothing. No one would ever respect her.

Then the mood would pass. She was Alma de Bretteville, a woman of destiny and, by God, she would fulfill that destiny. People would respect her not only in San Francisco but in all the world. Meanwhile, she had to go slow with Adolph. He'd come around eventually.

Her resolute mood sustained her when San Francisco was struck with the devastating earthquake and fire in 1906. People who were suddenly left homeless ran to Golden Gate Park, where a tent city quickly sprang up. Nobody seemed to know what to do. Alma did. Instinctively, and with ferocious energy, she helped organize community kitchens and ordered groups of dazed housewives to staff them. She directed the relief trucks with their loads of milk and fresh food to the tents where the kitchens were.

Next, she went up and down the park shouting for schoolteachers. She knew how important education was. She ordered the teachers to round up kids and get classes going again. Her commanding presence — all six feet of her — inspired confidence. If she couldn't persuade people with her winning smile, then she could intimidate them with a glare that defied opposition.

Adolph had his own problems during the 1906 catastrophe. Although his residence in Sausalito escaped harm, his parents' home on Van Ness Avenue was badly damaged. The magnificent Spreckels mansion, thought to be absolutely fireproof, was gutted when a careless maid left a third-floor window open. The curtains, ignited by the flaming wind, sucked the fire in. The family escaped injury, but it was too much for Claus. He lost not only his home but all of the Spreckels business interests that were centered in San Francisco. He never fully recovered from the blow. Adolph took on his father's responsibilities, in addition to his own.

Two years later, Alma abandoned her "go slow" policy, following an unusually severe bout of depression during which all her insecurities engulfed her. It was spring, the spring of 1908, and all around Alma everyone seemed filled with hope. Horse cars were running once more down Market Street, and cable cars were clanking up the Sacramento and Clay Street hills again. Two new theaters replaced temporary structures. Houdini was booked into one of them, per-

Adolph Spreckels had settled into a dignified maturity by the time he finally married Alma in Philadelphia in 1908. Newspapers reported that the couple were off on a world tour, during which they would visit "Dr. Nansen, the Arctic explorer and author..." Alma's mother, Mathilde, told reporters of her satisfaction with the match: "Mr. Spreckels and my daughter have been warm friends for years. I have frequently entertained Mr. Spreckels at my house and have been much impressed by his accomplished manners and courtliness. I believe it is the intention of Mr. Spreckels and Alma to include Norway in their honeymoon. While there, they will be entertained by Dr. Nansen, who always has regarded Alma as one of his favorite cousins."
(Photo courtesy Maryhill Museum)

forming his most spectacular magic act, escaping from chains under water in fifty-seven seconds. Market Street was full of sailors from the Great White Fleet anchored in the harbor. Women had left the days of "making do" behind them and were now promenading in the latest spring fashions imported from France by the City of Paris department store. Dainty waists topped pleated skirts whose hems barely touched the newly cobblestoned streets. Huge hats were skewered atop high pompadours, their brims drooping with "oddities in feathered effects." Businessman Randolph Hale was back on the luncheon circuit, getting citizens excited again about the idea of San Francisco hosting a world's fair to coincide with the opening of the Panama Canal. If people thought the idea had gone up in the flames that destroyed the city, Hale thought it was an opportunity to show the world how the city had recovered.

Everyone seemed to be making progress but Alma. It was time to put her plan into action. She knew that if she could convince A.B. to take her on a ship, he'd have to marry her. The nearer she could get with him to the East Coast, the closer she'd be to wedding bells.

Early in May, Adolph had to make a trip to the Spreckels sugar refinery in Philadelphia. He had never taken her before. Alma pleaded with him to go, she cajoled him, she threatened to break off their relationship. It is even conceivable that she thought about taking the same action she did against Charlie Anderson. She didn't have to. A.B. finally caved in.

According to their usual pattern for discretion, Adolph took the train to Philadelphia alone, leaving a ticket for Alma to follow him. Then Alma bought a ticket for her brother Alex, instructing him to follow them a week later. If she were going to be married, she needed someone to give her away, didn't she?

"Hell, I didn't even have to get to New York to persuade him to marry me," Alma confided to Anona Dukelow, her nurse-companion, years later. "Once he was away from that brother of his — J.D. hated my guts even before he met me — Adolph's opposition to marriage melted right away, and we were married in Philadephia. He was so happy, he agreed to take me on a year's honeymoon in Europe. We kept the marriage a secret for a whole month before some loudmouths we met accidentally in New York spotted us and the story got out. I heard it caused quite a commotion back home."[4]

"Commotion" was not exactly accurate. The tremors that the news caused would have registered, had there been a Richter scale in those days, greater than the shock of the earthquake two years previously. At breakfast all over town that Sunday, June 8, 1908, from

Nob Hill to South of the Slot, San Franciscans opening the morning papers rattled their cups and spilt their coffee when they read the headlines. There it was, in bold type, over the picture of a rotund, dignified, mustachioed man: "Adolph Spreckels Married to Alma de Bretteville. Millionaire in Europe With Bride After Secret Wedding in Philadelphia."[5]

The story was startling because of Alma's notoriety. The report was quick to recall that "Wife Awarded Verdict in Suit for Breach of Promise Seven Years Ago." Readers knew who she was; they knew who A.B. was, but they had no idea that the two of them knew each other. Not even his own family, outside of J.D., had heard of his attachment to Alma.

When a reporter told the news to A.B.'s nephew, John Spreckels Jr., the young man laughed and said, "That is a good joke on Uncle Adolph. He'll never marry."[6] It was also a good joke on young John and his brothers and sister, who had every right to think the estate of their ailing bachelor uncle would one day come to them.

According to the newspaper accounts, the couple was married "at the home of her aunt" in Philadelphia, with her brother Alexander giving the bride away. From Philadelphia, the story read, the couple went to New York, where they registered at a hotel before departing for Europe. It was there that friends of A.B.'s spotted them.

What did or did not happen in Philadelphia is not altogether clear. Alma had no aunt in that city, but Adolph did maintain an elaborately furnished apartment there for many years, which he used on his frequent trips to his sugar refinery. The couple did take out an Application for Marriage form on May 8, 1908, which is on record in Philadelphia. There is, however, no subsequent marriage certificate on record. Michael de Young's newspaper, the *Chronicle,* was quick to pick up this tantalizing bit of information and to report it prominently.[7]

Since the couple filed the first form, it is logical to suppose that they went through with the ceremony three days later in Adolph's — not some mysterious aunt's — apartment. And it is also possible that Alma, who always gave their wedding date as May 11, 1908, then decided not to part with the precious document she had waited so long for — not even long enough to get it registered. We can picture the tall, unblushing bride sweeping regally up the gangplank of the Cunard liner *Lusitania,* clutching the precious slip of paper proclaiming that she was, indeed, Mrs. Adolph Bernard Spreckels.

Alma's insistence on marriage had finally won over Adolph's better judgment. Knowing how much he loved her, perhaps he feared for the day she would leave him for a younger man and he would have to face his remaining years with a debilitating illness all alone. Perhaps, watching his brother J.D. relishing his grandchildren, he regretted having no children of his own. Perhaps the doctors were wrong, and there was no reason why he shouldn't father children.

But even if he gave in to his emotions, A.B. was still a cautious businessman. Before he signed the Application of Intent to Marry, he requested Alma sign a prenuptial agreement stipulating the amount of money to which she would be entitled should the marriage be dissolved for any reason. "I would have signed anything he put before me, I wanted to marry that man so badly," Alma told Anona Dukelow many years later.

The newlyweds were still in Europe six months later when Claus Spreckels died on December 26. Quickly, they made arrangements to come home.

"About that prenuptial agreement, Pet," Alma told Anona. "It didn't last very long. On the return voyage I got sick. Adolph was terribly upset and summoned the ship's doctor. He found out what was wrong. I was pregnant. Adolph was overjoyed. The first thing he did was to tear up the prenuptial agreement."[8]

While the fifty-one-year-old bridegroom was overjoyed, he was also very worried. He still hadn't shared his secret with his wife.

Chapter Notes:

1. Alma Spreckels, in a letter to Clifford Dolph, Maryhill Museum, January 3, 1949: "I went with my parents to Denmark when I was 23 years old."
2. Alice de Bretteville interview, Denmark.
3. Interview with Anona Dukelow.
4. Ibid.
5. *San Francisco Examiner,* June 7, 1908, p. 1.
6. Ibid.
7. *San Francisco Chronicle,* June 9, 1908, p. 2.
8. Anona Dukelow interview.

Little Alma, born in 1909, solidified Alma's social position as the wife of Adolph Spreckels and the mother of his child. (Courtesy John Rosekrans)

CHAPTER THREE

Alma Embraces Motherhood

 TO HER GREAT DISPLEASURE, Alma gave birth to three children over the next four years. If she had thought that one of the benefits of being an old man's darling was the fact that old men were not interested in raising children — *she* certainly wasn't — she was wrong about A.B. Once he held his first baby and saw that the little girl was perfectly healthy, his worries and fears about fatherhood subsided. He was ready to have more. He could afford a large family. The death of Claus Spreckels, and the subsequent lawsuits against his brothers for his inheritance, had added millions to A.B.'s fortune, as did the demise of his mother shortly afterwards.

In his jubilation over his firstborn, A.B. decided the baby should be called "Alma." Happy to be at what she thought was the end of her childbearing duties, Alma agreed her accomplishment deserved that kind of recognition. The baby, for the rest of her long life, would always be known as "Little Alma." The child had been born at A.B.'s Sausalito residence, in the village on the north shore of San Francisco Bay. Alma thought it was time they moved to the city. After all, she *was* Mrs. Spreckels now. She didn't have to hide out any more.

A.B. bought a house on Vallejo Street in Pacific Heights and moved his little family into it. The house was a tremendous step upward from where Alma had spent most of her life behind the store on Francisco Street. But she had other ideas in mind. The little girl who had delivered laundry through back doors and vowed one day to come through the front door of the most beautiful house in the city didn't have her house — yet.

A year and a half later, when Alma found herself pregnant again, she felt there was only one bright side to her predicament. She knew

33

she was getting closer to the house of her dreams. Adolph was so elated about having another child, how could he object to moving again when she found what she wanted?

She found the house early in December 1910. Alma told A.B. he could buy it for her for a Christmas present. It was the Jean Boyd residence at the corner of Washington Street and Octavia, across from Lafayette Park. It wasn't the Boyd house that caught Alma's fancy. It was the location. The site commanded the finest marine panorama in San Francisco — or *would,* once Alma got the obstructions out of the way.

San Francisco society, which still didn't take seriously the fact that Alma was really A.B.'s wife, soon received its first indication of the *outré* behavior they would come to expect from the new Mrs. Spreckels. Not only did she have her husband purchase and then demolish the Boyd house, but she also urged him to buy several others adjacent to it. Oh, no, she had no intention of uprooting the residents, she assured reporters. She would personally see to it that Mr. Spreckels moved the houses to another location down the hill.

Soon houses raised on stilts were a familiar — and irritating — sight along staid Pacific Heights. During the move, service on the Washington-Jackson cable car lines was disrupted, and traffic was a mess. Auto drivers muttered unprintable things about that Spreckels woman as they maneuvered through the tunnels formed by the stilts.

Alma ignored the wrath she was incurring. She was confident that when her new neighbors saw the house she was going to build, they would welcome the Adolph Spreckels family with open arms. What she had in mind was the kind of castle that Papa assured her would be worthy of the de Bretteville name.

Although it is doubtful that the Germanic Spreckels cared about building a French chateau, he gave his wife the Christmas present she wanted so badly. He hired architect Kenneth MacDonald Jr. and his young associate, George Applegarth, a graduate of the *Ecole de Beaux Arts,* to draw up plans for the mansion. Three years under construction, it turned out to be one of the grandest houses ever built in the United States. Before it was finished, Alma gave birth to her second child, a son, Adolph Frederick, and much to her disgust became pregnant a third time.[1]

The huge mansion was designed not only for the five Spreckelses plus their retinue of servants, but especially for entertaining in the grand style. The house seemed to march right up the Washington Street hill from Gough Street. At the lower end was the *porte cochère* with a large parking area. The main entrance was midway up the slope, with a flight of marble steps leading to a pair of wrought-iron doors topped with the Spreckels crest. The massive doors opened on the "parlor floor." Inside, an entry hall decorated with gold mosaics, set in Italian stone, stretched the entire length of the house, to where one could see the Pompeiian Court at the north end. The Pompeiian Court, a circular room, contained a fountain in the center, a ceiling painted with cherubs and cupids, and a breathtaking view of the San Francisco Bay, the Golden Gate, and the neighboring counties.

Bisecting the entry hall, running north and south, was the main hall. On the left was the reception room, a salon which was like the anteroom in a palace where one waited to be ushered into the throne room. The "throne room" at 2080 Washington was the ballroom, done in Louis XVI style, which spanned the full length of the west side of the house. In the center of the room, along the west wall, was a magnificent marble fireplace.

To the right of the main hall, next to the paneled den, was the living room, referred to as the "Italian Room." Designed as a departure from the French Renaissance style of the rest of the floor, the Italian Room had an ornate coffered ceiling. The floor-to-ceiling fireplace caused eyebrows to rise, not because of the cavernous opening, but because of the ornaments chained to each side of it. There, in colorful splendor, stood a pair of Nubian slave figures with purple loincloths and orange collars studded with rhinestones. Alma had a ready explanation for why they appealed to her. She said she found them in Venice on her honeymoon and fell in love with them. She told people they reminded her of her husband and herself, slaves to love.

Next to the Italian Room was the oval dining room. Adjacent to it, behind elaborately paneled doors, was a large pantry connected by a dumbwaiter to the hotel-sized kitchen in the basement. The basement, which one entered from the *porte cochère,* was so vast that Alma later converted it into two apartments and rented them out.

Upstairs were the family's intimate quarters. Off the main hall, which boasted a ceiling of Tiffany glass, were bedrooms for the three children, each with its own bath and dressing room. There was also a nurse's room, guest rooms and a large library. The east wing contained A.B.'s bedroom, bath and study, and Alma's bedroom, bath and boudoir. A private hallway separated the two suites. The top floor contained servants' rooms and a huge playroom for the children.

Since the mansion itself did not extend all the way down to the street below, there was space for rolling green lawns between the

*Adolph's pride in his son, born in 1911, is clearly evident. Fatherhood, coming
so late in life, transformed the former playboy into a devoted family man.
(Courtesy John Rosekrans)*

house and its mammoth garage, which faced Jackson Street. The garage contained a turntable in the center, making it possible for the chauffeur to maneuver each of the family's five limousines into its proper parking place. The cars, however, did not remain properly parked for long.

If her Pacific Heights neighbors were unhappy with Alma before she moved in, they were infuriated with her later on. She turned her posh garage, in the midst of one of the city's finest residential districts, into a rummage center for more than three decades, while she raised money for her various charities.

The house also contained an elevator, a necessity for A.B., who was finding it more and more difficult to walk. In July 1912, the family was vacationing at the Del Monte Hotel in Monterey when Adolph suffered a severe brain hemorrhage. Although his mind was not impaired, he was confined to a wheelchair or to walking with the aid of his valet and his cane. The elevator made it possible for him to enter or leave the house from the *porte cochère* entrance. The elevator was small, accommodating only three people, since guests to the mansion used the outside marble stairs to the parlor floor — at least they did until Alma ordered workmen to "yank them out and plaster over the opening" when she remodeled the house in the 1930s.

Alma was still unaware of the exact nature of A.B.'s illness. His "attacks" frightened her when they occurred, but reassured by Dr. Gallwey, she quickly shrugged off her fears. Too bad he was having so much trouble moving about, but then, most older people did, didn't they?

The night that her third child, Dorothy Constance, was born, she found out the shocking truth, the secret that A.B. could never bring himself to share with her.

"Many years later, Mother told me about what happened that night," said Dorothy. "Dr. John Gallwey had been at her side right up to the final moment of her labor. Then, just before her last contractions, there was a loud commotion in my father's bedroom."[2]

"Dr. Gallwey, come quickly," shouted A.B.'s valet. "Mr. Spreckels is having a seizure. I think he's choking!"

With but the briefest hesitation, the doctor abandoned his patient and raced down the hall. Later, after A.B.'s emergency had been attended to, and the new baby had made her arrival practically unassisted, the doctor tried to calm Alma's rage. He feared that what he had to tell her would only enrage her further.

She demanded to know why he had left her. What exactly was wrong with her husband? Bracing himself for the fury that was sure to follow, the doctor told her that A.B. was suffering from the tertiary stage of syphilis. Alma's face, an angry red a moment before, suddenly turned pale. Did that mean she had it too?

No, he hastened to explain. A.B. had been in a latent stage for many years. In that state, the patient usually ceases to be infectious. Quietly, he told her that A.B. had contracted the disease when there was no cure, before Dr. Ehrlich came up with his miraculous discovery.[3] The best he could hope for was that he would not infect her. He hadn't, and therefore her children were free of any symptoms.

The doctor explained that the disease affected Adolph's nervous system, resulting in locomotor ataxia, a degenerative disease of the spinal cord. It caused him to lose control over his muscular movements, mainly his walking. It was also the cause of the cerebral hemorrhages. Sorrowfully, the doctor told her, this would be her last baby. A.B.'s sex life was over.

Alma, thirty-two years old at the time, accepted the news philosophically. Everything had its price. Nothing in her life had ever come easily. She was also relieved. Now she understood A.B.'s reluctance to marry her. She had always thought it was because of her own inadequacies — that she wasn't good enough or educated enough or beautiful enough for him.

A woman of destiny, how ironic! Is this what she was destined for, the life of a celibate? Was that the price she had to pay? Would she have married A.B. if she had known this beforehand? Of course she would have! She loved him. She still did. Her heart went out to him because he had had to bear such a burden alone all these years.

But she certainly wouldn't have had children. Children made her uncomfortable. They took too much of her time, and she had better things to do. Now she was perfectly justified in living her own life.

With no reluctance, Alma promptly turned the care of her two daughters and son over to nurses, and later, a governess. Almost the only intimate contact she had with them was when she gathered Little Alma, Little Adolph and Dorothy to her side periodically to pose for pictures for the society section of the Hearst — never the de Young — newspapers.

While this kind of publicity was more favorable than the notoriety she had experienced earlier, it still did not make her any more palatable to San Francisco's socialites. It wasn't the way she looked that was irritating; she looked every inch a lady. She fancied lavishly beaded gowns for evening, but they were always black or white, and never *décolleté*.

Alma persuaded Adolph to buy her the imposing Jean Boyd house at the corner of Washington and Octavia Streets, as well as five other parcels to the north and east of the Boyd house, forming a single site 175 by 225 feet. Alma had the enormous Victorian houses moved to make room for 2080 Washington Street, one of the most striking landmarks in San Francisco.
(Courtesy Archives, San Francisco Public Library)

The white stone mansion, completed in 1913, was unlike any house ever seen in San Francisco. George Applegarth, trained at Paris' Ecole des Beaux Artes, designed the house to please Alma's taste for French grandeur. Not since the days of the railroad barons mansions on Nob Hill had anything so splendid been built in San Francisco. The scale of the house, with its porte-cochere at the right, was huge but beautifully balanced, with a splendid bronze-canopied entrance at the center. (Courtesy John and Adolph Rosekrans)

Right: The marble steps leading to the stately entrance are flanked by handsomely carved stone pillars and urns; the balconies are enclosed by cast iron railings and supported by by carvings of putti and garlands. Alma had the bronze portico and doorway removed in thed 1930s, when she converted the house into three apartments. Thenceforth the only entrance was through the side door, from the porte-cochere. (Courtesy Bancroft Library)

Overleaf: Alma gave her daughter a Christmas party in 1913, although the house was not yet furnished. Little Alma, to the left of center, wears a spangled dress fit for a princess and carries a wand, setting her apart from the more conservatively dressed guests. (Gabriel Moulin photo, courtesy Moulin Studios)

It was her behavior that distanced her from polite society. On the one hand, she felt she was above the rules that governed ordinary people. She was a de Bretteville, married to a Spreckels. She came from nobility. She could make her own rules. On the other hand, she felt inferior. Everybody knew she had once been poor and was uneducated. She yearned to be accepted by society the way the wives of A.B.'s brothers were accepted.

It was important to her to have a fine home, but she wasn't going to change herself into a pinky-raised, tea-drinking snob to live in it. She refused to pretend to like people she thought were bores. She was attracted to people who did interesting things. Otherwise, if they were stuffed shirts, she told them so and got rid of them. And so what if the rules said ladies weren't supposed to drink? That didn't apply to her. She loved a cocktail, and she could down many of them without showing any adverse effects. She also liked to take her shoes off when her feet hurt, and put her feet up on the nearest coffee table.

Alma was a great embarrassment to Eleanor Spreckels, Rudolph's wife, who never let anyone forget that she was born a blue-blooded Joliffe. Eleanor showed her displeasure with "that woman who was Adolph's mistress" when it was time for Little Alma to go to school. Alma wanted to enroll her daughter at Miss Burke's, the most elegant school in the city. It also was the school that Rudolph's two daughters attended.

"You let that woman's child in this school and I will remove my daughters," Eleanor threatened Barbara Burke, the headmistress. Miss Burke got the message.

"I'm terribly sorry," Miss Burke murmured politely to Alma, "to have to turn down your request. But I'm afraid confusion would result with so many Spreckels girls enrolled in the same school."

"I see my sister-in-law got to you before I did," stormed Alma. Humiliated, she was forced to settle for second best; she enrolled Little Alma, and later, Dorothy at the Sara Dix Hamlin School.[4]

If Little Alma couldn't get into the finest school, Big Alma was determined that her child would play a starring role in the finest Christmas party ever staged in San Francisco.

The Washington Street mansion was completed in December 1913, when Little Alma was not quite four. Although it would be another year before it would be furnished and the family moved in, the empty mansion formed a perfect backdrop for Alma's lavish production. It was her first large party, the first time she was able to indulge in her fantasies without regard to cost. Five years before, Alma had been a kept woman whose only parties consisted of dinners for two in private dining rooms. Now that she was Mrs. Adolph B. Spreckels, mistress to a huge fortune and the mother of three children, those children were going to have the kind of Christmas she had only dreamed about.

From the description of the party in the *Examiner,* we can see Alma, standing in the empty ballroom, issuing her orders to the floral designers like a general planning for a massive assault. She told them she wanted the whole house decorated in festoons of greens, shimmering with frost. "Tie the greens up with great bunches of gilded pine cones and gilt and iridescent balls of every color. Cover the chandeliers with silver bells and boughs iced with make-believe snow, and against the walls I want vases of poinsettias. And I want the biggest Christmas tree you can find. It's got to reach from the floor of the Italian Room up to the ceiling, do you understand?"

They understood. On Christmas morning the empty mansion was transformed into a magic wonderland. Little Alma was the star of the party. Dressed as a fairy princess, she held a gold wand in her hand. With it she assisted Santa Claus, who crept out of the huge fireplace. Santa was played by A.B.'s friend Samuel Shortridge (later U.S. senator from California). Little Alma took her role very seriously, indicating to Santa the order in which children were to receive gifts.

Later, to entertain the children, there was a troupe of clowns, a vaudeville show, a Punch and Judy show, an exquisite live doll who sang and pirouetted on the stage, and a Hawaiian band to strum exotic music.

In the evening, the grown-ups returned for a dinner dance. Alma, resplendent in a black velvet gown decorated with rhinestones and crystals, got her chance to act like the baroness and clap her hands for the liveried servants who waited table.

If the assemblage didn't include any of San Francisco's top-drawer socialites — they sent "regrets" — among those present were people Alma found far more interesting: writer Jack London and his wife, Charmian, local sculptor Earl Cummings, and the Persian minister to the United States. The latter entertained guests with a Persian variation of the tango. Another of the male guests donned women's clothes to mimic the live doll who had earlier entertained the children. Alma thought that sort of behavior was hilarious. As the guests left, each received a booklet showing pictures of the new house.[5]

A week later, Alma, flushed with the success of her first party, staged another one. This time it was an elaborate "At Home," on January 3, 1914. Dinner, with an eleven-course menu printed in French, preceded dancing in the ballroom to the strains of Hawaiian

Alma appears to have settled comfortably into the role of patrician wife and mother as Little Alma (left), Little Adolph (right) and baby Dorothy share a picture book. (Courtesy John Rosekrans)

and ragtime bands. Those bona fide socialites who couldn't restrain their curiosity dropped in long enough to get a good look at the mansion.[6]

Two days after the "At Home," 2080 Washington was the scene of yet another outrageously elegant function. This one was a stag party Alma planned to honor her husband's sixtieth birthday. From the butler's pantry she directed the affair. She watched A.B. presiding over the banquet table she had decorated so lovingly. At one end of the huge table, in a pool of water, floated a miniature of Adolph's famous yacht, the *Lurline*. At the other was a replica of the racetrack where he ran his horses. The harlequin waiters wore his colors, red, navy and white. Around the table sat a gathering of notable men in costumes ranging from formal dress to clown, hobo, Yankee farmer and French ambassador.

Dick Hotaling was dressed as a cafe girl. It was his liquor warehouse that had miraculously survived the 1906 earthquake and fire intact, and was immortalized in the doggerel, "If, as they say/God spanked the town for being over-frisky/How come He burned the churches down/And saved Hotaling's whiskey?"

At the appropriate time, Alma signaled for four husky waiters. Staggering under the weight of a huge birthday cake ablaze with candles, they marched into the room. The cake measured eight feet ten inches in circumference. Sam Shortridge acted as master of ceremonies, and Alma's sculptor friend, Earl Cummings, who was dressed as a ballet dancer, designed the bronze plaque which served as the birthday card.

As pleasurable as entertaining was for her, it barely tapped Alma's creativity or her enormous energy. She was a woman of destiny; she knew she was designed for more important things than presiding over fancy tables. But what?

Adolph understood her restlessness, her frustrations. He deeply regretted his inability to satisfy her sexual needs. He knew she would never turn to another man. When he did get her to go to dinner parties with his friends, her greatest delight was coming back to him and describing the entire evening for his amusement. She would snuggle up next to him on top of his large bed and read from her notes about what was served, what the latest gossip was, what witty things were said. She loved it when he called her his "Pet." Nobody had ever referred to her in those terms. It made her feel diminutive and cuddly and, most of all, loved.

Lloyd Howard, whose father had been a friend of A.B's since their grammar school days, recalled one of those "dates" A.B. had arranged for his wife. Lloyd was thirteen, and he was enchanted with

Alma that night in the spring of 1913 when she came to his parents' home. He was also very curious about the woman so many people called shocking.

"My parents gave a dinner party for the Spreckelses shortly after the birth of Dorothy. Adolph could not attend because he had had an attack. Alma was escorted by Ignatz Steinhart, the banker who gave the city the aquarium. She had on a white gown. She was inordinately beautiful at the time."[7]

The only thing shocking about her behavior was the wink she gave the boy when he stared at her as she jotted down notes in the little notebook she took periodically from her reticule.

In addition to keeping her busy socially, Adolph pondered other outlets into which he could channel Alma's energy. He knew of her passion for knowledge, of her love for art, and for the finest in eighteenth century furnishings. When it became apparent that none of those furnishings were available locally, he found the answer he was looking for. Much as he would miss her, he encouraged her to go to Paris to shop.

It didn't take much persuasion. A month later, in the spring of 1914, with no knowledge of the French language, Alma set out alone for the long journey across the United States and the North Atlantic. Her first priority was to select a bed for her new bedroom. Remembering Ashton Potter and the hard, damp ground where she was first bedded down, she was determined to find a very large and very comfortable bed. And because Alma loved to make outrageous remarks, we can hear her add, "What's Tessie Wall got that I can't get?"

Tessie Wall, known as the "Tinsel Queen of the Tenderloin," was the town's most notorious madam. She had a passion for antiques and fine furnishings. Tessie, who bought the draperies from J.D.'s mansion when Alma's brother-in-law moved to San Diego, boasted to the newspapers of owning a huge, gold French bed decorated with swans and cupids. Alma would go Tessie one better.

"I'm going to find me a bed that kings made love in," she vowed.

She found the bed, and she found much more. She found Loie Fuller, the dancer, and Auguste Rodin, the sculptor, and through them, she found a whole new direction to her life.

Chapter Notes:

1. He was renamed Adolph Bernard after A.B.'s death. *San Francisco Chronicle,* November 10, 1924.
2. Dorothy Spreckels Munn interview.
3. Dr. Paul Ehrlich discovered his arsenic compound, Salvarsan, for the treatment of syphilis in 1909.
4. Dr. Charles Albert Shumate interview.
5. *San Francisco Examiner,* December 25, 1913, p.7.
6. Menu, invitations, Spreckels Folder, California Historical Society.
7. Lloyd Howard interview, Dodie Rosekrans tapes, 1976.

The inimitable Loie Fuller, who single-handedly invented Modern Dance, dedicated her life to art and captivated all Europe. She then attempted to wrap it up and present it to Alma Spreckels. To a remarkable extent, she succeeded. (Courtesy Margaret Haile Harris)

50

CHAPTER FOUR

Alma Collides
With French Culture

LOIE FULLER TOOK ONE LOOK at Alma, the beautiful American who towered thirteen inches above her, and was immediately drawn to her. Not since Loie, who was a lesbian, first met Queen Marie of Romania when she was still a crown princess, had she been this excited about another woman. Loie was introduced to Alma at a dinner party at Ciro's, then Paris's most glamorous restaurant. The dinner was arranged by Mitchell Samuels, of French and Company, art dealers in New York. When A.B. alerted the firm that his wife would be in France on a buying trip, they informed their Paris representative, who immediately arranged a banquet in her honor.[1]

"La Loie," the *"Fée Lumineuse,"* the Fairy of Light, as the French called her, once delighted Paris with her dancing at the *Folies-Bergère.* Although, at fifty-three, she wasn't dancing herself anymore, she was still the toast of Paris with her troupe of young girls whom she trained in her technique.

She was born Mary Louise Fuller in a small town in Illinois, in 1862, although Loie liked to say it was 1870. That's the year she gave in her autobiography. She was raised in Chicago and became attracted to the stage in the concert saloon run by her father. But her first appearance on a stage, she claimed later, was as a temperance lecturer.[2]

She studied singing at the Academy of Music in Chicago, and moved to New York to embark on a career in musical comedy. Mary Louise became Louise and, finally, Loie. She played in vaudeville, stock companies and burlesque. Somewhere along the way, she was married briefly to the nephew of President Rutherford B. Hayes, Colonel William Hayes. Hayes, it was later learned, already had a wife. The "marriage," which was never consummated, was a disaster, and Loie sued him for bigamy. It was the first and the last time she ever had a romantic liaison with a man.[3]

Loie's career took a new direction when she danced in an obscure play called *Quack, M.D.* She had a tiny part in a hypnotism scene wearing a filmy costume. Deciding to steal the show, she wafted and twirled to soft music in a "Serpentine Dance," as dim filtered lights played over her body. At a time when the electric light was still a novelty, she captivated the audience. From then on, she devoted her life to the exploitation of color and movement.

Loie had a vivid imagination not only for the dance but also for creating her own publicity. She gave several highly romantic versions of how her art began. In an early story, she claimed the idea had come to her "quite by accident," when, in a play, she wore an old Hindu costume given to her by an Indian officer. In her autobiography, the Indian officer was changed to a London officer. Because she was so tiny (just over five feet), she kept stepping on her gown. "Mechanically I held it up with both hands and raised my arms aloft," she wrote, "all the while that I continued to flit around the stage like a winged spirit. There was a sudden exclamation from the house: 'It's a butterfly! A butterfly!' To my great astonishment, sustained applause burst forth."[4]

By the time she got to Paris, she also had a story for how she conceived the idea of using colored lights. She said she was inspired by the hues dropping from the great rose windows of Notre Dame upon her handkerchief, which she spread upon her knees to dry, for in her discouragement she had been weeping.[5]

The truth is Loie shed no tears in Paris. When she found upon her arrival in that city that an imitator was performing the serpentine dance at the *Folies,* she went to a performance, concluded the woman was no competition, and then persuaded the director to see her own version. She made her point and got the job. She opened at the *Folies* in November 1892, using four of her dances, "Serpentine," "Violet," "Butterfly" and *"La Danse Blanche."* Her performance was hailed as "a success without precedence in this theater," and she became the darling of Paris. She patented her designs, which called for attaching wands under her skirts containing 120 yards of the finest translucent, iridescent silk.[6]

As a result of her overnight conquest of Paris, Loie was invited everywhere. Her miserable French accent was considered "quaint," and her frank, open manner was called "amusing."

After her disastrous marriage to Hayes, Loie turned to women for her sustained relationships, the most significant of which was her long association with Gabrielle Bloch. "Gab," who dressed as a man, always wearing dark blue suits, fell in love with Loie when she first saw her dance at the *Folies Bergère*. She joined Loie's household soon after. She remained for nearly thirty years as companion, lover and business associate.

Loie's other long relationship was with Marie, queen of Romania. They met when Marie brought her children to see Loie perform in Bucharest in 1902. Over the years, Loie's company toured the Balkan States frequently, and a close friendship developed between the two women. The queen, a lonely Englishwoman trapped in an unhappy marriage in a foreign country, felt a great need for self-expression. Loie encouraged her to publish her poetry and the fairy tales she wrote for children. Despite the disparity in their positions, they shared much in common. They were both romantic; both loved to wear floating scarves and veils. Both loved color, mysticism, young protegees and lots of publicity.[7]

That night at the dinner at Ciro's, Loie looked at Alma, sitting next to her, and envisioned a long relationship with her, too. Mystic that she was, she could predict they were destined to be very close friends.

Alma had dressed very carefully for the dinner party. On her gown she wore a pair of diamond clips Adolph had given her to bolster her courage before she left home. Despite the grand entrance she made as she swept into the room, she felt very self-conscious and unsure of herself. There were people at the table who were famous in the art world. What were her credentials in this august assemblage?

She needn't have worried. When you have money, she was soon to learn, people take you very seriously, crediting you with wisdom you may or may not possess. She was readily accepted as a wealthy patron of the arts from California. By the time she gulped down her second glass of wine, any timidity she felt had vanished. She discussed the theater loudly and confidently with Mr. Hackett, the actor on her left. Leaning over him, she gave Dr. Cornelia Quinton, the director of the Albright Art Gallery in New York, advice on collecting. She pronounced her opinions about art, with the help of translators, for the benefit of the famous Spanish artist Anglade Camarosa, across from her.

But the most interesting person there, Alma thought, was the dancer sitting next to her on her right. Loie talked excitedly about the sculptor Auguste Rodin. "I have been friends with the Master since 1896, at the time of the French Exposition. I had my own theater just inside the Exposition grounds. Roche did the ceiling, in a

Above: Loie Fuller, born in 1862, was a truly liberated woman, an anachronism in the age of Queen Victoria. With her bare feet, streaming hair, and tie-dyed robes, she might have been photographed in Golden Gate Park in the 1960s. Opposite: Loie's troupe of dancers toured Europe, providing a refreshing antidote to the stuffiness of the times. Isadora Duncan, famous San Francisco expatriate, joined the troupe for a time, but later wrote that Loie's entourage of "beautiful but demented ladies" became too much for her. (Courtesy Bancroft Library)

beautiful shade of blue. I adored the Master's work, and I wanted to share it with the world. So I appointed myself his agent. In 1903, I took the first large collection of his work to America for exhibition in New York."[8]

Alma listened, fascinated. Recalling the incident later, in notes meant to be included in her memoirs, she wrote: "Loie told me no one would purchase them. They said they could buy a bronze for $25 at some department store. One of the pieces is now at the Metropolitan Museum in New York, *The Storm.*"

Loie insisted that Alma meet Rodin. But first she would help her new American friend shop for antiques. Alma noted the education in art that Loie gave her.

> I used to be a student at the Mark Hopkins Art School [but] I knew nothing of art and imagined that all things antique were worth owning. Loie Fuller and I became great friends and she taught me that ugly things were also made in the old days and you had to learn to distinguish. One must admire furniture with beautiful lines and workmanship.
>
> A friend of hers — then deceased — Gallé, manufactured inlaid furniture and glass for the masses, but he also made signed, unique pieces. Some of his works are now at the Arts Decoratif in the Louvre. I visited Gallé's son and bought a small collection of Gallé's signed pieces.[9]

In Alma, Loie recognized she had a pigeon, and she wasn't going to let her fly away. Loie decided to use Alma to promote Rodin in America, and in return she would promote Alma as a great patron of the arts.

Alma saw in this strange little woman a valuable ally. Not only was she learning a lot from her — Adolph would be so proud — but Loie was introducing her to many fascinating people. Loie was friends with everybody, from the famous astronomer Flammarion, to Professor and Madame Curie, to Empress Eugenie, now known as the duchess of Vendôme, the sister of King Albert of Belgium. Excitedly, Alma jotted down names in her little notebook so she could remember to tell Adolph all about her new friends when she returned home.

Best of all, Alma knew that Loie understood her. Loie told Alma she was a woman destined for great things, and that she, Loie, was the one Heaven had sent to show her the way.

Near the end of May, after she had been gone more than two months, Alma began to get homesick. She sent a postcard to her daughter, addressed to "The Spreckels Farm, Napa." She wrote, "My

Dear Little Alma, It is very warm in Paris today. Mother had a sleeping porch built for you at Napa. Do you sleep there? I hope soon to come home as I am lonesome for you all. Lovingly, Mother."[10]

Alma spoke so often to Loie about A.B. that the dancer felt she knew all about him. Especially about his love of horses and the sugar plantation in Hawaii. Loie sent Adolph a postcard, to the house on Vallejo Street, calculated to interest him. It was a picture of a lavish mansion and coachhouse. "This is the chateau of W. K. Vanderbilt. Here is his livery stable. Aloha. Loie."[11]

Alma's lonesomeness quickly passed and she stayed in France through the summer. It helped somewhat that she had family there. The first thing she had done when she arrived was to send for her cousin Pierre, the marquis de Bretteville, and his wife, Yvonne, who lived in the Loire Valley, inviting them to be her guests at the hotel. Not that she wanted to show off, but what's the point of being rich if you couldn't do nice things for people — especially your family?

Loie had so much to show her. She was particularly eager for Alma to meet Rodin. Alma wrote about it later. "Together we went to the Biron Palace where Rodin had his studio. It was July, and Rodin was sending a collection to the Duke of Windsor [actually, the Duke of Westminster] in London to be shown for some charity. We went to Meudon, his residence. He was away, and we peeked in and saw his collection of antiques."

Although she was disappointed at not meeting the great sculptor, Alma by this time was ready to return home. She had her tickets to go back via England, where she planned to visit with her former miniature-painting teacher, Myra Edgerly, who was living in London. But Loie did not give up easily. Early the next morning, she phoned to say that she had found Rodin. He was living in the country with his doctor.

> I said, 'Loie, I am leaving this afternoon.' She begged me to change my reservations to a later time. I did, and I sat up all night on the boat crossing the Channel. We went out to the country and met Rodin in the garden. He introduced us to his secretary. (Years afterwards I met her and she said, 'Do you remember me?' It was Malvina Hoffman.) Rodin was a little man of Norman descent. He had a long, white beard and wore a black velvet beret. Loie began telling him that I was Alma Spreckels and that my husband had some money to build an archway in Golden Gate Park (this was a fund left in a friend's will for such purpose), and she wanted him to allow us to have the *Gates of Hell*. He said, 'No, I cannot do that as they belong to *L'Etat.*'
>
> 'Well,' she said, 'Master, Mrs. Spreckels has a museum in San

Loie's graceful movements were enhanced by colored lights and yards and yards of flowing silk. (Courtesy Bancroft Library)

Opposite: Loie's troupe, here collapsed in little heaps, drew large audiences at the 1915 Panama Pacific Exposition in San Francisco, to Alma's great satisfaction. (Courtesy Maryhill Museum)

Francisco and I want you to let her have some of your works, and here is a photo of the museum.' And with that, she showed him a large photo of 2080 Washington St. I was on the spot, as I did not like to tell Rodin that Loie had a vivid imagination, and that it was our home.

He said, 'Softly, softly, Miss Loie. You leave the picture here and I will think about it.'[12]

When Alma finally left Europe, the continent was on the brink of war. "The first time we heard of the assassination of the Archduke of Austria [June 28], we were having tea in the gardens of the Princess de Polignac, famous composer and musician. Just before leaving Paris, there was a big show of aeroplanes outdoors on the Bois." By the time she arrived in New York on the *Majestic,* war had been declared.

Alma's first foray into French culture had been a success. Interviewed on her return, she filled the ears of reporters with news of the great quantities of tapestries, furniture and other antiques she had brought back for her new residence, as well as the number of distinguished people who had entertained her.[13]

"While I was in Paris, I was the guest of my cousins, the Marquis and Marquise Pierre de Bretteville, and a great-uncle Count de Brumer." There was no reason to tell the press they were *her* guests. "Among my most interesting experiences was a visit to the Chateau of Flammarion, the noted astronomer, and an afternoon spent with Rodin, the foremost sculptor of modern times."

Alma got in a dig at local San Francisco society when she let it be known that "most of my time was spent in the company of artists and men and women of achievements. I care little for the casual diversions of society."[14]

Of all the treasures Alma came home with, the one she prized most of all was a thank-you letter from Empress Eugenie, also known as the duchess of Vendôme. Alma had sent the woman who was once the wife of Napoleon III a "memento of happier days." It was a copy of an oil painting depicting Pierre de Bretteville's grandfather (Alma's great-uncle), General Louis de Bretteville, embracing Eugenie's son, the little Prince Imperial, at Napoleon's side, before Louis departed with his troups for battle. When Pierre, who owned the picture, showed it to Alma, she pounced upon this irrefutable proof of her family's importance. Pierre graciously — if reluctantly — let her keep it. Before Alma left France, she immediately had a copy sent to the duchess. The result, which Alma flourished before the press, was a tearful letter of thanks in which the duchess wrote how happily she herself remembered the general. What did it matter to Alma if the de Bretteville name meant nothing to local society? In Europe, they knew what her family stood for.

Two weeks after Alma's return, Loie rang the bell at the house on Vallejo Street, where the Spreckelses were still living. War or no war, Loie crossed the ocean (she made twelve crossings in all before the war ended), her suitcases stuffed with Rodin plaster molds and drawings. Ostensibly, she came to arrange for her dance group to perform at the coming Exposition. But her chief concern was to make sure that Alma's enthusiasm for Rodin's work didn't cool. It was Loie's dream to have a Rodin museum in the United States. She had to convince Alma it was her destiny to provide it.

While Alma was delighted to see her new friend, A.B. was less so. He took an immediate disliking to the strange, dumpy little creature wrapped in her eccentric clothing. In the next few weeks, A.B. watched disdainfully as his wife and the dancer huddled together, excitedly hatching their wild schemes. Loie, often carried away by her own enthusiasm, was not one to inspire confidence, especially in a man as pragmatic as A.B. Sensing his distrust, even possibly his jealousy, Loie realized she would get no cooperation from him, and she concentrated solely on Alma.

She convinced Alma that her desire to become a great art patron would be enhanced if she became involved in French and Belgian war relief work. Help these countries now and there will be no end to their gratitude later, Loie reasoned. Then, when the time came for Alma to seek favors for the museum she was destined to build, she would have the love and the support of all of Europe.

If Alma could understand the wisdom of such advice, A.B. certainly couldn't. To the man who was educated in Germany, the whole idea of taking sides with Germany's enemies when America was neutral just didn't make sense. But Alma, her big heart already touched by Loie's stories about starving women and freezing children, innocent sufferers who had absolutely nothing to do with the war, was determined to become involved.

In the short time they were together, the two women began making plans for a giant fund-raiser for French war relief. They called it a "Tombola." Alma described it years later in a letter to Clifford Dolph, director of Maryhill Museum in Washington: "It is really a raffle, but I got away with the illegality by calling it a 'Tombola.' Many people would rather give articles when they will not give money."[15]

Loie promised to get all her friends in Europe to send things, and with what Alma could collect in America, they could raise enormous amounts of money by raffling the gifts off. Loie implored

Alma to include Belgium in the fund-raising effort. Poor, dear little Belgium was in such a bad way!

She reminded Alma that although Germany had signed an agreement not to cross Belgian soil in order to attack France, the Germans quickly broke that agreement once war was declared. King Albert spurned the Kaiser's offers of huge sums of money for the privilege of entering Belgium, and prepared gallantly to lead his troops against an invasion of his tiny country. It looked as if the duchess of Vendôme's brother and his people were in for a long, bitter struggle.

Before the little dancer went home, Alma took her to see Arthur Putnam, whose work Alma had been collecting. Putnam was a local self-taught sculptor. He learned to carve animals while working on ranches and in abattoirs. With a few deft slices of his knife into clay he could make animals spring to life. Just when his sculptures, especially his pumas and jaguars, were beginning to gain him international recognition, he was struck by a brain tumor in 1911. After an operation for its removal, Putnam was left with a useless left arm and left leg. He could never again sketch or model the magnificent animals that brought him fame.

The sculptor and his wife lived in a shack out at the beach, near where Alma was born, in very impoverished circumstances. He drank continually to block out his pain and his bitter memories. Alma visited him frequently, taking with her baskets of food. Before discussing business with him and giving him any money for the molds he still had, she would thrust the food at him and command, "Eat first."

Loie was enthusiastic about Putnam's work and offered to take fourteen of his plaster molds, as many as she could carry, back with her to France in her suitcases, now empty of their Rodin pieces. She promised to have them cast by Rudier, Rodin's *fondeur*, and get them back in time to be displayed at the Exposition. Alma agreed to pay all expenses. (Later, after Rudier cast them, Loie brought them back in December, and Putnam was awarded a gold medal for them at the Exposition.)

Loie also carried back to France from that August visit $7,200 of Alma's money, part of it for the Rodin drawings she had brought over, the rest as a deposit for six sculptures she had convinced Alma she ought to have to begin her Rodin collection. A.B. kept Alma on an allowance — a very generous allowance — and from it she was able to scrape together the money.

To Alma, who just a few short years before had walked to work in order to save a nickel carfare, that check seemed like an extraordinary amount. But to Loie, who envisioned making Alma the owner of the greatest Rodin collection in America, this did not look like a very promising start. Alma knew from experience that going slow with Adolph was the best procedure to follow. She was not going to ask her husband for more. She was sure she could make him come around eventually. She always had.

After Loie left, Alma turned back to entertaining. While she might have told reporters that she cared little for those "casual diversions of society," she didn't altogether abandon them. As soon as the rest of her French purchases arrived (including her green velvet canopied bed with the gold swans) and were put in place, Alma moved her family into 2080 Washington. Then she and A.B. opened their house to the international celebrities who were flocking to San Francisco for the upcoming Exposition. Alma, like the city, was ready to entertain the world.

She entertained for the Duke de Montpensier, who sailed through the Golden Gate on his yacht in the fall of 1914. He was brought to tea by Jules Clerfayt, the San Francisco agent for the Trans-Siberian Railroad, who was also connected with the Belgian consulate. Clerfayt's wife, Lita, was a friend of Loie's and Queen Marie's. She would soon become Alma's devoted friend for life.

There was the party for Sam Hill, a wealthy railroad man from the state of Washington and worldwide advocate of good roads, who was brought to dinner at 2080 by one of A.B.'s customers, a Seattle wholesale grocer. When Alma found out that Hill was a friend of King Albert of Belgium, she told him about her wonderful friend, Loie Fuller. She promised to have Loie call on him on her return to America.

The prince and princess of Siam were the Spreckelses' guests at an elaborate New Year's reception. To make the exotic couple feel at home, Alma asked all the guests to come in Oriental costume. The result was total confusion; it was difficult to tell the localites from the visiting Chinese, Japanese and other Asian commissioners to the Exposition. Nevertheless, the *Examiner*, writing about the Spreckelses' party for the Siamese royalty, stated, "The reception had that world-wide cosmopolitanism which lifts such an evening above cursory frivoling."[16]

A month later, the Panama-Pacific International Exposition, the most beautiful of all expositions, opened on February 20, only nine years after the city had lain in ruins as a result of the 1906 earthquake and fire. Located on what had recently been swampland, the Fair was bathed in beauty. A 435-foot Tower of Jewels, with its sparkling rays of rubies, emeralds, sapphires and aquamarine bril-

*Christmas 1915 found Alma, wearing
her favorite dress, entertaining a group
of elegant ladies at 2080 Washington
Street. Her grave expression is
curiously at odds with "The Living
Doll," in a short skirt, sitting on the
arm of her chair in the embrace
of another guest. Today's San
Franciscans may be surprised to see
how easily "drag" fit into the social
scene in 1915. Transvestism neither
surprised nor offended Alma, who had
known artists and "Bohemian" people
since her adolescence. (Gabriel Moulin
photo, courtesy Moulin Studios)*

liants, glowed majestically over the Court of the Universe, with its colossal statues depicting the nations of the East and West. This was flanked by the radiant North and South Gardens. The poignant loggia of the Palace of Fine Arts was reflected in a misty lagoon. There was the Court of Abundance, with its lavish Spanish decorations, and a Court of the Four Seasons, with its recessed fountains and sculptures, and so much more.

All this was on the outside, competing for attention with what was to be seen inside the buildings, described as a "university of current information." Inside, Henry Ford operated an automobile assembly line which turned out eighteen cars a day; inside was a working exhibit of the U.S. Mint, and a glass-enclosed school for children of the Exposition's staff, presided over by Maria Montessori of Italy. In one building, you could use the transcontinental telephone, or listen to New York with headphones on your ears and hear the reading of each day's headlines from Manhattan newspapers. You could watch moving pictures in the exhibit halls and, wonder of wonders, you could go for a ride in an aeroplane.[17]

With all the excitement at home, it would have been easy for Alma to forget the war in Europe, a continent and an ocean away. But dedicated Francophile that she was, Alma couldn't forget. Even if she wanted to, there was Loie to urge her into action. In a letter dated December 12, 1914, Alma wrote to her new friend: "I have received your message. It has sunk deep down into my heart. Follow your plans, I will give the Rodins to San Francisco. *Come,* and we will carry out the great relief work together for France, which we both love so much — France, the country of my forefathers! And we shall, as you say, include that great little country, Belgium!"[18]

The ubiquitous Loie had been working feverishly ever since her visit to Alma to get some of Rodin's sculpture for her. So many factors worked against it. There was Rodin's agreement with the French foreign office that his work should be sold only to governments or museums — and by now it was clear to the Master that Alma didn't fit either category. Then, too, the only finished works available had been ordered years before by foreign states.

Loie was persistent. Once she knew how eager her American friend was to own his sculpture, she set to work convincing Rodin. He was no longer in Meudon. When France declared war, the Master fled to Italy. Loie went after him with Alma's check. She got his permission to let Alma acquire the pieces on exhibit in London for the duke of Westminster's benefit. Then she returned to Paris to get the government's permission for their release.

Her job was made easier when France, which previously had

canceled all plans to participate in the San Francisco fair, reversed itself. Three months before the opening day of the Exposition, in November 1914, Charles Moore, the fair's commissioner general, made a surprise visit to M. Albert Tirman, the French minister of commerce, begging him to reconsider. Moore pointed out how valuable the morale effect would be to every Exposition visitor. It would show, as nothing else could, the gratitude of the French people to the people of the United States for the money that was being poured in to aid the wounded and destitute since the war began. Tirman agreed.

Moore arranged for the French artifacts to be sent aboard the U.S. Navy collier *Jason,* which would be coming back empty after delivering a cargo of toys and other Christmas gifts to the children of the warring nations. As a U.S. government vessel used for coaling its ships, the *Jason* would not be subject to search and seizure.

When Loie heard there was to be a French exhibit, she knew Rodin's works would form a major part of it. But the idea of sending the Master's sculpture over in the hull of a ship used for carrying coal was, to her, unthinkable. Besides, she wanted to get them to Alma as quickly as possible. She knew she could count on her rich American friend to pay the shipping expenses. She made many visits to the Quai d'Orsay to the Ministers of the Beaux Arts and the Foreign Office to get permission for the early release of a Rodin collection.

A memo, dated *"Vingt-quatre Decembre, 1914,"* authorized Loie Fuller *"d'apprendre les oeuvres que elle a achetée et payée"* five of Rodin's works: *The Age of Iron, The Thinker, Rochefort Bust, The Siren,* and *The Prodigal Son.* When she got that permission, she cabled a one-word message to Alma, ("Success"), packed forty-eight boxes and crates with Rodin drawings and casts, and set sail again for America.

The idea for a museum — not exclusively a Rodin museum — had been growing in Alma's mind ever since her return from Paris. While Loie might have planted the seed, Alma was too strong-willed to be the instrument for anyone else's desires. This was something she herself wanted. Loie had tapped into an idea embedded in Alma's subconscious mind since her visit to Copenhagen, long before she was rich or dreamed she could ever own an art collection.

Alma began to see the establishment of a museum as her mission in life. Now that she had the means to do it, she felt it her responsibility to bring art to the people who otherwise might never see it. A museum would not only reflect the grandeur of art and architecture, it would also, in its tastefulness and refinement, reflect favorably on the de Bretteville-Spreckels name. Indirectly, of course. She had no intention of putting her name on it the way de Young put his name on that tacky warehouse in Golden Gate Park full of stuffed birds and miners' picks. She'd show his snotty daughters what a *real* museum should look like. She would create a whole cultural center for the arts — as fine as anything in Europe.

Of course, Alma couldn't build the museum herself. Not on her allowance. She would have to have A.B.'s support, and, since he and his brother were so close, it wouldn't hurt to have J.D.'s support, too. She approached both of them while she and her husband were visiting J.D. at his home at San Diego, shortly after her return from France.

San Diego was now as much a Spreckels bailiwick as San Francisco. Ever since Adolph's brother first sailed into the little town in the southernmost part of California, in 1887, to pick up provisions on his return from a yachting trip to Hawaii, he had been intrigued with the possibilities of developing San Diego into a full-fledged city. When the town fathers enticed him with a harbor franchise for wharves that did not yet exist, to handle the shipping that was not yet attracted to that matchless bay, he accepted the challenge. He would do for the economy of San Diego what his father had done for Hawaii.

In less than fifteen years, by 1902, with A.B. as his "fifty-fifty partner" in all his ventures, J.D. not only built his wharves, he built and owned the city's municipal railway, an electric company, and much of the downtown real estate, on which he developed hotels, office buildings and two newspapers. Branching into the surrounding communities, he took over the del Coronado Hotel when it was facing bankruptcy, established a second resort near it called Tent City, and bought an undeveloped island in the harbor, called North Island, which would later prove to be a financial bonanza when the Navy purchased it for an air base. The same devotion and commitment the Spreckels brothers felt for San Francisco they now felt for San Diego.

When Alma broached the idea of a Spreckels-financed San Francisco museum to J.D., he was strongly against it. He was not fond of the woman who had seduced his brother into marrying her. He considered her a fortune hunter. She had lavished enough of his brother's money building that effeminate French castle they lived in. Now she wanted to squander more on a French museum. What did she know about building museums of *any* kind? To J.D., who strove to be the very quintessence of refinement, the idea that his loud, eccentric sister-in-law could do anything that would reflect credit on the Spreckels name was preposterous. As diplomatically as possible, he expressed his opposition.

A.B. went along with him. It was true his wife had no experience with that sort of thing. Alma suggested putting the museum in San Diego if that would change their minds.[19] It didn't. But if J.D. considered the matter closed, he underestimated his sister-in-law's determination. In one city or the other, Alma knew she would eventually have her museum. She would let the matter drop — temporarily.

On the train ride back from San Diego, Alma was uncharacteristically quiet. Clutching the cablegram from Loie, with its message of "Success," she decided to wait until the statues arrived before continuing her campaign.

Chapter Notes:

1. Written account by Alma Spreckels, Jean Frickelton papers.
2. Margaret Haile Harris, *Loie Fuller, Magician of Light,* Virginia Museum, Richmond, Va., April 1979, p. 16.
3. Clara de Morinni, *Chronicles of American Dance,* New York, 1948, pp. 202-220.
4. Loie Fuller, *Fifteen Years of a Dancer's Life,* Boston: Small & Maynard & Co., 1913, p. 28.
5. Janet Flanner, *Paris Was Yesterday,* New York: Viking 1972.
6. Harris, p. 18.
7. de Morinni, op. cit.
8. Written account by Alma Spreckels, op. cit.
9. These pieces are now at the Maryhill Museum, Maryhill, Washington.
10. Alma Spreckels Papers, Archives of American Art, Smithsonian Institution, Gift of Dorothy Spreckels Munn.
11. Ibid.
12. Written account, Alma Spreckels, op. cit.
13. *San Francisco Examiner,* August 5, 1914, p. 9.
14. Ibid.
15. Maryhill Museum correspondence, Spreckels papers, January 10, 1949.
16. *San Francisco Examiner,* January 4, 1915, p. 7.
17. Bernice Scharlach, "The Unforgettable Exposition," *California Living, San Francisco Examiner,* March 9, 1975.
18. Frontpiece, pamphlet: "For Five Friends", Spreckels papers, California Historical Society.
19. Barbara Roberts, unpublished U. C. doctoral thesis, 1976, from an interview with Elvin Howard, Senior Guard, CPLH.

Auguste Rodin's The Thinker, *first of the sculptor's works Alma bought for San Francisco, has stood in the courtyard of the Palace of the Legion of Honor for almost 70 years. (Courtesy Fine Arts Museums of San Francisco)*

CHAPTER FIVE

A Blessing to All Humanity

WITH EVANGELIC ZEAL — and Loie's help — Alma threw herself into fulfilling her mission. Like her statue in Union Square, she stood poised, her hands outstretched. With one hand she was ready to bring French art and culture to raucous San Francisco. With the other, she was going to send back aid and succor for "the starving women and children made homeless by war." Her father, anticipating the luster her endeavors would add to the de Bretteville name, called her "a blessing to all humanity." San Francisco society had less flattering ways to describe her.

But we must digress to pick up Loie, whose machinations were so closely interwoven with all of Alma's efforts. Loie beat the *Jason* to the Golden Gate by nearly a month. Triumphantly, she returned with the five Rodins that had been at the Duke of Westminster's exhibit in London, plus one from her own collection. Alma immediately called a press conference to display the works "obtained at enormous labor and expense." She was photographed next to *The Thinker,* with headlines that proclaimed, "Mr. and Mrs. A.B. Spreckels Bring Treasures Here," and "Choicest of All, The Thinker, Will Be Presented To This City." The collection would remain at 2080 only until the French Pavilion at the Exposition opened.[1]

Despite the impression the news stories gave that the Spreckelses had purchased the entire collection, all Loie had was Alma's $7,200 down payment. Alma could only commit A.B. to *The Thinker,* which he had agreed to give to the city, and *The Genius of War,* sometimes called *The Call to Arms,* from Loie's own collection. Alma persuaded her husband to buy that one for her, because she had great plans to use it in her war relief effort.[2]

To celebrate Loie's coup, Alma staged at 2080 Washington Street

71

the "greatest celebration of art ever held in the West, and at the same time, one of San Francisco's most brilliant social functions," according to the newspapers.[3] Guests of honor were the French commissioners to the Exposition, including Albert Tirman, the minister of commerce; architect Henri Guillaume; and Jean Guiffrey, commissioner to the Beaux Arts.

For the enlightenment of her other guests, a gathering of local men and women prominent in art and literature, Alma asked Loie to lecture on the works of Rodin. The tiny woman, engulfed in her draperies, stood before a canvas screen set up in the Louis XVI ballroom and illustrated her remarks with a slide presentation of the Master's works.

"When our day shall belong to the past, when generations have come and generations have gone, the immortal works left by Rodin will remain, and his genius will stand like a giant in the storm — unshaken, unmoved," she prophesied. "Rodin, the magician who has brought out of human nature the best and crystallized it into bronze, is the apostle of simplicity, and has shown the world that only the true simplicity is truly great."

When Loie finished her slide presentation, the lights were turned on. Alma walked slowly over to a covered statue and, with a dramatic flourish, unveiled her bronze, *The Genius of War.*

It was more than just Loie's own enthusiasm for Rodin that made Alma such a devotee of his work. Even if Alma could not appreciate the Master's message, that we create our own despair by seeking unrealistic goals (nothing at this point in her life seemed unrealizable), she could respond to his artistry. The girl who had once posed in the nude understood Rodin's total and unprejudiced celebration of the human body. She could grasp the meaning of his controversial *Age of Bronze,* which depicted a nude young man so real, so full of vigor, that Rodin detractors accused him of casting directly from life instead of creating an original work. A large woman filled with great strength herself, Alma felt drawn to the powerful proportions of his works. Most of all, because of her own nature, she understood his bluntness and candor. To Rodin, there was nothing ugly in art, only that which was false.

The second unveiling of the statue came four weeks later, when *The Genius of War* became the ingenious centerpiece of a million-dollar project Alma concocted.[5] Her idea was simple. She would make one million photo copies of the sculpture, which she described as "the call of a winged victory to a humanity rising up for battle," and sell them as raffle tickets for a dollar apiece. Thus she hoped to raise a million dollars for the "relief of wounded soldiers on European battlefields." The prize was to be the statue itself. "Should the winner prefer funds," she announced grandly, "he will receive a sum of money and the statue will be presented to San Francisco." There is no indication of anyone having won the prize, nor of how much the scheme raised, but the dollars-and-cents value of the publicity it engendered was considerable. And the statue was presented later to the city.

Ingenious, too, was the way that Alma combined her war relief efforts with her determination to prove to A.B. and his brother that she was fully capable of organizing a museum. The same day she revealed her million-dollar-raffle plan, she also announced that her former residence on Vallejo Street was to be turned into "a Temple of the finest arts." (In an attempt at modesty, she told reporters, "I prefer to call it my 'studio.' ") The nucleus for her temple-museum-studio were the gifts that were pouring in for her Tombola, the drive to raise money for the French and "that great little country, Belgium."

Alma had thrown all her energy into soliciting for valuables. Didn't she show San Francisco how to entertain the world? Now she would show those society women what fund-raising was all about! By now, others were entering into relief work. The recognized organizations for aiding those countries were the Red Cross and Herbert Hoover's Commission for Relief in Belgium and France. But Alma wasn't about to work for them. She would head her own group, *give* the orders, not take them, cut through all the rigmarole and get things done!

Accordingly, she launched her "Three F's Campaign." A brochure, written in Loie's florid prose, flooded the city. It extolled the "wonderful work of Mrs. Alma de Bretteville Spreckels for civilian victims of war in France and Belgium." In convoluted terms, it explained that the three F's were the initials standing for "For Five Friends."[6] Listed were the charities to be aided, and it was noted — in large block letters — "it is for these combined works, founded by *women*, and carried on by *women*, that this [campaign] has been organized."

But Alma did not discourage the help of men. Although the fund was "originated by Mrs. Spreckels of San Francisco," it was under the patronage of "Kings, Queens, Presidents, Ambassadors, Ministers of State, Army and Navy, Diplomats, Notables, Consuls, Authors, Composers, Painters, Sculptors, Clubs, Colleges, Society, the People and the Clergy of the World."

Even the pope appeared to give his blessing in the full-page picture of His Holiness, Pope Benedict XV. The brochure also

Rodin's The Call To Arms, *(full view opposite, detail above) stood in Alma's grand ballroom for several years before it went to the Legion of Honor Museum. The Legion of Honor now holds 106 works by Rodin, the largest collection outside France; of these, 96 were gifts from Alma Spreckels and her family. (Courtesy Fine Arts Museums of San Francisco)*

contained pictures of Alma and her children, Loie and her dancers, and, in a full-page spread on page one, Alma's treasured painting of her great-uncle, General Louis de Bretteville embracing Napoleon III and his infant son.

Opposite Alma's favorite painting was a reproduction of the letter she sent to Loie which kicked off the Three F's Campaign. In it, Alma wrote, "I have received your message. It has sunk deep down into my heart... *Come* and we will carry out the great relief work together for France, which we both love so much. France, the country of my forefathers! And, we shall as you say, include that great little country, Belgium!"[7]

Alma figured she would need about ten thousand objects for a successful raffle. With all the ferocity of a pointer hunting for game, she pounced upon likely contributors. Phoning to Detroit she got Henry Ford out of bed at 6:30 one morning to solicit — successfully — a Model T from him. At precisely what time she roused the former president of the United States, Theodore Roosevelt, is not known, but he responded with an autographed copy of his book, *Hunting the Grizzly Bear.*

William Howard Taft and the current White House occupant, Woodrow Wilson, sent autographed pictures. The new friends Alma had made in France, Madame Curie, Anatole France, Camille Flammarion and the mayor of Bonne, also sent autographed pictures or books. She coaxed A.B. into donating a thoroughbred racehorse, and a rancher friend gave a prizewinning Holstein heifer. Before she was done, a year later, she had collected not merely the ten thousand objects she needed, but double that number.

While the hyperbolic brochure with the publicity it engendered certainly did not endear Alma to San Francisco society — they were finding the flamboyant, hard-working woman harder and harder to take — it did have beneficial effects everywhere else. Gifts began to pour in. They were beginning to clutter up the parlor floor of 2080. That was when, in a flash of inspiration, Alma decided to turn the Vallejo Street residence into her "studio."

Besides housing the gifts, the studio would serve another purpose. By confining her activities to a locale other than her home, Alma could keep all the commotion that swirled around her away from her ill husband. Earlier, when the milk wagons and other delivery vehicles that rumbled up the steep brick hill between Washington and Jackson Streets disturbed A.B.'s rest, the city obliged by putting large, circular concrete planters down the middle of Octavia Street to slow the traffic. They are still there. Alma knew that by being away from her home from early morning to late at night, she would be kept apart constantly from her young children. But since they were not in her care even when she was at home, she felt no qualms about leaving them.

The French Pavilion at the Exposition opened in April. When Alma took A.B. to the dedication ceremonies, she knew she wanted the entire Rodin collection, and she wanted it housed in a permanent building just like the temporary replica of the Palais de la Legion d'Honneur, built by the Parisian architect Henri Guillaume for the Exposition.

Guillaume had constructed, in only three months' time, a copy of the Parisian Palais de la Legion d'Honneur, originally the Hôtel de Salm, built in the year of the French Revolution for the prince of Kalm-Kirbourg. The fortunes of the prince fell with the revolution, and the palace was sold to Napoleon in 1803. Here the emperor founded the Order of the Legion of Honor.

Alma, pushing A.B. in his wheelchair, approached the pavilion through a triumphal arch, flanked by double rows of Ionic columns, with figures of Fame, in low relief, occupying the spandrels. She saw the lateral peristyles and extended wings connecting the front portico with the main part of the pavilion, and forming a deep court in front of it. There, in that magnificent setting, in the center of the court, sat the awe-inspiring bronze figure of *The Thinker*. She decided there could not possibly be any other setting than this for the brooding, three-times-larger-than-life figure.

Gazing at the magnificent sculpture, Alma told A.B. about the story she had heard in France. When Clemenceau, the great statesman, wanted to do some deep thinking, he would go to Rodin's studio, where the Master was then working on the statue. He begged the Master to let him remain in the atelier because the suggestion of thought emerging from that clay was so powerful. Alma, speaking softly, said she could feel it, too.

Guillaume knew what he was doing when he placed *The Thinker* in this setting, she thought. She owed it to Rodin to exhibit it in the same way. Deeply moved, A.B. agreed with her. Alma's heart was filled with gratitude to her husband, this wonderful man who could make her most exalted dreams come true. He was going to build her museum for her; now she had to work on getting the Rodins to fill it.

When Loie, with her dancers, returned to prepare for their performance at the Exposition in June, she begged Alma not to let the Rodins be returned to France. In notes meant for her memoirs, Alma wrote: "She enthused me to acquire the five Rodins, *The Thinker*, in gigantic size ordered by Switzerland, *John the Baptist, The Age of Iron,* the bust of Rochefort and *The Prodigal Son.* Rodin was going to let me have a collection loaned to the duke of Westminster.

"I went to Raphael Weill, White House Department Store owner, and he said, 'I don't think you ought to purchase them as you can't buy something you know nothing about.' "

Weill had his own reasons for giving Alma this advice. Probably because *he* knew something about Rodin — he was a Frenchman himself — and he resented Alma's domination of the scene. Fortunately, Alma sought other advice:

"Dent Robert was the publisher of the *San Francisco Examiner,* and I phoned him and asked his opinion if the five Rodins should be acquired for San Francisco. He said, 'If you can get even one, it would be marvelous.' "

That decided it. Those Rodins were not going to go back to France.

Alma hated to ask A.B. for the money, after he had already promised to build her the museum. Besides, she knew how he felt about Loie. She took her problem to May Slessinger, her friend from art school days. May had a beau who was very rich, David Bachman, the grandnephew of Levi Strauss, the jeans manufacturer. In addition to his inherited wealth, Bachman was a successful stockbroker. The only reason he and May were not married was that Bachman suffered from a severe heart problem, chronic myocarditis. (When they finally did become husband and wife seven years later, in 1922, it was in the hospital on his deathbed.)[8]

May took Alma to Bachman. Alma wrote a memo on the visit: "He was going to lend me the money on my note and then said he might die and it would look queer for him to lend me the money. I finally borrowed the money from John D. McKee, of the American Trust. Then I confessed to Mr. Spreckels and he paid for them, but said, 'Don't do that again, as you will destroy my credit.' "

Alma's involvement in her museum plans didn't slow her Tombola activities. Like her mother, she could handle many projects at once. Even Loie was impressed. Writing to Mme. Dalmier, wife of the French Minister of Arts for Belgian Relief, Loie noted: "France is indeed fortunate to have in San Francisco such an indefatigable worker as Mrs. Spreckels. She is up at 6 a.m. sending out 50 to 100 letters before breakfast. I wish France could see her. She is her own secretary and writes and sends out letters on our work all the time." Then Loie, remembering her own priorities, added, "Nothing is done for our friends without sacrifice, so what I am doing is to help make Mrs. Spreckels become a great woman who will bring good to France later on, for little by little we shall have Mrs. S. become a great art patron and when she is free to spend her fortune she will understand how and where to do it."[10]

If Loie was impressed with Alma's letter-writing — and the results it was bringing — A.B. was equally impressed with her ability to organize a museum. He saw what she could do when she threw open the doors to her Vallejo Street studio on May 29, 1915.

In a welcoming speech, Alma announced the intended purpose of the studio was to be "a museum to house Rodin's bronzes, as well as an institution which is intended to encourage the endeavors of California painters and to develop and promote international art in all the thousand and one phases."[11]

The Genius of War had been moved from 2080 to the entrance foyer of the studio. The winged goddess seemed to fly right at you, according to one observer. To the right was the Rodin Room, filled with original drawings from which the sculptor had worked. In the same room stood Rodin's *Hand,* called "a perfect specimen of bronze anatomy." There was also a California Room, which featured the work of local artists. Alma gave Arthur Putnam's animals a room of their own. An Oriental Room was filled with rare Chinese and Japanese art.

The walls were hung with the autographed pictures of European kings and queens, and Pope Benedict XV. The most prominent portrait in the room was the oil painting of General Joffre by Jacquier, signed by the French generalissimo himself, "Joffre, 15 Fevrier, 1915." (Alma had postcards made of this picture and sold them at a dollar apiece.) And displayed where lovers of books could handle them were "priceless volumes by the world's masters and leaders of thought containing their autographs."

Among her guests that evening was Charles Freer, a nationally known art critic and collector, attracted to San Francisco by the Exposition. Casting an expert eye about him, Freer predicted that here was the nucleus of a collection destined to raise art on the Pacific Coast to a new level.[12]

That was not the way San Francisco society evaluated the evening. Alma had raised *bad taste* to a new level, was their unanimous opinion. What people talked about and remembered for years afterwards was not what Alma had done on the inside, but what went on outside — the scandalous entertainment she provided that night on the lawn. All over town, people gossiped about the Black Opal Dance performed against the white satin sheets. White satin *bed* sheets. Satin sheets from the bed that kings had made love in. Who but Alma would dream of such a thing? But then, they whispered, what else would you expect from that outrageous Spreckels woman?

Viggo de Bretteville, whose aristocratic ideals inspired Alma to fulfill her destiny, finally called her "a blessing to all humanity." (Courtesy Kjeld Storm)

Mathilde Unserud de Bretteville, who bore six children, baked pastries and took in washing to support her family, bequeathed to Alma her pragmatism as well as her beauty. (Courtesy Kjeld Storm)

The entertainment had evolved innocently enough, when a bene-factor from Australia, Percy Marks, contributed a black opal to the Tombola. In an attempt to promote its sale, Loie choreographed an exotic routine for her dancers, performed on a stage set in the garden outside the studio. Alma had the sheets strung on a line across the garden as a backdrop. Against them, Loie bathed the gracefully cavorting children in rays of colored lights.

Loie staged another unconventional dance a few weeks later when she and her troop performed at the Exposition. She lay as the deceased Elaine, the lily maid of Astolat, floating on a barge in the lagoon of the Palace of Fine Arts, while her "maidens" and one local boy, Joe Paget-Fredricks, did a dance of mourning in and out of the colonnades of the palace and on the surrounding lawns.

For over a year, until the Tombola was brought to its successful conclusion the following March, Alma's studio was the setting for teas and lectures and other affairs to promote her war relief fund. As gifts arrived that were destined to be sold, she got the city's merchants involved. When the French government sent over numerous sets of books illustrated with French works of art, Alma piled them into her Rolls-Royce and motored downtown to get the cooperation of the leading bookstores to sell them.

When a collection of beautifully gowned dolls arrived from France, she placed them in the lobby of the Fairmont Hotel and in the two department stores run by local Frenchmen, her friends Raphael Weill (the White House) and Paul Verdier (the City of Paris). When she received a collection of paintings donated by French artists, she was quick to get a similar donation from California artists and then hold a preview showing of both. She raised extra money by having tea served daily in her studio by Chinese girls, a custom out-of-town visitors found a delightful novelty.

The Panama Pacific International Exposition closed on December 4, 1915. At the stroke of noon, Charles Moore, commissioner general of the Exposition, read a toast from President Woodrow Wilson, which was given around the world at the same moment: three o'clock in New York, eight o'clock in the evening in Paris and five o'clock in the morning in Tokyo. It proclaimed that the Exposition, in its motive and objective "was eloquent of the new spirit which is to unite East and West and make all the world partners in the common enterprises of progress and humanity."[13] From the top of the Tower of Jewels, an American flag, a wreath, and an Exposition banner descended on a long, slanting cable over the heads of the crowds assembled in the Court of the Universe; doves were released and the beautiful Exposition was over.

When the French Pavilion closed its doors, Alma collected her Rodins, which she now fondly referred to as "my children," and installed them in the salon of 2080 Washington. She and A.B. had promised them to the city, and until Guillaume could return and build her museum, she would enjoy them in her home. Meanwhile, she continued with her efforts to alleviate suffering.

On Saturday night, March 11, the Tombola came to an end, and there was great excitement in the city. Crowds began to assemble in the Palace Hotel by noon that day despite the fact that the drawings were not scheduled to begin until the evening. Policemen kept order as people flocked into rooms adjoining the main ballroom to see some of the more costly gifts that were displayed.

Alma fussed over last-minute details. "Go out and buy the biggest Kewpie doll you can find," she told one of her helpers, peeling off some money from the large roll of bills she was now accustomed to carrying. "We'll put the doll behind the steering wheel of the Model T. It'll give the Lizzie some life!" She straightened the reins on the full-sized model of the thoroughbred racehorse, Nezib, with a noble blood line. She would have trotted the horse itself into the hotel had the management not protested. She threw a Spanish shawl over a grand piano "to give it more charm, Pet," she explained to another admiring minion. She modeled an ermine neckpiece, carried a diamond stickpin around on a pillow, in a last-minute push to sell tickets, and lectured on the fine points of several oil paintings to all who would listen.

When the drawing began in the hotel's main ballroom, two stalwart police officers guarded each side of the stage from which names were called, and an officer stood at each door to keep the surging crowds in order. Alma, after freshening up in the suite she took for herself in the hotel, reappeared in a black velvet gown and ermine wrap to acknowledge the congratulations she received on the success of her efforts.

She was also present a few days following, when the thousands of remaining Tombola gifts were displayed and raffled off in the huge new Civic Auditorium, the only place large enough to display them. When the final results were in, Alma's fund had reached not just the $10,000 goal she had set for the Tombola, but over $18,000.

She was moved to tears by the bouquet of flowers from a Polk Street florist, delivered to 2080 the following morning. It was from her father. Written on the back of one of Viggo's engraved calling cards, the message read, "Most cordial congratulations! May God keep you in his holy guard and strengthen you to be in the future what you have been in the past — *A Blessing to All Humanity*."[14]

She was certainly not regarded as a blessing to San Francisco society, who gathered in the same hotel four nights after Alma's Tombola. She was conspicuously absent from the invitational affair at the Palace Hotel Thursday night, when all of the city's elite congregated for the annual Mardi Gras Ball. The affair had a garden theme, with socialites artfully dressed as "flowers or bugs." There were ladies attired as the pink rambler rose, a Dolly Varden bouquet, larkspurs, jonquils and all manner of insects. Mrs. George Cameron, one of the de Young sisters, came as a whole cherry tree, and the queen of the Mardi Gras Ball was Lady Bug Mrs. C. Templeton Crocker, sister-in-law of the chairman of the other Belgium relief fund.

Alma showed her contempt for the whole affair by leaving town. Right after the success of the Tombola, she and A.B. went to their del Coronado Hotel for a "brief rest."

A week following the Mardi Gras Ball, the children of the "flowers and bugs" had their own fancy-dress afternoon party at the Fairmont, also by invitation only. Its theme was "birds," and twittering among the throng were the children of Eleanor and Rudolph Spreckels, Little Eleanor Spreckels (a parrot) and Claudine Spreckels (a blackbird). Uninvited were the children of Alma and A.B. Spreckels.

Alma wasn't going to allow her children to be entirely overlooked. The day before the "birds" party, she and A.B. made the official presentation of *The Thinker* to the city. The spectacular Rodin bronze that thousands had viewed in the French Pavilion during the Exposition was unveiled by "the Master and the Misses Spreckels on 'Favorite Point' in Golden Gate Park, March 21, 1916."[15] That, to Alma's thinking, was a hell of a lot better for her children to do than getting dressed up as some stupid birds!

More hurtful to Alma than her constant rejection by San Francisco society was the fact that now she was being snubbed by the Belgian consul, M. Francis Drion, the man representing locally the very country she was trying so hard to help. Alma's heavy-handed approach to fund-raising offended Drion. When she first spoke to him about "starving women and freezing children suffering so helplessly," he accused her and Loie of exaggerating. Now that the suffering was a known fact, he threw his support behind Herbert Hoover's group, the Commission for Relief in Belgium and France, known as the California Commission. It was headed in San Francisco by Mrs. William Crocker; her assistant, Mrs. Vernon Kellogg; and what Alma referred to scornfully as "that Burlingame crowd."

Right after Alma's successful Tombola ended, the California

Commission staged its big fund-raiser, an Open Air Market, in Union Square, a place sacred to Alma. She was terribly upset from the moment A.B. came home from a Park Commission meeting and told her the women had asked permission to use the square. Three hundred women, well known in San Francisco social life, including the Belgian consul's wife, sold everything from vegetables to works of art from gaily decorated stalls flying the red, yellow and black Belgian colors.

"Many of the cakes and cooked viands were the products of the chefs in the wealthy homes, and gowns were sold at a ridiculously low figure, disregarded by their owners for some trivial objection," the newspapers noted.[16] The used-clothing booth was presided over by Mrs. Francis Caroland, the former Harriet Pullman, the railroad heiress. She owned the one-million-square-foot French chateau, Carolands in Hillsborough, the ultra-chic enclave in wealthy Burlingame.

Even animals were pressed into service. There was a monkey, trained to accept no donation under ten cents, and there was a booth presided over by the elegant Mrs. Frederick Kohl, where she displayed her beagle hounds both in person and as the stars of her home movies of the Hillsborough hunts. No opportunity to raise money was overlooked, including the one that was most galling of all to Alma.

How she must have fumed as she read, "Mrs. William Crocker and Mrs. Vernon Kellogg did not overlook a single detail in the raising of money. Even the chairs that fringed the Dewey monument in the center of the square were rented to weary shoppers for five cents per half hour." Imagine, those women with their behinds to her statue! A.B. mollified Alma somewhat when he pointed out to his "Pet" that it took three hundred women to raise a total of $8,000, while she, practically unaided, had raised $18,000.[17] Later, she would not let this fact be lost on the Belgian queen!

Locally, her accomplishments were not overlooked by the members of the Indoor Yacht Club, a fun-loving civic booster organization "advocating and encouraging yachting but without experiencing the terrors of the sea... and avoiding the use of water except for bathing purposes."

The all-male club conferred upon Alma an honorary life membership for being "in the foreground in all movements that have for a purpose the alleviation of the suffering of mankind... Practically unaided, she collected some twenty-odd thousand prizes and sold a corresponding number of tickets. She worked day and night giving up all her time and neglecting her own personal duties... She has

*Adolph Frederick Spreckels (later renamed Adolph Bernard Spreckels Jr.)
at age five gave no sign of the deeply troubled adolescent he was to
become, nor of the misery he was to cause to himself, to his mother,
and to his six wives. (Courtesy Maryhill Museum)*

just lately given to the City of San Francisco a collection of the famous sculptor, Rodin...There is a great career in store for this estimable lady, and the time is not far off when public appreciation will dedicate to her the love she deserves."[18]

The IYC was right when it predicted a great career in store for Alma, and also when it spoke of her neglecting her own personal duties. But it was wrong about the time not being far off when the public — or her children — would give her that love. The public, at least that part of it she most wanted to impress, rejected her, as we have seen. Her children were growing up resenting her because she seemed to find her projects more important than they were.

"The love the children should have given to their mother was going to their governess," said Mrs. Dukelow, Alma's nurse and companion in her last years. "Mrs. Spreckels told me that Little Alma once bought the governess an expensive watch as a birthday present and charged it to her mother."[19]

Little Alma, who inherited her father's love of horses, had ambitions to become an expert equestrienne. Her mother was seldom there to encourage her.

"My childhood was anything but happy," recalls Dorothy Munn. Her brother was a bully who loved to pick on her. She shared little in common with her sister, who was four years older.

Little Adolph, whose parents doted on their only son, was an undisciplined, sensitive, headstrong boy. He had a tendency to things scientific, which, guided into proper channels, might have led to his becoming a doctor, a desire he later expressed to his daughter, Lois. Instead, it led to cruel experiments on small animals and children. Once, he asked for and was given a home tatooing kit. He made a game of chasing his young cousins through the house with his ink and needles, trying to experiment on them.[20]

Alma would leave the children with Fraülein Buhler, the German governess A.B. had selected for her sense of discipline. Buhler adored Little Adolph, whose charm and good looks quickly won her over as he later won over each of his six wives. In Fraulein Buhler's eyes Adolph needed little discipline because he could do no wrong.

The boy displayed a curious hostility toward his mother. Who can say what resentments tore at him? Perhaps he heard the whispers about Alma's being a "wicked woman" from his schoolmates at Potter's Boys School, a block away from 2080. He seldom displayed any affection toward Alma, and their only interchanges were shouting matches.

Often, to be doubly sure the children were well taken care of, Alma would leave a de Bretteville sister-in-law in charge. The children — particularly Adolph — were quick to see that neither the governess nor the relative had any real authority over them.

A.B. was shielded from any unpleasantness and saw the children only during their supervised activities. Being at home a great deal of the time, he adored to watch them at their dancing lessons and other lessons. They grew up loving their father and their governess, but not being able to understand their mother.

If Alma wasn't a good mother, she had a medal for being a good godmother. The medal was presented to her by Loie Fuller. Loie had returned to Europe after her dance tour was completed. But in 1917, just before America entered the war, she was back. She brought with her the large gold medal, a gift from the Seventh Regiment of the Belgian Artillery, who had named Alma the regiment's "godmother" in recognition of her services to the Belgian cause.

Loie also brought Alma a signed photograph of Queen Marie, in gratitude for what Alma had done to secure aid for Romania. Loie liked to bring her friends together, especially when she felt there could be some mutual benefit. The way she had brought Alma and Rodin together, she now enlarged the circle to include Queen Marie. The queen knew all about Loie's rich American friend with the big heart who was doing so much for Belgium and France, and she was quick to solicit Alma's support for Romania.

When Romania entered the war on the side of the Allies in 1916, it found itself caught in a vise between Germany and Russia. Three months later, the Germans took over Bucharest, Romania's capital, and began to systematically plunder the country. There were no medical supplies. When Loie told Alma that doctors were reduced to using sawdust to bind up wounds, Alma's heart was touched. Thereafter, she elevated Romania to the status of a "great little country," along with France and Belgium, and raised money for medical supplies for them. Thus, a relationship was established between Queen Marie and Alma long before they met personally.

After leaving San Francisco, following the performance of her dancers at the Exposition, Loie went to Seattle where she visited Sam Hill, the "good-roads man," the friend of King Albert, whom Alma entertained during the fair. (The friendship between Sam and Alma had since grown to the point where she and Adolph named him godfather to their son.) Loie was impressed with the "castle" Sam was building on a bluff above the Columbia River Gorge. He owned seven thousand acres of adjacent fruit and ranch land where he intended to start a Quaker colony. The castle was to be his family residence. Loie thought it would make a splendid museum, one not only honoring Rodin but Queen Marie, too. Of course, she would have to arrange for Sam to meet Marie and then, well, who knows?

Sam went to Europe shortly after Loie's visit. When he met the queen of Romania, it was, for him, love at first sight. The queen wrote in her diary after the meeting, "Mr. Hill has singled out Albert and me as the two sovereigns that are worthy of upholding, and he is going to uphold us with his tremendous power [as a] great financier and idealist combined. There are... curious and magnificent beings upon this earth, and sometimes one suddenly, most unexpectedly, stumbles upon them."[21]

It was also unexpected, except to Loie, that the quartet — Alma, Loie, Sam and Queen Marie — would find themselves together in Sam's remote corner of the United States nine years later.

After Alma received the photograph of the beautiful Queen Marie, she immediately penned a thank-you note. "Your Majesty, your thought of others at such a time as this has touched me deeply. I have told Loie that while I am tied by home and family duties, I will help in the work all I can and these lines are to declare to Your Majesty how my heart goes out to you in the great sacrifices you are making and the horrors you are enduring for the benefit of others, for your people and for us all and for Humanity. Devotedly yours, Alma de Bretteville Spreckels."[22]

Once America was in the war, Alma's "home and family duties" did not deter her from even greater war relief efforts. With the successful completion of the Tombola, Alma's Three F's Campaign was replaced by the "Commission for Aid — Civil and Military — France and Belgium." She designed a new letterhead with a new set of officers. She designated Senator Hiram Johnson as the honorary president and Sam Hill as honorary vice president. She took for herself the job as treasurer. Across the bottom of her new stationery was the message: "Under the High Patronage of Her Majesty The Queen of the Belgians and Mme. Raymond Poincaré." The latter was the wife of the president of France.

Alma's response to Drion and to the efforts of Herbert Hoover's California Commission was to intensify her own efforts. Those efforts were shortly to provoke the wrath of the Belgian government. Listening to her husband discuss the necessity of securing more outlets for the distribution of his sugar, Alma saw a way to expand her own operations. What she needed was the help of some organization that had branches outside of San Francisco — a men's service club like the Indoor Yacht Club, which appreciated what she was doing. Unfortunately, the IYC was limited to the city. She wanted to expand into the six western states, and why not Hawaii, too? Going through the list of groups that could be of help to her, she decided upon

Dorothy (left) and Little Alma play a game with their father in the garden: Little Alma is about to crown her father king, echoing the royal theme that runs through the family history. (Courtesy John Rosekrans)

the Rotary Clubs, who had affiliates in all those places.

The following week, Alma got herself invited to their luncheon meeting. We can see her, dressed in her most becoming suit, smiling her most persuasive smile, ordering them to become "God Fathers" for the Milk Fund for the Belgian orphans. She held up an empty milk bottle. "This is how you'll do it. You will notice the band on this bottle with its message, 'Drop a Penny, we need many.' I want to see these bottles positioned all around populated areas such as theaters, markets, pharmacies, etc. And not only in San Francisco, but in every city in the West where there is a Rotary Club. Together, we can perform the greatest humanitarian effort ever attempted. And isn't that what Rotary is all about, gentlemen, to help humanity?"

Roaring their consent, the men of Rotary expanded Alma's bases throughout California and into Oregon, Washington, Utah, Nevada, Arizona and across the Pacific to Hawaii. She deputized her brother Gus and her sister, Anna, to oversee the collections.

By now, Alma was solidly identified in the public's mind with Belgian aid. When she organized a May Festival at the Fairmont Outdoor School, the papers noted that "much of Mrs. Spreckels' patriotic endeavor is under the patronage of the Queen of Belgium."[23] When a group called the San Francisco Committee for Rebuilding Homes in France was formed, Alma, who immediately donated $1,000, was described as "one of the first women in California to become identified with the organized relief of Belgium after its invasion, the work she initiated here in its behalf being acknowledged in letters sent to her by King Albert and Queen Elizabeth."[24]

Alma's aggressiveness did not find favor among others toiling in the same vineyards. She was particularly annoying to Consul Drion. The first shot in the war between Alma and Belgium was fired in San Francisco.

Chapter Notes:

1. *San Francisco Examiner,* March 28, 1915, p.2.
2. A "Memorandum of Agreement," signed by Loie and Alma, dated May 14, 1915, lists the purchase of five works, and an option to buy another by July 15, 1915.
3. *San Francisco Examiner,* April 1, 1915.
4. Ibid.
5. *San Francisco Examiner,* May 3, 1915, p. 1.
6. They were: Civilian Aid of France; the Appui Belge; the Ambulance Train of these two organizations; the Widows and Orphans of Writers, Artists and Sculptors, and the Friends Ambulance Unit Society.
7. Pamphlet in the Alma Spreckels File, California Historical Society, San Francisco.
8. *San Francisco Chronicle,* Nov. 22, 1922.
9. From Frickelton Papers, although Frickelton, for reasons of her own, made a vain attempt to cross out the May Slessinger episode.
10. Spreckels Papers, Loie Fuller to Mme. Dalmier, undated, New York Public Library, Lincoln Center.
11. *San Francisco Examiner,* May 20, 1915, p.3.
12. Ibid.
13. Ibid.
14. Jean Frickelton papers.
15. Minutes of the Recreation & Park Commission for April, 1916.
16. *San Francisco Chronicle,* April 8, 1916, p.8.
17. *San Francisco Examiner,* March 23, 1916, p.5.
18. *The Main Sheet,* April 10, 1916, p.7.
19. Anona Dukelow interview.
20. John Rosekrans, Jr. interview.
21. Hannah Pakula, *The Last Romantic,* New York: Simon and Schuster, 1984, p. 340.
22. Spreckels papers, Loie Fuller Collection, Library of the Dance, Lincoln Center, November 1, 1917.
23. *San Francisco Examiner,* May 30, 1918, p.9.
24. Ibid., February 15, 1918.

King Albert and Queen Elizabeth of Belgium made a world tour in 1919 to thank all those who had raised money for Belgian war relief. All except one. (Coutesy San Francisco Chronicle)

CHAPTER SIX

Alma's War with Belgium

ALMA DID NOTHING to hide her contempt for Consul Drion. As she wrote to Loie, "Belgium is not well represented by their Consul here. He is a neurasthenic. I go to quite a few social functions here and also many of the foreign consuls come to my home. They all laugh at him and say that he is always complaining about how sick he is and that he eats more than anyone else at all the lunches and dinners he attends."[1]

Whether he suffered from nervous prostration or not, one thing the consul was sick of was Alma Spreckels. So was Mrs. Vernon Kellogg, of the California Commission. Their displeasure with the woman who was soliciting funds so contentiously for Belgium soon reached the ears of Baron de Cartier, the Belgian ambassador to the United States. Early in June 1918 Alma received a letter from Baron de Cartier informing her that her Milk Fund collections must be terminated. Alma was furious. In a letter dated June 27, 1918, to the Countess Van den Steen, lady-in-waiting to Belgium's Queen Elizabeth, she poured out her ire.

> You will never know what I have been through. Countess Van den Steen, I have been stoned for Belgium, the Germans have insulted me, your own Belgian Consul here has refused to endorse me because he is afraid of some of the women of the other Committee. In fact, I have been treated like a PICK POCKET! You can believe me that I don't have to beg anybody to do charity for them. I only did it because I loved Miss Fuller, I respected and admired Her Majesty, and of course, I wanted to try to do something for poor Belgium and the little children, and of course, I have French blood in my veins — it is the Call of the Blood. I am sending to you a report of the monies sent to you to date. We will have to continue to send the money direct to the Queen,

because of the people out here connected with the California Commission who keep trying to cast discredit on my work. Remember, I wrote to you that I secured the Rotary Clubs to become God Fathers for the Milk Fund. We had the work established in six states and Hawaii, and expected to have big returns for you. Very suddenly I received a letter from Baron de Cartier telling me that he was going to appoint college girls to do this work, and that he did not want me to have charge of the Fund. Mrs. Vernon Kellogg...had gone to the Baron de Cartier in Washington — she had become very jealous of my work — and she got him to give her charge of the Milk Fund. However, I believe that everything is coming out all right...I am very glad to tell you that negotiations are being carried on between the California Committee and myself to reach an amicable understanding. I am trying to show Mrs. Vernon Kellog that I only want to help Belgium, and that I do not want anything else.[2]

Alma's way of making everything come out all right was to launch a feverish letter-writing campaign to all her influential friends urging them to intervene on her behalf. The next day, to the honorary president of her organization, Senator Johnson, she wrote: "I am mailing you under separate cover copies of letters and telegrams that have passed between Baron de Cartier and me...I do not think I will do any more work than I have already put in those six states, but I want Baron de Cartier to realize that I have done a good and noble work with the purest intentions. Everything has been done in a most business-like manner above criticism. I would appreciate, dear Senator Johnson, anything you can do to aid me."[3]

She wrote to one of her vice presidents, Judge H.A. Melvin, on July 7, beseeching him to get de Cartier at least to endorse the work that her Commission for Aid, Civil and Military, France and Belgium, was doing in California. The baron refused. He replied to Judge Melvin, "The official endorsement of the Belgian Legation has been given to the California Committee which represents in California the Commission for Relief in Belgium under the chairmanship of Mr. Herbert Hoover."[4]

The news that de Cartier had not only taken away her Milk Fund drive in the six states but also refused to endorse her work in California was a bitter blow, but Alma would not give up. The avalanche of letters continued. She had Eugene Fritz, secretary of her organization, write to de Cartier demanding to know "why Mrs. Spreckels' methods have not been satisfactory." Once again, de Cartier reviewed all the previous correspondence and went on to say:

"Notwithstanding her formal promise, and the other indirect

assurances [to stop collecting], Mrs. Spreckels started anew to place milk bottle stands, making it extremely difficult, in some places, for the Gamma Phi Beta Sorority to carry out their work... I felt obliged to withdraw my endorsement from Mrs. Spreckels' work and I requested Mr. Drion to inform her of my decision."[5]

Undaunted, Alma kept right on helping Belgium. When she collected the next $5,000, she wrote to the Countess Van den Steen, instructing her to "arrange that the [money] sent through Her Majesty's graciousness, may be given to Mlle. Gabrielle Bloch, for her Ambulance Service of the Aide Civile et Militaire Belge.

"We are indeed glad to be of service to all. We want Her Majesty to also administer parts of the sums sent to Her for the orphanages which she herself supports. We are striving our utmost to accomplish great things for Her, but German propaganda is meeting us everywhere, causing misunderstanding between friends which makes everything difficult, but Her Majesty can count on me to make every sacrifice to keep everybody friends."[6]

Shortly after the Milk Fund debacle, the Belgian queen felt obliged to disassociate herself from Alma. Again it was Alma's overzealousness in her desire to raise funds, this time for the queen's orphanages, that caused trouble.

The scandal broke when a Miss Ruby Hulin, a California writer, sent a colorful bit of journalism to a Los Angeles newspaper following an interview with Alma. The writer quoted Alma, talking about the queen's orphans, estimating that there were forty thousand orphan children in Belgium and that they were herded together in a fortress named California. The queen, the article went on to state, had given Alma her personal permission to beg for aid, and then telegraphed her thanks.

Whether Miss Hulin bothered to check her facts, or whether she wrote from the impressions that Alma gave, is not clear. The Los Angeles papers printed the article verbatim. It was then clipped by people who opposed Alma and forwarded to the queen. Elizabeth quickly withdrew her royal support from Alma's fund-raising efforts.

Alma immediately sent a cablegram to the queen apologizing for the story, which she declared was a complete fabrication, probably the work of Baron de Cartier. She got no reply. As Loie told her later, "Your telegram practically declared war between you and de Cartier. Nobody could undo it with him. He is your most difficult enemy... An open quarrel ties the hands of the queen who is not mistress in her own country."[7]

Undaunted by the lies and exaggerations of people she said were out to discredit her, and with A.B. standing firmly behind her, Alma renewed her effort to prove that she only wanted to help Belgium — with or without the queen's endorsement. In another letter to the queen's lady-in-waiting, she wrote, "If the work which my brother, Gus, and I have created and organized throughout Western US and Canada is not interfered with and taken away from us, I will take the responsibility to realize through my organization the $100,000 pledged to you in the book for the work of the Duchess of Vendome."

Whether the queen responded to that communication is not known, but what is known is that Alma made good not only on her promise to raise $100,000, but she charged ahead to make another $15,785.83 beyond that![8]

The following October, in 1919, when the king and queen of Belgium made a tour of the United States to thank all those who worked so hard for the relief of their country, Alma could hardly wait until they reached San Francisco. Surely she would be given a medal for what she had done. What other woman in San Francisco had worked as hard or as successfully as she had? No matter what differences she had with Baron de Cartier or Consul Drion, how could they overlook the fact that she had raised more than $133,000 (including the funds from the Tombola), besides the food and clothing and medical supplies her committee had sent over?

Before the arrival of the royal pair, there were stories in all the newspapers about their personal lives. Alma was delighted to know that King Albert, prior to ascending to the throne of his uncle, King Leopold, had a great interest in ships and had visited shipyards in France, Great Britain, Italy, Germany and the Scandinavian countries to learn all he could about ocean carriers. Alma would tell him all about A.B.'s Oceanic Steamship Company.

And the queen — despite her rebuff, Alma was fully prepared to love her. She was so well educated and so talented! Not only was Queen Elizabeth a physician who used her M.D. degree to full advantage when she cared for the wounded during the war, but she was also an accomplished musician, a lover of the arts and a renowned horsewoman. Alma just knew there would be immediate rapport between them.

Alma read with mounting excitement of the plans made for welcoming King Albert and Queen Elizabeth. They were only going to spend twelve hours in San Francisco, following their visit to Santa Barbara. During those twelve hours, there would be an official welcome in City Hall, followed by two luncheons, one for the king and one for the queen. The king was to be honored at the Palace Hotel by some men's clubs including the Rotary. The queen's luncheon, at the St. Francis, was to be sponsored by "women who were active in Belgian relief work during the war."

After the luncheons, the queen was scheduled to hold a reception "open to all ladies who are or have been members of any of the organizations that have in any way contributed to the Belgian charities in this country during the war." Alma was sure this was the time when she would be decorated. All the slights and the hurts and the embarrassments she had experienced in the past five years when she worked so hard for Belgium would be obliterated in that glorious moment when she received the Queen's Medallion.

The queen wired ahead from Santa Barbara to ten women, inviting them meet her in private audience on her arrival. Alma received no telegram. Heartbroken, she phoned Dr. Clampert, the chaplain of the "Grizzlies," the famed 363rd California Battalion who had fought in Belgium. Dr. Clampert knew how much Alma had done for Belgium. And so did Bryand Whitlock, the U.S. ambassador to Belgium, who was traveling with the royal party.

"Dr. Clampert...asked me to get a full report of our work ready," Alma wrote to Loie afterwards. "I had a stenographer come up. Mrs. Whitlock was a friend of Dr. Clampert. He visited them in Le Havre. He said that the Whitlocks knew that a great deal of help was being sent over by Mrs. Spreckels of San Francisco to Free Belgium. They had heard about it and knew all about it...Dr. Clampert told me for the first time that when he returned with a letter from Her Majesty, Consul Drion refused to read it and said, 'We have the Burlingame Set helping, and that is all we need.'

"The Consul has yet to find out that the biggest Set in the world is The People..."[9]

Continuing her campaign to get the queen's attention, Alma tried sending flowers. She had them delivered to the queen's suite right after her arrival. "I sent the Queen some orchids with a letter of admiration and sent the letter to the Princess Chimay asking her to see that the Queen read it. Also I sent the Princess some orchids. I never heard from them."[10]

Alma decided against going to the queen's luncheon. Not when she hadn't been asked to sit at the head table. But of course that was impossible, with the queen flanked by Mrs. William Crocker, Mrs. Drion and Mrs. de Cartier. Instead, she bought a ticket to the king's luncheon, sponsored by the men of the Rotary Clubs. *They* knew what she had done for Belgium.

Herbert Hoover presided over that affair. Alma bore him no malice. "When he entered, we all stood up — even the King," Alma wrote to Loie.[11]

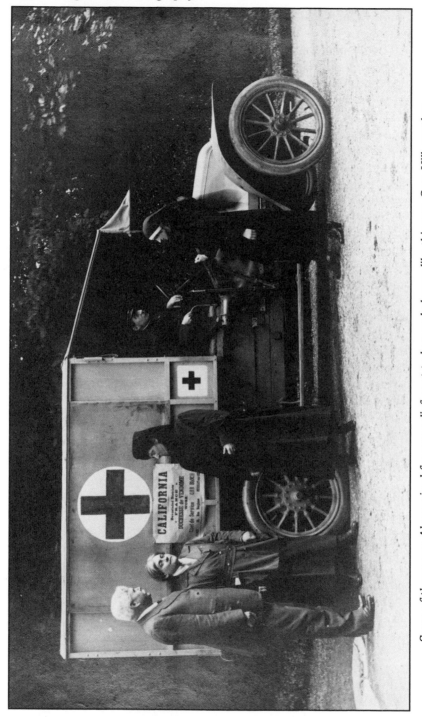

Some of the money Alma raised for war relief went to buy ambulances like this one. Sam Hill, another relief contributor, is at left, with Gabriella Bloch, Loie Fuller's lover. The sign credits the Duchesse de Vendôme, Alma's friend, and reads "Chef de Service: GAB Bloch." (Courtesy Maryhill Museum)

After lunch, Alma tried again. "My name was sent up to Count Oultremont asking for a private audience with Her Majesty," her letter continued. "I never intended to ask for that, but I met the Washington representative of the tour in the [hotel] Manager's office and he said if I liked, he would arrange a private audience. He sent my name to the Count and word came back that she could not grant it.

"I have a friend here, a Countess Von Moltke from Denmark … she stayed over in San Francisco just to see what the Queen would do. How disappointed she was! She said she knew royalty and she was sure that the Queen would take my hand in hers and before everybody kiss me and thank me warmheartedly for all that I had done or else send for me privately to see her."[12]

Since the queen was ignoring her, Alma decided to continue on to the king's reception following his luncheon. The fact that she had no card to get in didn't stop her.

> I just went in with a crowd who had cards. I would never have gone even to that audience … but I had taken the money from the public and it would look strange for me not to go. The mayor [Sunny Jim Rolph] said in front of everyone to King Albert that I was the one who had done the most in the whole of California for Belgium. Afterwards, I met the mayor in the lobby of the hotel and he said, 'I meant every word that I said to King Albert. You deserve more than I said.' And he said that he would tell the King about it again on his ride in the park with the King if he could possibly mention it again.[13]

Alma couldn't resist telling Loie about some of the women whom the queen *had* decorated:

> Miss Sarah Harker was a *paid* person. Mrs. [Vernon] Kellogg received one dollar a year and expenses, but she was paid by the Food Administration and what about expenses. She also stated to me that she had refused to meet Her Majesty on one occasion and that she did not care to know her. Mrs. James Ellis Tucker, her husband borrowed $500 from my husband two years ago so that he could go to Washington and get a position, he has never returned the money. As for the other women, with the exception of one, the public has never heard of them.[14]

To Loie's consoling comment that the queen would probably send Alma a medal after she returned to Belgium, Alma responded:

> She need not derange herself to do so. All San Francisco knew, in fact the entire Pacific Coast from Vancouver, B.C., down to San Diego [knew], what I have done for Belgium. All San Francisco

waited to see what [the queen] was going to do.

The Queen could never do anything now to make up for her public neglect of me... Fortunately for me she decorated so many people who never did anything for Belgium that the decorations meant nothing to the California people... I was at a dinner party on Friday night and met Admiral and Mrs. Palmer there. She told me of her private audience with the Queen and how the Queen kissed her little girl. Her husband was decorated. The King decorated the man in Santa Barbara from whom he borrowed his house, also the Head Detective who took care of their tour. All these decorations have been given great prominence in the American papers.

Don't forget I was the Queen's friend in front of the whole world. I am sure Marie, Queen of Romania, would never have done that to me. I received her Medal, and look how little I did for her!

I could keep on writing, but I am glad I live in a Republic. That is my answer to it all. My ancestors worked for Royalty for ages but thank God I live in little old United States![15]

After her public humiliation, Alma retreated like a lioness to lick her wounds at the del Coronado Hotel. It didn't take her long to rebound. All she needed was another project. A few months later, she was writing to Loie: "I want to forget all the unpleasantness and work hard now for the museum for my city. I am glad it is to be in San Francisco... I have very great and strong reasons for not putting it in San Diego. Two hearts were not with me in it..."

The two hearts were J.D.'s and Adolph's. Her brother-in-law, aware of the controversy Alma could generate, once again emphatically declined her offer. A.B. just as emphatically wanted the museum in San Francisco. Since he promised his wife he'd build her museum, he decided it was better to do it close to home. That way he would see more of her, he could observe what was going on between her and the unpredictable Loie, and he could maintain some financial control. But Alma was not about to abandon San Diego without leaving behind some display of her generosity. Appealing to Loie for help, she continued:

"How I wish I could get something for San Diego, too. Those ladies I met yesterday love their little museum here. You know all these empty buildings are here [from the San Diego Exposition in Balboa Park, following the Panama-Pacific International Exposition]. I told the ladies I would get something from Bartholome for their museum, and something for Santa Maria... If you could get a tapestry and a Sèvres for San Diego — oh, I wish you could — I would make a branch of our museum in San Diego. It would be a big advantage to France to have this French art in the southern part of California. Also, how much would a third set of Arthur Putnam's first models cost?"[16]

Alma's bitterness was replaced with enthusiasm for the task that lay ahead of her: the building — finally — of her own museum. The girl who came in through the back doors, who worked so hard for war relief and experienced nothing but rejection, was about to come through the front door of an enormous project that would surely earn her the love and the respect that she felt were rightfully hers. She was about to fulfill her destiny.

Meanwhile, Auguste Rodin, the sculptor who also knew the pain of rejection, the Master who had struggled for fifty years against poverty, abuse and ridicule for his unconventional ideas before he was finally recognized as the world's foremost sculptor, died in Paris in November 1917. Alma had never seen him again after that first meeting. By now she had acquired a total of thirteen of his masterpieces, all of which were in the ballroom at 2080 Washington. She owned one of the finest private collections of Rodin's works in the country.

Happily, she looked forward to the day she could share her "children" with the world.

Chapter Notes:

1. Spreckels papers, Loie Fuller Collection, Lincoln Center Library of the Dance, October 28, 1919.
2. Alma to Countess Van den Steen, June 27, 1918, Loie Fuller papers, Lincoln Center.
3. Alma to Senator Johnson, June 28, 1918, Ibid.
4. Baron de Cartier to Judge Melvin, July 9, 1918, Ibid.
5. Baron de Cartier to Mr. Eugene Fritz, August 16, 1918, Ibid.
6. Alma to Countess Van den Steen, July 4, 1918, Ibid.
7. Loie to Alma, February 6, 1920, Ibid.
8. Alma to Loie, October 20, 1919, Ibid.
9. Alma to Loie, October 28, 1919, Ibid.
10. Ibid.
11. Ibid.
12. Ibid.
13. Ibid.
14. Ibid.
15. Ibid.
16. Alma to Loie, June 25, 1920, Ibid.

Marshall Foch, commander of the French army, was one of many illustrious Europeans who inscribed pictures to Alma after World War I was over. (Courtesy Maryhill Museum)

CHAPTER SEVEN

Alma Captures France

PATRIOTISM — PURE AMERICAN patriotism — was the way Alma convinced her Teutonic husband to spend a million dollars for French culture. Of course, her goal was to introduce French art to America, and she knew Loie's goal was to erect a shrine to Rodin, but she packaged those aims inside a red-white-and-blue flag. The museum would be a memorial to the California boys who gave their lives defending their country.

How fervently A.B. bought the package is apparent in the statement he delivered to the Board of Park Commissioners when he made his formal offer at their meeting on January 5, 1920. He declared it was the purpose of "my wife and myself to contribute to the beautification of our native city something not only beautiful in itself, but also something devoted to patriotic and useful ends: something which might be dedicated as a suitable memorial to our brave boys who gave their lives to their country in the Great War, and also lend itself, as a home of art and historical treasures, to promoting the education and culture of our citizens, and especially the rising and coming generations."[1]

Along with his offer to build a museum, A.B. sent a check for $320,000 "to be used for and to insure the completion of the building." He noted that "upon completion of the building it is the intention of Mrs. Spreckels to offer to you as a nucleus of the art treasures to be housed therein a valuable collection of sculptures and other works of art by famous artists."

The museum actually cost A.B. over a million dollars to build. That fact came out after his death, when in a codicil to his will, dated September 12, 1923, he revoked a sum of money he had originally left to John McLaren, Golden Gate Park superintendent, for the beautification of the park. Explaining his action, A.B. wrote, "I do this for the reason that the cost of construction of this memorial has far exceeded the original estimates made therefor, and I feel that the expenditure in excess of $1 million is all that I should make for such a public purpose."

Alma chose Alta Plaza Park, six blocks west of 2080 Washington, as the original site for her museum. Shortly after A.B. made his formal presentation to the city, she described the site in a letter to Loie as "the finest part of the residence district. People are saying, how did you ever think of such a splendid place? Adolph is crazy about it. He just loves it. People have telephoned, wired, written and personally thanked us.

"When it is finished," she vowed to Loie, "I will declare publicly all you have done for it. I would not be worthy of the name de Bretteville if I did not give justice where justice is due... To a few, I have mentioned your part in it and they are so surprised. How can they expect *me* to have done what I did alone? People are so stupid. I am here in the West, 6,000 miles away where they do not realize the great importance of what Rodin and all means. However, I do it because my soul cries out to express itself and something in me loving art must come out.

"The site donated by the Park Commissioners is two square blocks on Jackson Street between Pierce and Scott. It is hilly in the back. I have chosen the exact spot with Applegarth." George Applegarth, the architect who built 2080 Washington, had agreed to work with Guillaume on the museum. "It will be 100 feet back from the sidewalk. Mr. McLaren, the Park superintendent, loves Adolph and he is going to make the grounds around it beautiful. Also he is going to make the Court of Honor lovely, too.

"Adolph and I cabled Guillaume the news last week but we have not heard from him yet. Mr. Raphael Weill is crazy about it and has sent word to me several times offering to help... Many other wealthy people have sent word offering to help."

Since one way of helping, to Alma's mind, was to purchase paintings for the museum, she continued: "Now, *listen*. What is Bartholome's scheme about paintings? Could he send the list and some stories about them? People naturally want to know what they are paying 200,000 francs for. Perhaps I can interest someone."

In the ten-page letter, written in January 1920, Alma gave her friend the latest news about Arthur Putnam, whom she had been supporting for some time with a monthly check, as well as a list of other people to whom she was giving financial support. About Putnam, she had this to say:

I went to see him yesterday and arranged to take many of the plasters for the Museum. I suppose that some must have been lost in transit by the American Express. However, he has duplicates. Poor Putnam. So far he is the only California artist who has offered to present something to the Museum. He is a wonderful man. Oh, if you could see him, it is pitiful. Really, he is worse and he can hardly walk. Only for me I guess he couldn't get along. He has given me his Cave Man in plaster and an Indian head, life size. I am going to have a Putnam Room. There will be quite a few plasters.

Then Alma wrote about her cousin, Marquis Pierre:

Loie, you wrote that Pierre was without a position. Why couldn't I pay him a monthly salary to represent me, you two to work together. I can't afford to give him as much as I would like to. You see, my Father has to be taken care of. You see, I had to pay his doctor $2,000 or else go to Court — and it was a French doctor, too. All the other doctors were willing to swear for me in Court they would only charge $250 or $500 at most, but my lawyers did not want me to go to Court nor did I like Father to go as he isn't just right at times. A.B. paid it, but he takes $500 a month out of my allowance till it is paid, so I feel it keenly. I asked Adolph to raise my allowance, but he wouldn't. I must pay nurse, doctor, auto upkeep, laundress and cook for Father. There are five people in his house at present besides cook and nurse. Then I help two families in Denmark, there is Putnam every month, and there are a whole lot more that I could tell you about but I won't tire you...Now Loie, I will give Pierre $100 a month, that will be 1000 francs. Will you work with him? I will give it to him for one year and also when I can afford it, I will give more...Could he not represent the Palace in Paris? You know, Loie, he is my cousin and you know he has suffered a lot. [Pierre had been a prisoner of the Germans during World War I.] It would be wonderful if he could as my cousin represent me and help ...Loie, it is wonderful that I have gotten Adolph to give $320,000 for this work in the face of unkind opposition of people very close to him who tried to spoil it and almost did. I cannot write it but will tell you when I see you. I want to go slow with Adolph...I wish I might go over to France. Would it do the Museum any good if I did? Please answer this seriously as otherwise I want to remain here to be with Adolph who has been wonderful doing this in face of advice and adverse criticism of the project by others near him and absolutely standing by me and it. I also want to be here while the building is being constructed.

Loie's response to Alma (February 6, 1920) was to give her a

*The inscription on this picture reads "Pour Mme Adolphe Spreckels: M. Curie,
I. Curie." Marie and Pierre Curie had shared the Nobel Prize in physics in
1903; she won a second Nobel in chemistry in 1911. Mother and daughter
Irene signed the picture to Alma, who must have enjoyed showing it to her
friends in San Francisco in support of her claim that she cared only for
people who were accomplished. (Courtesy Maryhill Museum)*

lesson in diplomacy. Loie was trying to work quietly "as to the best way of getting the [French] government to announce to you their donations of the Gobelins and the Sèvres...because you see I do not wish to appear to ask for it as if it were a bargain upon which you were making the museum." Which was exactly the impression Alma was creating by bombarding with cablegrams everyone she thought might be helpful.

Loie's letter continued:

> I am very careful that there be no mistake especially on your part. Guillaume came, and to my utter astonishment, he told me that with your cablegram to him he already went to see the chief of the cabinet who happens to be a particular friend of mine. Guillaume had only been able to get the chief to consent to 'examine the question' of a gift.
>
> Today I went to see the minister myself, and took Mr. G. with me, and I obtained his promise [that the gifts would be made] in the presence of Guillaume.
>
> Now I am going to see Pierre tomorrow, but Mr. G. tells me you've already written to him to work with Pierre for the museum. If Pierre and I are going to represent you here, you must send every letter and every communication you have to make through us...You see, you cannot have so many heads of things...I am more glad than I can tell you that you will have Pierre in this work, and I think it is a splendid idea that you will send him $100 every month. I shall take the news to him with the greatest joy.

In her next letter to Alma, Loie's joy had quickly evaporated.

> When I was about to tell Pierre you were going to name him your representative and give him $100 a month, he tells me you have already engaged him and sent him two months' at $150 a month. I am glad, delighted over it. But why ask me if I approve of the idea when it is done? It was only a pretense asking me if I thought it was what you ought to do. That's the way you do things, right or wrong. And when it's wrong, somebody has to fix it...You will not avoid difficulties unless you are more straight. I refer to your working directly through three of us here before we are together asking each of us to approve of the other.[2]

Alma shrugged off Loie's criticism and ploughed ahead on her project. Of course she was being straight. How could she be more straight? Diplomacy was to her just another word for pussyfooting around. You have to work as hard as you can to make something this tremendous come about. Being so far away, you have to send letters and cablegrams and keep after so many people, or else nothing would get done. This was costing her husband a great deal of money — something Loie could not appreciate — and Alma was going to see that the money wasn't wasted.

Even with her very limited business knowledge, Alma was aware that her husband could very comfortably afford such a munificent gift. The vast scope of the empire owned jointly by J.D. and A.B. had been demonstrated six months before, on May 22, 1919. That night, 350 Spreckels company employees representing the various Spreckels interests staged a "New Home Party" at the Commercial Club for the two brothers, to celebrate the company's move to its new headquarters in the recently completed eight-story Oceanic Building, with a penthouse, at 2 Pine Street. To add to the festivities of the evening, everyone wore a decorated paper hat — even the nattily uniformed firemen from Spreckels, the sugar city near Monterey. The hats, made from used sugar cartons, designated the Spreckels interests "on land and sea" for which the guests worked.

The Spreckels interests, in addition to the sugar companies (Spreckels Sugar, U.S.; Western Sugar, Hawaii; Pampanga Sugar, Philippines) and the mighty Oceanic Steamship Company, also included investment companies (J.D. & A.B. Spreckels Securities, Monarch Investment Company). There were railroad companies (San Diego Electric Railway; San Diego and Southeastern; San Diego and Arizona, which they owned with the Southern Pacific Company; the Pajaro Valley Railroad and the Point Loma Railroad); utilities companies (Coronado Water Company; United Light, Fuel and Power Company; Olympic Salt Water Company); two daily newspapers (the *San Diego Union* and the *San Diego Tribune*); hotels and resorts (Hotel del Coronado, the Coronado Country Club, Coronado Tent City, San Diego Hotel and the Golden West Hotel, Mission Cliff Gardens, Mission Beach Company); banks (First National Bank of San Diego, Bank of Coronado); real estate holdings (San Diego Land Department, Spreckels Theater Building, Union Building, all in San Diego; and the 7th and Hill Building, Los Angeles), as well as some miscellaneous properties such as the Pacific Commercial Warehouse and Lurline Baths in San Francisco, the historic Ramona's Home in San Diego and the Spreckels Salvage Tire Company.[3]

A.B.'s wealth also included the princely profit he made in 1916 when he transferred his and Alma's interest in 640 acres of oil land in the McKittrick Hills district near Bakersfield to Standard Oil. His Tanforan Racetrack in Burlingame and the Tia Juana Racetrack, just across the border from San Diego, were both flourishing.

Then there was North Island, in the San Diego harbor, which J.D. bought in 1901 and used mainly for hunting. Condemned by the government in 1917, the island was used as an Army and Navy aviation training base. The condemnation act provided that "the question of compensation can be settled at a later date." When the war was over, the Spreckels brothers were compensated to the tune of $5 million, plus interest, or a total of $6,098,000, on an original investment of $20,000.[4]

Edward Kallgren, who joined the Spreckels Company in San Diego in 1916, and was later transferred to San Francisco when the Pine Street building opened, recalled the early days in the new Oceanic Building. "A.B. had a beautiful office, paneled all in mahogany. Young Adolph — he must have been eight or nine at the time — would take a tennis ball and bounce it on those precious walls. He got away with it, but I used to think, 'God, what a spoiled brat!' A.B. had a nurse with him every hour of the day and night. His mind was very clear and he was very popular. People liked him."[5]

Kallgren remembers his first meeting with the boss's wife. "I was told Mrs. Spreckels had been given some very poor tickets to a horse show and I was to go to her home to see about exchanging them for something better. When I got to 2080, I was ushered in by a uniformed character to her bedroom. It was as big as my whole house. There was this large, beautiful woman pacing up and down, obviously outraged. She was talking to herself. 'To think they would give me, Mrs. Alma de Bretteville Spreckels, such cheap tickets!' She was acting like a queen — like she thought she was royalty. Well, I had my little say, took the tickets, and was able, fortunately, to exchange them for better ones."

Loie's response to Alma's "answer-me-seriously" query about whether she should return to France or "remain with Adolph who has been wonderful" was an emphatic "Come and bring $20,000 with you." In addition to what Alma could get donated or loaned from the French government, there were many other things Loie wanted her to buy for the museum. Early in May 1920, four months after A.B. announced his gift, Alma left for Paris to line up French support for the museum. She got it. Soon after her arrival, she was guest of honor of the French government at a reception in the salon of the Grand Palais, "in recognition of her services in behalf of French art, and the French cause during the war," according to a newspaper account.[6] The reception was attended by "members of Paris society, by high officials and distinguished artists."

Unlike San Francisco society, French society adored Alma. They found her bluntness disarming. If her manners were coarse, her wish to promote French culture in America was genuine. She so charmed her friend the duchess of Vendôme, France's highest-ranking noblewoman, that the duchess was moved to write a letter to A.B. about

Above: Architect George Applegarth's drawing of the proposed California Palace of the Legion of Honor Museum, to be built in Lincoln Park. The design was adapted from that of the Palace of the Legion of Honor in Paris, of which Alma became a member when the French government decorated her for her war relief work. The interior incorporated the most advanced ideas in museum construction: walls 21 inches thick, made with hollow tiles to keep temperatures even, an $85,000 heating system which washed the air passing through it. The builder used 7,000 cubic yards of concrete and a million pounds of reinforcing bar. All materials were of the best quality, which is why the original plumbing fixtures still work after 66 years. (Courtesy Bancroft Library)

Facing page: George Applegarth, the architect, is shown as a student at the Ecole des Beaux Artes in Paris before 1906. He designed the Spreckels house at 2080 Washington Street, as well as many other important buildings in San Francisco, including the Clift Hotel. (Courtesy Mr. and Mrs. J.J. Applegarth)

about "dear and sweet Mrs. Spreckels," pledging to "help as much as I can with real enthusiasm for your museum, collecting works of art which will represent a little of our French soul and spirit."[7]

When Alma returned home in August, she reported jubilantly to the waiting press that "Gobelins tapestries donated by the French Republic and rooms furnished by royalty of Europe" would adorn the California Palace of the Legion of Honor, which she and her husband were erecting in Alta Plaza.[8]

Later, when she was alone with Adolph, she gushed over the tapestries in more detail. She told him there were four of them — absolutely priceless — about Joan of Arc. It had taken two men four years to weave each one of them!

There was lots more, she reported excitedly. The French government promised to give a comprehensive collection of Sèvres vases, and a large collection of war medals and ancient coins. The duchess of Vendôme pledged to furnish a room, to be called La Salle de la Duchesse de Vendôme, enlisting the aid of fifty of her friends among the old noblesse, each of whom would donate a work of art.

While Alma was ecstatic over the progress made in that visit, there was one thing she was not happy about: the location of the museum. Later that night, when she finally climbed into her green velvet canopied bed that kings had made love in, she worried that the day might come when there would be need to enlarge the museum. You couldn't do that at Alta Plaza Park.

The next morning, she had A.B.'s chauffeur drive her around to all the parks in the city. The most beautiful one was Lincoln Park, and the ideal site within it was Inspiration Point.

Inspirational as that idea was, it offered what seemed to be insurmountable difficulties. Lincoln Park was the site of the city's only public golf course, and Inspiration Point was in the vicinity of the putting greens for the seventeenth hole. Alma could anticipate the furor that was sure to erupt if that sacrosanct ground were disturbed.

Another problem was the remoteness of the site, referred to as Land's End. The city proper lay far to the east; the area was surrounded by sand dunes and there were no roads, except one in the military base, the Presidio, connecting it to the rest of the city.

Those difficulties provided just the kind of challenge Alma needed. Restrictions that applied to ordinary people did not apply to her. Predictably, when news got out about the new location of the museum, a howl went up among the city's golfers. Alma quieted them with the announcement that she had secured the services of a famous golf course architect, W. Herbert Fowler, who would redesign the seventeenth hole.

Once the Park Commission approved the new site, Alma made plans for an elaborate cornerstone laying on February 20, 1921. She sent invitations to representatives of all the Allied nations of the World War, to the top brass of all branches of America's land and sea forces, as well as to leaders of civic, religious and patriotic organizations. The enthusiastic response was just as she expected.

On a beautiful, sunny Saturday afternoon, thousands of people gathered on the spot, which seemed like the top of the world with its command of blue water and rolling green hills. Old Glory streamed in the salt winds from the Golden Gate, and its colors were echoed in the banners carried by the long files of blue- or khaki-clad men. Cassassa's band played the anthems of the two countries whose friendship was to be further cemented in the building about to be erected.

Alma, looking elegant in a severely tailored dark suit and white blouse with a sable scarf flung around her neck and a flowered hat perched on her head, sat between A.B. and a scowling J.D. They listened to speeches paying tribute to the brothers' generosity and to their countless achievements in finance and trade.

Then eleven-year-old Adolph Jr., solemnly attired in a navy Eton suit with its white round collar underscoring the cherubic expression on his face, took in hand the gold shovel, a gift of John McLaren. A reporter at the scene noted that "the handle of the implement bent cruelly beneath the vigorous plunge" of the boy.

Next came the laying of the cornerstone itself. Alma supplied the first trowel of mortar. Mayor Sunny Jim Rolph extolled her as the woman "whose love of beauty and art is the mainspring of a work that will grow greater with the years."

Into the cornerstone box were placed some panoramic views of the city; photographs of the ocean and surroundings taken from the building site; portraits of Alma and Adolph and their children; a poem by Rudyard Kipling, "When Earth's Last Picture is Painted"; a program of the day's ceremonies; and the flags of America and France, made from California silk. Just before the box was closed, the roar of an airplane droned overhead. The plane swooped down and landed on the sand dunes, and the pilot rushed over with the February 19 copy of J.D.'s newspaper, the *San Diego Union.* Then the box was closed and the cornerstone was sealed.

The program concluded with a chorus of thirty male voices singing "La Marseillaise," followed by the entire assemblage singing the "Star-Spangled Banner."

Among that assemblage was Clay M. Greene, a well-known poet and playwright, and a Bohemian Club friend of A.B.'s. So moved was

Alma was able to pluck Marshall Joffre and his entourage out from under the noses of San Francisco society during their visit in 1921. Shown above are Marshall Joffre with Sam Hill, one Harry Stibbs, and Colonel Grant, grandson General U.S. Grant, visiting the site of the museum Adolph was to build for Alma as a memorial to the California boys killed in the war. (Courtesy Maryhill Museum)

Greene by the afternoon's ceremonies that he wrote a poem dedicated to A.B. and Alma titled, "The Ground-Breaking." One stanza, about young Adolph, whose future looked so promising, seems particularly poignant in view of the wasted life the boy was later to lead.

> *And when their son turned that first spade of sod*
> *I saw their faces flush with love and pride*
> *That one with rocky path of life untrod;*
> *With no hope unfulfilled nor whim denied,*
> *Had done his mite for those who rest with God,*
> *And who in spirit smiled on that hillside.*

The gold shovel came into use again in December when Marshal Foch visited San Francisco for thirteen whirlwind hours on a triumphal transcontinental tour, as the guest of the American Legion.

Entering the city at the Ferry Building at the foot of Market Street, the French hero stepped through a replica of the Arc de Triomphe which straddled Market Street. It had been designed in Foch's honor by local artist Haig Patigian. The great center shield bore the national insignia of France draped with huge American flags. On the shield was a massive wreath with garlands of flowers and greens in honor of the man who led the victory in the war that everyone believed was the last the world would ever have to fight.

Although it wasn't on his agenda until Alma put it there, Le Marshal's tour of the city included a stop at the museum site. Following a visit to the wounded at the Presidio hospital, Foch and his party were driven around the curving highway, past Fort Point and above the Golden Gate to Lincoln Park. Then, according to Alma's hastily made plans, Foch and his party were taken from their limousine and marched through a double row of uniformed cadets to the future site of the museum. There she presented him with the gold shovel, its handle straightened. A tree was lowered into place, the Marshal tossed a few shovelfuls of earth upon it, and Little Alma, whose turn it was to appear beside her mother in the spotlight, presented Foch with a bouquet of purple lilies.

When Marshal Joffre and his wife made their visit to the city four months later, Alma staged a third performance of the gold shovel ceremony. The Joffres were the guests in this country of Alma's friend from Washington, Sam Hill, who was touring the West with them. Alma, much to the chagrin of the city's noted socialite hostesses, took over one whole day of the four-day California tour. She gave a luncheon for the Joffres, a reception in the afternoon, and that night she arranged a dinner to be held at the home of Alma's brother and sister-in-law, Alex and Clarisse de Bretteville.

Sure, Alma could have given the dinner for the Joffres at the Spreckels mansion. But she wanted to show that Burlingame set a thing or two about the de Brettevilles. Even a man as distinguished as Le Marshal knew enough to pay his respects to the American branch of a noble French family!

Soon after the Joffres' departure, Alma made plans for her own return to France. With a target date for the opening of the Legion of Honor little more than a year away, to coincide with the national American Legion convention in San Francisco in the fall of 1923 (the date was later postponed for another year), Alma was eager to get as much exposure — and as much art — for the museum as possible.

Alma left her ailing husband and her children and, with enormous energy, embarked on a six months' tour of Europe. She asked Clarisse de Bretteville to oversee her children at home, and to spend the summer with them and her own children at the Napa ranch. She was very fond of Clarisse, the sweet, very pretty wife of Alex.

Clarisse's parents were English-born Jews, and her father was a men's custom tailor. She and Alex met when he came to have some suits made. Their marriage was a shock to San Francisco society, but they were used to surprises from Alma and her family. Alma thoroughly approved of Clarisse. Alma had no objections to a person's religion, whatever it was. She only objected to people who were snobby and pretentious. She admired people who were educated, and people who she felt admired her and understood what she was trying to accomplish. Clarisse fit those categories. Clarisse's only ambition was to be a good wife to Alex and good mother to her two sons. She did not criticize her sister-in-law for her unique lifestyle. Instead, she tried to be as supportive as she could, which, in this instance, meant spending the summer with all the children at the Napa ranch.

Alma sailed for Paris early in April. She took her brother Oscar and his wife, Maud, with her. Let them see how she was treated in France!

Alma's mission this time was to expand upon the publicity she received for her museum on the last trip. Having already secured the promises of gifts, now she was after a place in which those gifts could be seen before they left France. What better way could there be to encourage others to contribute?

"Of course, Dear, the perfect place would be the Paris Palace of the Legion of Honor," wrote Loie, "except that no foreigner has ever been granted such permission."

That decided it for Alma. She would settle for nothing less than the Paris Palace. She'd really give Oscar and Maud something to talk about when they returned!

Two months after she arrived in Paris, Alma cabled home her success in obtaining "a portion of the Paris Palace of the Legion of Honor for a display of art objects collected in Europe."[9] Just as she had hoped, the collection was to be enlarged to include the uniform and sword that Marshal Joffre wore at the Battle of Marne, and two notable medal collections, one from the French government, and the other a series of eighty medals forming the history of the war from 1914 to 1918.[10]

While it is true that much of Alma's success was due to the help she got from Loie Fuller, a great deal of it was due to Alma's own forceful personality and the lavish manner in which she entertained.

For example, there was the June party she gave at the Théâtre de Champs-Elysées the night Loie presented one of her light, color and dance creations, featuring the American dancer Anieka Yan. Following the performance, Alma took her guests to supper at the Hôtel Plaza-Athenée, where Marshal and Mme. Joffre and the Grand Duke and the Grand Duchess Cyril of Russia were her guests of honor. Others included the curator of the Louvre; a sprinkling of French nobility; her friend Baron Bertouch-Lehn, who entertained her on her first visit to Denmark when she was still A.B.'s mistress; and government officials from Romania, Denmark, England and the United States. She did not leave out her friends from the 1915 Exposition, Albert Tirman, and Henri Guillaume, the French architect of her museum. And, in a gesture typical of her egalitarianism, she also invited members of the Peixotto family, Sephardic Jewish friends from San Francisco who were vacationing in Paris. Edgar Peixotto was a California painter; his father had once been the U.S. envoy to Romania.

Alma loved including friends from San Francisco. Let them see how popular she was and how the French loved her. Let them carry that message back home!

Two former San Franciscans, permanent fixtures in the Paris art scene, who were never included in Alma's parties were Gertrude Stein and Alice B. Toklas. Indeed, there is nothing to indicate that Alma ever met them. Gertrude Stein and her friends like Picasso and Modigliani represented an art movement Alma regarded as reprehensible. She called it "Communistic," saying, "The screwy art of today is done on purpose...to make the people miserable and dissatisfied."[11]

From Paris, Alma sent a postcard to her son. The picture on the front was Drouais's *Enfant et Chat*. On the reverse side she wrote: "Mother wishes she could have your portrait done like this.

*Queen Marie of Romania, beautiful granddaughter of Queen Victoria, sits
in the throne which she designed and later replicated for Alma. Her four
children are (from left) Princesses Marie (Mignon), Elizabeth, Ileana,
and the future King Carol. (Courtesy Maryhill Museum)*

From your loving mother."[12]

After putting Oscar and Maud on a boat for home, Alma left Paris for her first personal meeting with Queen Marie in Romania. The queen received her at Sinaia, the summer palace.

Alma adored Queen Marie. She was brilliant, she was beautiful, she was talented, and best of all she was democratic. She embraced Alma as a friend! Imagine, she gushed to A.B. later, being the house-guest of a real queen in a real palace and being treated as a treasured friend! Alma's gratitude knew no bounds. Nevertheless, she was there for a purpose, to get art objects for her museum, and Alma, overwhelmed as she was, never lost sight of her goal.

The queen, writing of the visit later, said, "Mrs. Spreckels interested me in her Memorial to the 3600 California boys who were killed in the Great World War...I promised [her] that I would reproduce a Byzantine Golden Room much as I have at Sinaia, Romania, and in there I would put a Collection of Royal Souvenirs such as the Model of my Crown and the Original Gold Mantle which I wore at the Coronation of King Edward and also at the Coronation of the Czar of Russia, and also a collection of Personal Souvenirs of the different Crowned Heads of Europe. Also a collection of Golden Byzantine Furniture made under my supervision."[13]

Alma's visit was shorter than she would have liked because she had unexpected work to do. Shortly before she left Paris for Sinaia, she had received an exciting message from Washington. It informed her that she had been appointed by President Harding to be a special envoy of the U.S. Labor Department to investigate the conditions of women in industry in Europe. She took her appointment very seriously. While she knew she owed the honor to A.B.'s old friend, Sam Shortridge, now a U.S. senator from California, she also knew the appointment was more than just ceremonial. The Department of Labor, a cabinet department, was less than ten years old, and its Women's Bureau was much newer than that. The Women's Bureau, in the process of formulating rules and regulations, was eager to learn what was going on elsewhere in this pioneer effort.

Alma wrote in her preliminary report, "I was in Paris when officially notified of my appointment. My prior engagements were such that I was not able to make as comprehensive investigation of the conditions...as I desired or as the scope of my duty required. I visited Romania, Serbia, Italy and England, but my time was so limited that I made but cursory observations in these countries."[14]

Nevertheless, her seven-page report contained not only her observations but specific suggestions including eight-hour working days for women, maternity leaves and benefits, attention to hygienic environments, and "obedience to many rules and regulations having for their object the health of girls and mothers." Everywhere she went, Alma, the former stenographer who entered the working world at the age of fourteen, was impressed with what her sisters in the work force were now doing. "Due to the loss of men in the great war, many more women are now employed in manual labor than formerly and they show aptitude and ability which are astonishing," she wrote.[15]

Alma concluded her report stating, "I beg to suggest that many of these rules and regulations, set out in the accompanying volumes and printed matter, might well be adopted and observed in our country. The physical welfare of women engaged in day, and particularly night, work is of vital importance.

"I am sure you realize that the strength of our nation depends on the welfare of our women who are fast entering into the many fields of industry..."

In the last month before Alma returned home in October, she sent for Clarisse to be her guest in Paris. Although Clarisse had never been to Europe before, it probably took some persuasion because she was not wont to leave her children.[16]

By this time, Alma was beginning to miss her own children. In another postcard she wrote, "My dear little Son: In about six weeks I will be home if all goes well. I am longing for all of you. Kiss Papa and Little Alma and Little Dorothy from Mama. I send you love and kisses. Affectionately, Mama."[17]

Perhaps the invitation to Clarisse was prompted by Alma's desire to thank her sister-in-law for taking charge at Napa that summer. But Alma, who was so adept at getting other people involved in her projects, may have wanted Clarisse's help in the matters at hand. Somebody had to do the legwork and gather those "accompanying volumes and printed matter" from the French Ministry of Labor, which Alma referred to in her report, and to underscore the pertinent articles. Who better than the devoted Clarisse?

When Alma and Clarisse returned home, they stopped in Washington where Alma, accompanied by Senator Shortridge and her very impressed sister-in-law, called on Secretary of Labor James J. Davis to deliver her report. Marching ceremoniously into his office in her Paris finery, all six feet of her more regal than ever since her visit with Queen Marie, Alma first intimidated, then disarmed and certainly impressed Davis, as his letter following her visit indicates.

After congratulating her on "the very fine report," and assuring her that "it will be of valuable assistance to the Women's Bureau of this department in their work in carrying on the welfare of women in industry," he went on to say, "I need hardly add that I enjoyed immensely the personal visit I had with you at the time you submitted your reports. It was no less profitable than interesting."[18]

But Alma and her mission did not generate universal approval. The kind of outrage mere mention of her name could evoke is apparent in the "related documents" that are filed along with her report in the National Archives.

One is a letter from a woman in New York, a Mrs. M.J. Simmons of the Hotel McAlpin, who demanded, "Will you kindly put me in touch with the man who appointed Mrs. Spreckels to investigate certain conditions in Europe?"

The other is a letter to Secretary Davis from an irate woman in San Francisco, one Grace C. Ross, who, upon learning that Alma was to consult him on "Europe's condition especially France," wrote somewhat hysterically, "Tell Mrs. Spreckels that as an American her duty is to her own country, and that duty is to show France we will not submit to any more hypocrasys [sic] and the next time we will not listen to any more of her [Mrs. Spreckels'] lying pleas."

A quick response from the Labor Department hastened to explain the purpose of Alma's visit and to add that "Mrs. Spreckels' appointment was not for the purpose of extending aid in any manner to foreign governments at the expense of our own. In fact, her appointment was on a purely nominal salary; and her services given gratis to the American people. She received not a penny in wages nor any contribution toward expenses incurred."

On the train trip home from Washington, Alma's mind was at work expanding the plans for her Paris Legion of Honor exhibit. Why not make it a two-way street? Not only would she display the French gifts at the spring show, she decided, but she would also collect and bring back with her to Paris the best work of American artists. She would ask both U.S. President Harding and French President Poincaré to be patrons!

When she arrived in San Francisco on October 12, 1922, after six months in Europe, Mayor Rolph, the city's board of supervisors and the leaders of the local French colony were on hand to greet the woman who was the friend of presidents and queens. Also present with their customary bouquets of flowers were Alma's two daughters. They had come to regard their mother as that lady who stopped between trips to visit their home.

During the few months that Alma was in residence at Washington Street before returning to Paris in the spring of 1923, she took on another project. In addition to running an international art exhibit, she organized a drive for clothing, blankets, sheets and other necessities for the refugees of the devastated districts of the Ardennes in France.

In a typical solicitation letter, this one addressed to Dr. Harry Tevis of Santa Cruz (January 2, 1923), she wrote in part, "Twenty villages in that district are the personal care of the Duchess of Vendôme. I, myself have just visited these villages and know the great need and suffering. The Duchess is doing all within her power... but there is so much to do. The Duchess has been so kind to help me with my Museum. She, with fifty of the ladies of France, having donated an entire French room (of the Periods of Louis 14th, 15th and 16th and Napoleon 1st), so you may see she is almost one of us and takes a great interest in our fair San Francisco... All freight charges to France will be defrayed by me."[19]

The exhibit at the Paris Palace of the Legion of Honor was opened with full fanfare in April 1923. Alma was disappointed that President Harding himself didn't find it important enough to drop everything in Washington to attend. Instead, he sent Ambassador Myron T. Herrick to present a message of felicitation to French President Poincaré. Alma was delighted at the large turnout and the huge amount of interest shown in the American part of the exhibit. She said later, "I think the great men of France, and the great women also, were more interested in the collection of California art... than in any other part of the exhibit. The beauty, the majesty of the California redwoods carry a very marked charm to the eyes accustomed only to old-world flora."[20]

Back home, magazines were reporting that "all the greatest of France were there. Parisians present say they have never seen such marvelous homage paid to anyone as Mrs. Spreckels received."[21]

After the exhibit closed, Alma stayed on to enjoy the heady atmosphere of postwar Paris, which was undergoing an exciting entrance into the age of the flapper. Restricting corsets were becoming a thing of the past as clothing loosened, waistlines dropped and skirts rose from ankles to calves. Watching a group of young girls giggling over the new styles in a boutique on the Rue St. Honoré, Alma had a sudden desire to see her oldest child.

Little Alma was now a teenager and a high school student. During the brief intervals when her mother was at home, the two fought incessantly. Once, the fight was over a young man with whom the girl insisted on going out, over her mother's objection. Unable to stop her any other way, Alma simply ripped off the girl's dress as she prepared to leave the house.[22]

In an effort to establish better relations between them, Alma decided to send for her daughter to spend her summer vacation with her. It didn't have the desired effect. To the girl, being with her mother, whether at home or abroad, meant being trotted out for photographs with Alma's celebrity friends. She felt she was being used. Her mother was a stranger to her.

Alma found her eldest child to be as strong-willed as she herself was. Shouting matches between the two of them became their standard form of communication. They had nothing in common to discuss. Little Alma hated the French, could work up no enthusiasm for art and was bored with her mother's friends. The two agreed only on one thing — they could not get along.

While all of France may have paid homage to Alma, she couldn't understand why she got only defiance from her daughter.

Chapter Notes:

1. John Rosekrans papers.
2. Loie to Alma, March 19, 1920, Ibid.
3. Edward Kallgren interview.
4. Elretta Sudsbury, *Jackrabbits To Jets, A History of North Island,* San Diego, 1967.
5. Edward Kallgren interview.
6. *San Francisco Examiner,* May 28, 1920, p. 11.
7. Henriette, Duchess of Vendôme, Princess of Belgium, to A.B. Spreckels, July 22, 1920, John Rosekrans papers.
8. *San Francisco Examiner,* August 9, 1920, p. 9.
9. *San Francisco Examiner,* June 9, 1922, p. 5.
10. Ibid.
11. Letter to Clifford Dolph, January 3, 1949, Maryhill Museum.
12. Spreckels Papers, Archives of American Art, Smithsonian Institution, Gift of Dorothy Spreckels Munn.
13. Queen Marie to Alma Spreckels, John Rosekrans papers.
14. National Archives, Washington, D.C., Record Group 174, Department of Labor, Office of Chief Clerk, file 156/13.
15. Ibid.
16. Charles de Bretteville interview.
17. Spreckels Papers, op. cit.
18. James L. Davis to Alma Spreckels, October 1922, John Rosekrans papers.
19. Tevis Family Papers, Bancroft Library, U.C. Berkeley.
20. *San Francisco Examiner,* August 8, 1923, p. 15.
21. *Overland Monthly & Out West Magazine,* March 1924, p. 103.
22. Edith de Bretteville Walsh interview.

Alma, in severe but stylish dress, posed on the steps of 2080 Washington Street in 1921. (Courtesy Archives, San Francisco Public Library)

126

CHAPTER EIGHT

Queen of the City

 ALMA SAT AMONG THE Gold Star Mothers two months later when the American Legion, holding its national convention in San Francisco in October 1923, came to affix a plaque to her uncompleted museum honoring the California dead "who gave their lives that we might be free."

The night before, the Legionnaires had whooped it up during their parade through downtown. In the city where Prohibition had few supporters, people lining the streets laughed and cheered as the veterans marched behind a float, the "S.S. Bootlegger," a "rum-runner from St. Helena, where the good grapes grow," as it rolled up Market Street, escorted by a platoon of mounted police.

This morning, as the survivors of the War to End All Wars honored the eternal memory of their dead comrades, their mood was somber. A speakers' stand, set up in the Court of Honor, was decorated with greens and tricolored bunting. Alma was full of sympathy for the Gold Star Mothers, many of whom had given two, three and even more sons to the cause of civilization. With them sat the amputees, the blinded, the shell-shocked and the other wounded representatives of the Disabled American Veterans. National American Legion Commander Alvin Owsley affixed a plaque which read: "That Men May Not Forget, the Living Legion, in convention, speaking comradeship with the dead again, voice their love for those who gave their lives that we might be free."

Since A.B. could not stand up to speak before an audience, Senator Shortridge did the honors. Despite Alma's newfound feminist awareness, it did not occur to her — or to anyone else — that she speak on her husband's behalf. But if her tongue was silent, her mind was racing ahead.

It was probably at these ceremonies that Alma conceived the idea for her Book of Gold, a project that would take her the next eight years to complete. In the days before computers made the task easy, she decided she would find the names and hometowns of each of the 3,600 boys from California who were buried on French soil. Her intention was to record the information in a book and dedicate it to their mothers. She wrote about the project years later in a letter to Clifford Dolph. She wanted Dolph to use the information as leverage in securing Portland bank president Frank Belgrano as a member of Maryhill Museum's board of trustees. Belgrano, a former American Legion national committeeman, had been present that day at the dedication of the plaque.

"I had the military records searched for the names of the California boys who died in France," wrote Alma. "It took years. The names of the boys are in this book and messages to the Mothers of the Heroes who died for their Country. Signed by the greatest people in France, including Marshals Foch and Joffre. The book is now at the entrance of the California Palace of the Legion of Honor.

"At an official function given by the American Legion at the Civic Auditorium, I think Mr. Belgrano was Grand Commander, I presented The Book to the Gold Star Mothers and they presented it to the L. of H. Palace. Go over and show this photo to Mr. Belgrano and tell him you are going to frame it and hang it at Maryhill Museum."[1]

The huge, gold moiré-covered book, with its ivory cross overlaid upon it, resembled a giant family bible. All the pages were heavy parchment. The list of names and all the messages inside were done in calligraphy. Loie Fuller, who jumped in enthusiastically to get the greetings from the French generals and statesmen, wrote to Alma that "you were a great woman to make [the book] dear, and that work alone here will open ways for you to reach paths not trod by others."

The Book of Gold, resting on its pedestal, occupied a conspicuous place inside the entrance to the museum for nearly a quarter of a century. It was retired to the Legion of Honor archives at the start of World War II. In 1923, with the museum in its final stages of completion, Alma turned to a new building project, the remodeling of A.B.'s ranch at Napa, where she had spent many clandestine weekends before their marriage. The ranch, which A.B. had originally purchased in 1898, contained the finest accommodations for the breeding and training of racehorses. But the ranch house itself, though comfortable and pleasant, was hardly in keeping with Alma's new concepts of what a country estate should be. With A.B.'s indulgence, she ordered the house demolished. In its place, workmen began construction on a new 57-room mansion which Alma would soon fill with costly antiques and paintings. In the manner of the French chateaux, she created "apartments" within the building so that each of the children would have his or her own quarters.

Most of the land was fairly flat, but there were rolling hills for horses to graze, a prune orchard, hen houses and riding paths. With the addition of a swimming pool which Alma ordered to be built, her remodeling would make the ranch an even more delightful summer place for children, as well as a showplace for grown-ups. A.B., pleased with what his wife was doing, promptly christened it Alma Villa. Unfortunately, he would never live to see the job completed.

While work was going on in Napa, Alma sat still long enough to have her portrait painted by Richard Hall, whom she met in Paris, where he had painted many of her friends in the nobility. By this time, some of the furnishings for Queen Marie's "Romanian Room" had arrived, and Alma chose the intricately carved, high-backed, silver-and-gold-inlaid throne chair as a fitting prop.

In a brocade gown under a mantle of sables, she graced the throne with regal dignity. In a canvas seven feet high by five feet wide, the artist painted Alma at the zenith of her power. Behind her were the honors and the love bestowed upon her by the French. Ahead, she could anticipate the tribute that was sure to come with the opening of her museum. Despite the fact that she was now in her forties, the beauty of her face and her figure, which earlier had made her the delight of photographers, painters and sculptors, was still very much in evidence. The artist faithfully reproduced all that, and accurately portrayed her determination in the firm set of her jaw. But he caught something else. He caught in her eyes a look of wistfulness reflecting the pain of past hurts and hinting at the insecure woman under all her bravado.

Richard Hall also did a portrait of Clarisse, in which he captured the essence of Alma's sister-in-law, the homemaker, seated contentedly with her two sons.

Alma staged a large tea for more than two hundred and fifty people, ostensibly to honor the painter, but in reality to unveil before San Francisco its new Queen of the City. A large buffet table, done in gold colors with garlands of daffodils and masses of spring flowers in large, polished brass bowls, graced the ballroom at 2080 Washington. Mrs. Lita Clerfayt, now home from Paris, where she lived for several years after her husband died, and Mrs. Edgar Peixotto helped Alma greet guests. Lita, a well-loved figure among the city's elite, was as gentle and soft-spoken as Alma was coarse and loud.

*Alma's daughters dressed as royal French pages for the lavish ceremonies
staged by the American League of Penwomen to honor Big Alma in
1924. It is not hard to see which daughter enjoyed herself more.
(Courtesy Archives, San Francisco Public Library)*

It was probably her presence that was responsible for so many of the socialites in the crowd, among them Eleanor and Rudolph Spreckels.

If San Francisco society didn't get the message about the city's new reigning queen, the local chapter of the American League of Penwomen certainly did. Two weeks later, before five hundred people, they acknowledged Alma's sovereignty in elaborate ceremonies in the Gold Room of the Fairmont Hotel. In a French setting of the period of Louis XV, the Penwomen staged a series of tableaux honoring her "in recognition for the service that Mrs. Spreckels is rendering in advancing art and letters on the Pacific Coast."[2]

In the opening tableau, Alma, wearing a lace-draped gown of white satin and a large black picture hat, was escorted to the "throne of honor" by two costumed pages. One of the pages was her reluctant daughter, Little Alma. The flower girl, whose duty it was to strew petals in the "Queen's" path, was shy little Dorothy.

Outside the hotel, floral tributes rained from the sky, dropped by a squadron of five Army airplanes. Inside, the felicitations of the Army, Navy and the city of San Francisco were expressed by General Morton, Admiral Simpson and Mayor Rolph. Even President Harding sent his tribute to the occasion via a special representative.

All this adulation didn't turn Alma's head away from her duties. Her immediate priority was to get rid of the man appointed as the museum's first director, Arthur Upham Pope, the only credentialed museum director available at the time. Pope's claim to fame was as a celebrated Persian scholar.

"What the hell good is that kind of expertise in a *French* museum?" she demanded of Herbert Fleishhacker, who as president of the Park Commission had appointed him. When she learned that Pope had never visited Persia and had always wanted to go, Alma presented him and his wife with one-way tickets to that country, and then had him replaced with Cornelia Sage Quinton, director of the Albright Art Gallery in Buffalo, and her friend since that 1914 Paris dinner where Alma had met Loie Fuller. Before Dr. Quinton left New York, Alma had a job for her to do. In a letter to her, dated June 10, 1924, Alma wrote:

"I almost wired you to go to the Metropolitan Museum and make an investigation of how they run the educational part of the Museum. I want the Board of Education to co-operate with us here. Perhaps they will give us something in their budget. If you are still in New York, will you get all the literature and their system. I notice that they have 30,000 slides and that they lend them all over the state ... and that teachers and public school children get in free at all times.

"I am trying continually to make friends for the Museum. It has been a great deal of work and I will be glad when you arrive as I have been carrying on the burden alone. I lost one year through the Popes..."[3]

Alma suffered a far greater loss when, on June 29, 1924, six months before the opening of the museum, A.B. died. He had been ill with a cold for several weeks. When it progressed to pneumonia, Alma decided to get the children out of the house. "We were making too much noise and Mother didn't want to disturb Daddy's rest," Dorothy recalled. "I was sent to Fallen Leaf Lake with Aunt Clarisse."

Little Alma, who loved to be around horses, was sent up to the Napa stock farm with her older cousin, Edith, daughter of Walter de Bretteville. "We rushed back as soon as we got the news," recalled Edith. Aunt Alma was so distraught."

Alma arranged for her son to go on an automobile trip with his uncle and cousins. Fortunately, the motor party was equipped with a radio receiving set, and calls for the boy were broadcast from sending stations in the Bay Area.

A.B. died during the night; the official cause was a cerebral hemorrhage. When young Adolph arrived home the next morning, Alma turned to her only son for comfort. Instead of responding to her tearful hug, the boy pushed his mother away, screaming with anger.[4]

"You bitch," he shouted at her. "You deliberately sent me away so I would never see my father again!" All the bitterness he felt toward her, all the whispers about her, all the sniggering of the boys at school, came rushing out in a torrent of invectives. Alma, unable to speak, stood there, ashen, as her son ended his tirade by shouting hoarsely, "You whore! Everybody knows you're nothing but a whore!"[5]

The funeral was delayed until the arrival of J.D. He had been on his yacht, the *Venetia,* going through the Panama Canal on his way back from the Republican National Convention in New York when he got the news.

A.B.'s death left Alma devastated. She felt completely alone with three children she hardly knew. Her adored A.B.! Gone was the man who had been husband, father and mentor to her, who had snatched her from a mediocre existence and enabled her to become an international celebrity. Her A.B., the man who called her his "Pet," the man who stood by her and her ideas even against the advice of his brother and his best friends. She felt the irony of the fact that he had not lived long enough to see what his money and her work had produced. Despite all her bluster and pretentions, underneath it all she was a self-conscious, uneducated, insecure woman who needed the support — both moral and financial — that A.B. had always lavished upon her. "Everything I know I learned from my husband," Alma told Anona Dukelow years later.

Although A.B. had left her alone, he also left her "one of the wealthiest women in the West," according to Attorney William I. Brobeck when he revealed A.B.'s will, which was reputed to be around $15 million, the equivalent of more than $100 million in 1990 dollars. With the exception of a $100,000 bequest to charities and several gifts to friends and business associates, one half of the estate went to Alma and the other half to the three children.

A.B., knowing Alma's propensity for spending money on art, left her the money in trust. He knew the influence Loie had over his wife, and how nothing could stop Alma once she made up her mind to possess something. According to the terms of the will, "one half of the net income from the estate is to be paid at practical intervals to Mrs. Spreckels as long as she lives, her share to go to the children upon her death. The income from the remaining half of the estate is to be accumulated for the children and paid to each in equal shares as she or he reaches legal age. When the youngest of the children becomes of age, the principal of the trust estate is to be equally divided among them."[6]

Leaving his wife's money in trust was unquestionably the wisest move A.B. could have made. While it was a source of much irritation to Alma, it also provided her with what she considered an ironclad alibi for turning down pleas for money. "You know, Pet," she'd rasp, "I'm in trust!" For four years after A.B.'s death, she had to make do on $25,000 a month drawn against that trust. In 1930, during the Depression, she agreed reluctantly to a reduction to $12,500.

That will, over the years, was to be challenged constantly in the courts by Alma and by the children. In 1931, when Alma had gone through a total of $1,700,000, she went to court to have this sum charged against the estate that would ultimately be divided by the children, rather than against her half of the estate.

When little Alma married Jack Rosekrans before she became of age to inherit her share of the estate, she sued on grounds that if she were legally old enough to marry, she should be legally old enough to assume her inheritance. The Spreckels family would be back in court again in 1948, when Adolph Jr. filed suit against his mother and sisters for mishandling of his father's fortune.

A.B.'s will also provided an income of $250 a month for life for Alma's older sister, Anna de Bretteville. It was probably the only

When Adolph Spreckels died in June 1924 his brother J.D. came at once from San Diego; Alma met him at the Southern Pacific station. The Spreckels-owned San Francisco Call *noted that their sorrow was lightened by their affectionate greeting. (Courtesy Archives, San Francisco Public Library)*

steady income she had. Inordinately proud of her noble name, Anna never found anyone worthy of changing it in marriage. After A.B.'s death, she went to Europe, where she moved in with another de Bretteville, Carl, an uncle only slightly older than herself.[7]

With astonishing naivete, Alma completely misunderstood A.B.'s bequest to Anna. She believed her husband did it only to please her. Alma was very protective of her family and in one fashion or another had seen to it that they were all taken care of. When her brother Oscar lost an arm in an industrial accident, she had A.B. give him a job in San Diego supervising rental properties the Spreckels Company owned there. When Walter's over-fondness for women caused problems in San Francisco, she sent him to Napa, where A.B. made him superintendent of the breeding farm. When Gus, who persisted in chasing after nonexistent gold mines and oil wells, got into financial binds, she was quick to provide him with money. She even took care of Alex, the one brother who didn't need her help. After A.B. died, she insisted that Alex leave his job as vice president of the Union Iron Works in order to represent her interests as vice president of the J.D. and A.B. Spreckels Company, although he had no knowledge of the sugar business.

What Alma failed to realize was that A.B. left the bequest to Anna out of gratitude to her for moving into his home and replacing her sister in all the wifely duties Alma was seldom around to perform. "Love to the children, Anna and you," Alma would write on postcards mailed from Europe. So intent was she on her museum-building that she completely failed to imagine the results when two lonely people are thrown together in close proximity.

While it was rumored that Anna was actually A.B.'s mistress for some years before his death, that does not seem likely in view of his impotence. But she was on hand to feed his fantasies, and for this, in a modest way, he showed his gratitude.

A.B. had hoped that his son would one day take over the Napa ranch. In his will, he instructed the trustees to retain the ranch until the termination of the trust, when his son "shall have the right to take the property as part of his share of the estate and at a reasonable value."

Alma went to court early in November to have little Adolph's name legally changed from Adolph Frederick to Adolph Bernard, "so that he may bear the name of his father." The court granted her petition.[8] It didn't matter to her that her son would bear the same name as his cousin, Adolph Bernard Spreckels, J.D.'s grandson, who was several years older, and who was the reason Alma's son had been named Adolph Frederick in the first place.

Alma had long since dismissed her son's actions the night of his father's death as just his way of showing grief. The boy, not yet thirteen when his father died, had always been a difficult child. She remembered when Mr. Clark, the tutor A.B. had hired to instruct him, quit after calling the boy "uncontrollable." She ignored Clark's emphatic suggestion that she get psychiatric help for him. She knew why he was uncontrollable: "He has a temper because he had a bad fall when he was little," she told the tutor.[9]

It wasn't her son that caused her sleepless nights. It was worrying about the museum. She was sure it would be a failure. Without A.B.'s support, her bouts of depression returned. J.D. was right: what did she know about how a museum should be built and what should go inside it? For all her good intentions, wasn't she, after all, just an uncultured, uneducated woman? She didn't care so much about the opinion of the Burlingame crowd — nothing she could do would get their approval — but what about The People? She was doing this for them. Papa taught her about *noblesse oblige*. She had a duty to people who worked so hard to feed their families that they never had time or money for anything else. Alma wanted a place for them to go which, without costing anything beyond streetcar fare, would enrich their lives.

Alma, who was not at all religious, even went so far as to ask God's help. "I do not feel that I am building this building at all," she used to say. "I just happened to be the instrument and I ask God each day and many times each day to help me to do it right."[10]

She did it right. The first to have their lives enriched were grammar school children. Like the children's party held at 2080 Washington before the family had even moved in, the first affair at the museum was for kids. On November 2, 1924, hundreds of children, some accompanied by teachers and parents, were loaded into buses at the foot of Lincoln Park and deposited at the entrance of the Palace. The children were captivated by de Chauvannes's *The Poor Fisherman*, the Joan of Arc tapestries, and the bright colors in galleries devoted to the collection of works by French painters such as Gauguin, Matisse and Cézanne, on loan from the Louvre. Alma read with satisfaction the response of Aaron Altman, director of art in the public schools, who appointed himself guide that morning. He enthused to reporters that "a new epoch seems to have begun for art... No normal boy or girl can behold these without some quickening of the pulse and the stirring of the imagination."[11]

Two days later, on Election Day, November 4, 1924, San Francisco voters who may or may not have voted in Calvin Coolidge as the new U.S. president overwhelmingly approved City Charter

Amendment No. 28, thereby formally accepting the California Palace of the Legion of Honor. Acceptance meant the city would pay administration costs, and upkeep of the building and grounds. The museum would be run by its own board of trustees, of whom the park commissioner was to be a member, and Alma (although it was never spelled out) would always be honorary president. On the same day, the voters also passed Charter Amendment No. 29, by which the city accepted the de Young Museum.

To compare the two museums — even to call the de Young a museum — was laughable to Alma. If there were any doubts about who was bringing culture to San Francisco, all you had to do was to read the *Chronicle* that week about what was big news at the de Young. Their idea of a work of art was a portrait of a member of the Vigilantes donated by a Mrs. Charles Coham. As for decorative arts, how about that latest acquisition, the bronze tablet commemorating the hundredth anniversary of the Detroit Lodge, No. 2, Free and Accepted Masons?[12]

The night before Armistice Day, Alma hosted a reception to preview the Legion of Honor. Gowned in majestic black velvet, she received her guests in the rotunda of the Palace. Her only jewelry was a magnificent string of pearls each the size of a bird egg, A.B.'s last gift to her. At her side were her three children; her brother-in-law J.D.; her cousin, Marquis Pierre de Bretteville, and his wife, Marquise Yvonne; and her brothers Alexander and Oscar, along with their wives.

Of all those close to her, only Loie was missing. Despite what Alma had promised Loie about "declaring publicly all you have done" and "giving justice where justice is due," the little dancer was absent. She was on tour in England with her troupe of young girls. Certainly she could have arranged to be present had Alma sent for her, as she had for Pierre and Yvonne. Alma did not, perhaps because she felt A.B. would not have wanted it, or, more likely, because she felt tonight was hers, and she wasn't willing to share the spotlight with Loie.

Guests, passing through the receiving line in the Court of Honor, walked in awe through the galleries. So fabulous was the museum, so unlike anything that San Francisco had ever seen, that even the *Chronicle* voiced its praise. "The elite of San Francisco's world of fashion, art and wealth had the pleasure of a private view of the loan collection of masterpieces and also enjoyed a leisurely survey of the California Palace of the Legion of Honor at a reception Monday night given by Mrs. Spreckels." "Graced by the presence of the official representatives of the French government, M. Albert Tirman,

Construction is almost finished on the splendid California Palace of the Legion of Honor in this 1924 photograph. (Courtesy Archives, San Francisco Public Library)

counsellor of the State [of France] and M. Jean Guiffrey, conservateur of the Louvre, it was one of the most impressive occasions in the history of the new and greater San Francisco," reported the *San Francisco Examiner.*

There were more than seven hundred works of art exhibited in the nineteen galleries on the main floor, the first five of which were "International Rooms" displaying the Romanian, Serbian, Polish and Belgian gifts Alma had collected on her European tours.

Two galleries were given over to Alma's Rodin collection, which now contained thirty-one pieces. (She did not give the collection to the museum at this time; she lent them.) Here, for the first time, art lovers in western America could see two exact-size copies of his masterpieces in the Louvre, *The Age of Iron* and *John the Baptist.* They could study his controversial bust of Rochefort, and his heads of Hugo and Balzac, and a half-dozen heads of lesser-known figures.

The next most important sculpture exhibit was that of Arthur Putnam's animals, which, as Alma had promised, were displayed in a gallery of their own. The collection of jaguars, pumas, pythons, wild boars and humans, equally primitive, for which Alma had given the ailing Putnam $5,000, were cast in bronze by the same foundryman who had worked for Rodin.

Putnam's biographer, Julia Heyneman, writing about it in her book, *Arthur Putnam, Sculptor,* said, "California owes Mrs. Spreckels a great debt for the fine imaginative conception to which alone the preservation, in permanent form, of so much of Putnam's finest work is due."

Another gallery contained the loan collection of priceless French paintings from the Louvre. Included were masterpieces by Corot, Cézanne, Degas, Gauguin and Van Gogh, painters whose works had never before been seen in the western United States.

The duchess of Vendôme had a gallery of her own devoted to the gifts and loans she collected from her friends, and the two garden courts contained examples of French architecture. In addition, there were galleries devoted to the Gobelins tapestries, to the Sèvres collection, to French sculpture (including Alma's Riviere collection, with his masterpiece, *Le Roghi*), French furniture and French costumes. One gallery was given over to "souvenirs of French America," and one room was designated as the "Alma, Dorothy, Adolph Jr. Room," in which Alma donated a collection of rare Egyptian art given in the name of her children. And in the rotunda there was the huge pipe organ, donated by J.D. in memory of his brother, standing as a promise that music would always play a prominent part in this monument to culture.

Opening day of the California Palace of the Legion of Honor, on Armistice Day, November 11, 1924, drew crowds to Lincoln Park to see Rodin's Thinker *and hear speeches in the courtyard, then to view 700 works of art in 19 galleries, the most important exhibit ever assembled in California. The museum was a memorial to California servicemen killed in the Great War; luckier survivors stand between the columns of the courtyard. It was also a memorial to Adolph Spreckels, who paid for it. And it was a triumph for Alma, who had brought French culture to San Francisco and was now the queen of arts in her home town. She was also the richest woman in western America. (Courtesy Archives, San Francisco Public Library)*

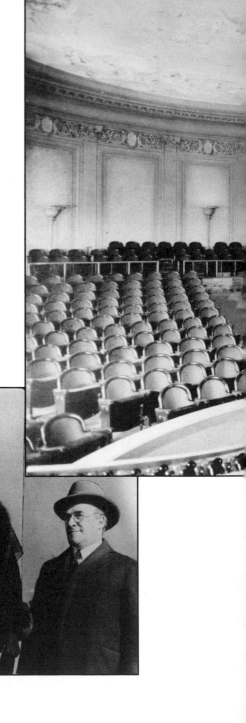

Above: the round theatre with its ceiling fresco brought music into the Palace of the Legion of Honor. Excellent acoustics and sight lines, as well as beautiful decoration, make it one of the finest small theaters in California. Restored in 1988, it is now called the Florence Gould Auditorium. Opposite: Alma's guests at the opening were A. Tirman, French Counselor of State (left), and Jean Guiffrey, celebrated conservateur of the Louvre Museum. The Burlingame crowd could hardly argue with that. (Courtesy Archives, San Francisco Public Library)

On the terrace level, guests viewed the offices and library, a small tea room and kitchen, a large room that would later be known as the Porcelain Room when Alma filled it with a rare collection of porcelain, and the exquisite rococo Little Theater, seating four hundred. The theater, with its round ceiling painted by a renowned Portuguese muralist, was a perfect setting for plays, lectures and chamber music.

Almost as gratifying to Alma as her brother-in-law's gift of the organ was the fact that Mrs. William H. Crocker, Alma's former adversary, was so impressed with the new monument to culture that she was moved to lend a piece from her own collection, Millet's *Man With Hoe.*

While the exterior of the building was a faithful rendition of architect Henri Guillaume's copy of the original Palace of the Legion of Honor, the interior was unique. No building in the world at the time was more fitting for the purpose for which it was erected. A.B. had seen to that. He had sent architect George Applegarth to Europe to inspect the architectural shrines in the Old World so that he could incorporate in the building the latest museum display techniques.

The lighting effects were the finest to be had anywhere. Not only were soft overhead lights used, but also, for the first time, side lighting. Oak flooring was laid with a matte finish instead of a polished surface to avoid the tiring effect of walking on slippery floors. The floors were stained dark brown to prevent any reflection of light on the glazed pictures. All the air in the building was washed through atomizers to free it from dust, and then heated and carried to the rooms at an even temperature throughout the year. The heating was accomplished without the use of unsightly radiators in the galleries.

The next day, November 11, 1924, all of San Francisco paused to celebrate the sixth anniversary of the armistice that supposedly ended war forever. While offices and public buildings were closed, observances included parades, feats of daring in the air and on the land, solemn rites at military cemeteries and a gala dance at night. But of all the observances that day, the most spectacular was the dedication of the California Palace of the Legion of Honor, the building meant to "honor the dead while serving the living."

By ten o'clock in the morning, over a thousand people, coming by streetcar, special buses and private cars, had gathered on the brow of the hill where the magnificent museum overlooked one of the most beautiful natural settings in the world, the Golden Gate, the entrance of the Pacific Ocean into the bay of San Francisco. The ceremony was held in the open Court of Honor. Sunny, blue skies smiled down on Rodin's masterpiece, *The Thinker,* brooding in the midst of the seated audience.

Alma sat on the rostrum, dressed in funereal black, her face covered by a long widow's veil. She knew the busybodies would criticize her costume as being theatrical, since she had long since put away her widow's weeds. Damn it, she thought, I'm wearing this out of respect for A.B. The night before she had been too caught up in all the excitement, all the glitter of the evening, to think about him. But now, listening to the words of praise for the gift of "the late Adolph Spreckels and Mrs. Alma de Bretteville Spreckels," tears sprang to her eyes. Oh, how she wished A.B. could be sitting beside her, his hand over hers, seeing what his Pet had accomplished!

Senator Sam Shortridge, looking very statesmanlike in his cutaway coat and top had, declared it "a masterpiece of architecture, which inspires admiration. This Palace of the Legion of Honor is to be the home of art. On its walls hang the glory of painting. In its galleries stand the pride of sculpture. From its stage will be unfolded the genius of drama, and through its spacious halls heavenly music will calm the troubled spirit and lift the soul to its thoughts of God."[13]

Then, M. Albert Tirman, now Counsellor of the State of France, speaking in French, added his praise. "Everything in the present ceremony gives to it a high significance. The magnificence of the gift made to your beloved city, the stately proportions and general artistry of the monument itself, its fitting dedication to art, a dedication which, by the will of its founders, is expressed in the form of an exposition of French art — all these things, together with the choice of that day of days on which to celebrate the inauguration, combine to render this time and this ceremony immortal..."[14]

Tirman lamented the fact that "the founder of this monument is no more with us," that "inexorable death has taken Mr. Adolph Spreckels from our midst at the very moment when he was about to witness the consummation of that work toward which he had bent his labors for many years." Then he went on to make a public announcement, not entirely unexpected by Alma. Under her veil, the widow was smiling proudly.

"The French government has not failed to acknowledge the worth and the moral significance of such a work. I am exceedingly pleased to inform you that the President of the French Republic has bestowed upon Mrs. Alma de Bretteville Spreckels the Cross of the Legion of Honor."

Sunny Jim accepted the museum on behalf of the city; the commander of the American Legion gave a tribute from the veterans, and Rev. Alexander Stevens of Grace Methodist Church pronounced

Arthur Putnam's Hurdler *(top) and* The Mermaid *(below) are two of nearly two
hundred works by the San Francisco sculptor in the collection of the Palace
of the Legion of Honor. Alma and Loie arranged for his works to be
cast in bronze in France, at the same foundry used by Rodin.
(Courtesy Fine Arts Museums of San Francisco)*

*Arthur Putnam in his studio in 1903. Alma was his faithful patron for years,
giving him a monthly stipend from her $7,200 allowance. In 1911 Putnam
underwent surgery for a brain tumor, after which he suffered constantly;
Alma gave him encouragement, sympathy and money to keep going.
(From* Arthur Putnam, Sculptor, *by Julie H. Heyneman.
Courtesy San Francisco Fine Arts Museums)*

the benediction. Taps were sounded at three minutes before noon in honor of the heroic dead, and the Olympic Club chorus ended the ceremonies with the singing of the *Star-Spangled Banner.*

The new Chevalier of the Legion of Honor, on the arm of Police Chief Daniel O'Brien, lifted her veil, winked broadly, gave the chief a nudge with her elbow and led the assembled multitude inside her building.

Despite all the public adulation she received, Alma, true to form, was the center of a controversy only one week later. The controversy surfaced when it was discovered that something in addition to Rodin's *Thinker* had been provided for in the Court of Honor. On the exterior wall of the museum, behind the curled back of the figure immersed in thought, Alma had instructed the architect to build a pre-need crypt. The crypt had two niches, one for Adolph and one for herself. Now that the building was completed, she wanted to have A.B.'s remains removed from the cemetery and placed in his niche.

Because San Francisco Health Department ordinances ruled against any human burials within city limits, she asked her friend Supervisor Eugene Schmitz (in 1907, as mayor, he had been jailed for corruption) to prepare an amendment to the city burial ordinance. Feeling confident it would all be accomplished quietly and successfully, Alma left town after the opening for a week's rest at the del Coronado. But nothing in which Alma was involved was ever done quietly. News of her request leaked out, and once the press got hold of the story, the amendment became the target for loud opposition. It promised to be a long, drawn-out battle. Informed of the situation, Alma cut short her vacation, rushed home and sent a letter to the board of supervisors. She demanded, in a complete about-face, that the amendment be rescinded. The tone of the letter, which reads like a formal business communication, sounds suspiciously as if it might have been dictated by J.D. to smooth over another of his sister-in-law's gaffes. Without J.D.'s insistence that the matter be dropped, to protect his brother's good name, it is doubtful Alma would have given up so easily. The letter read:

> Gentlemen: Shortly after the death of my late husband, Mr. A.B. Spreckels, some of his friends suggested that it would be an appropriate thing in view of the early completion of the California Palace of the Legion of Honor and his position as a member of the Park Commission for more than twenty-eight years, to make provision in the Court of Honor of the Palace for the permanent disposal of his remains.
>
> I entertained the same view and consented that this might be done.

Upon my return from the south, I learned from the public press that some opposition to the proposal had been manifested, and that the subject is likely to become a matter of public controversy. At the time I gave my consent, I did not anticipate this possibility and I would deplore, above all things, having the matter become the subject of public discussion.

While, therefore, I appreciate the kindly sentiments of those who suggested it, and of his dear friends and associates, official and otherwise, who have been active in arranging it, I must request that no further effort in that behalf be made under any circumstances.

I am sure you will appreciate the spirit in which this is written. Sincerely, Alma Spreckels.

The matter was dropped; A.B. remained in his grave next to his mother and father in the Spreckels mausoleum in Colma, and Alma was ready to forget her grief by turning to a new project.

Chapter Notes:

1. Alma Spreckels to Clifford Dolph, Spreckels correspondence, Maryhill Museum.
2. *San Francisco Examiner,* February 18, 1924, p. 1.
3. California Palace of the Legion of Honor archives.
4. Ulla de Bretteville Awl interview.
5. Dorothy Munn interview: "He called my mother a whore many times."
6. John Rosekrans papers.
7. Alice de Bretteville interview.
8. *San Francisco Chronicle,* November 10, 1924.
9. Dorothy Munn interview.
10. Frickelton Papers.
11. *San Francisco Examiner,* November 2, 1924, p. 12.
12. *San Francisco Chronicle,* November 10, 1924, p. 3.
13. *San Francisco Examiner,* November 12, 1924, p. 1.
14. Ibid.
15. *San Francisco Chronicle,* November 25, 1924, p. 13.

Alma's favorite portrait, painted by Richard Hall in 1924, shows her sitting in Queen Marie's throne. She gave the painting to Maryhill Museum in 1946 because the Legion of Honor refused to display it. (Courtesy Anona Dukelow)

CHAPTER NINE

The Second Royal Rejection

 NOW ENTIRELY ON HER OWN, Alma dropped the widow's weeds and adopted briefly the mantle of "business tycoon." Her first move was to order a shake-up of the Oceanic Steamship Company, of which she was now vice president. Three of the company's oldest employees were fired in a reorganization designed to move the steamship company into Oriental trade. "A woman's hand is at the helm," declared the newspapers.[1]

Whether that hand at the helm was effective or not soon became a moot question. With the death of J.D. the following year, 1926, the Oceanic Steamship Company was sold. J.D.'s children had as little regard for Alma as their father had. Alma didn't think very much of them either. The only matter on which both sides agreed was that the two estates should be liquidated as soon as possible.

"They hired two of the nation's largest accounting firms, Price Waterhouse and Haskins & Sells, to represent each side," said Edward Kallgren. "They spent $360,000 in accountants' fees in one year, and the two firms didn't accomplish anything except to check up on each other. The first thing they liquidated was the steamship company, and the two San Diego newspapers, the *Union* and the *Tribune* were next. Eventually, the only things they kept were the del Coronado Hotel and the sugar companies."[2]

The sale of the properties had the desired effect of bringing in a great deal of cash to the heirs. Having all that money left Alma very restless and very unsure. She had only her brother Alexander to advise her. Alex, a handsome fellow who towered above his six-foot sister, was a conscientious man who wanted to fulfill his role as Alma's advisor wisely. She regarded him as an employee — and an annoying one at that, especially when he wanted to restrain her spending. Since both of them were very excitable people who exploded easily, arguments between the two were frequent and loud.

Alma had always loved a cocktail since the days when Charlie Anderson took her to the Trocadero. Now she was drinking in earnest. Edward Kallgren remembers visiting her one afternoon shortly after the liquidation, when she asked him to bring over some old movies he had taken at a Spreckels Company picnic in Idora Park in Oakland, back in 1919.

"I was ushered into 2080 Washington and Mrs. Spreckels asked if I wanted a martini. The butler brought in a pitcherful. Well, in an hour and a quarter, we each had about five glasses. She was quite mellow, and I was a captive audience. She went to the phone and called the president of United Sugar Refinery, demanding to know the price of the stock. Spreckels Sugar had a half interest in the beet part of the company, and I guess she wanted to show me she was on top of things."

By the summer of 1926, Alma was ready to relinquish the role of business tycoon and try a fling at being the merry widow. Loie had been urging her for some time to establish a residence in Paris. Once, when Loie found her a beautiful apartment near the Arc de Triomphe, she begged Alma to lease it, but that was while A.B. was alive and it didn't seem right. Now she was ready.

"I was thirteen and a high school freshman at Miss Hamlin's when Mother took us to France that summer," recalls Dorothy Munn.

In order to get Little Alma, now seventeen and graduated from high school, to go back to Europe, Alma invited her friend Lutie Ireland to spend the summer with them. Adolph, who was almost fifteen, brought along his friend from Potter's Boys School, Jack Gage. Alma also took her maid, Gertrude, and her brother Gus with them.

"It was my first trip to Paris, and I was so excited," said Dorothy. "But we spent only one night there, at the Astoria Hotel. The next day, Mother dumped all of us, with Uncle Gus and the maid, at the Normandy Hotel in Deauville. It was a horrible summer. Poor little me, being the youngest, I was left out of everything. My brother was such a cut-up. He was misbehaving dreadfully in the hotel, and my sister was pining away for Jack Rosekrans, whom she met when she was fourteen or fifteen. When we got back to Paris at the end of the summer, we were taken to this big chateau in Neuilly. Mother had bought it while we were gone!"[3]

Alma's idea in buying the chateau was to settle the children in Paris. No reason why Dorothy and Adolph couldn't attend French schools, and a year in Europe for Little Alma before she made her debut would add polish to the girl whose major preoccupation seemed to be participating in horse shows.

Only a few months prior to the trip, Little Alma was injured in a fall at the Los Angeles National Horse Show during the jumping sweepstakes. Her horse, Domino, refused to take a barrier and crashed into a rail. Little Alma's knee was caught between the rail and the saddle. At her scream, a doctor ran to her aid and bandaged the knee. Limping but smiling bravely, she climbed back into the saddle to await the judge's decision. She took third place.[4]

Alma was enjoying herself thoroughly that summer, as she always did in Paris. She was a celebrity there. When her limousine rolled down the Champs-Elysées someone on the street would always recognize her and wave. She loved to entertain and to be entertained by her royal friends and the members of arts groups.

There was also, this year, a feeling of romance in the air. Alma, at age forty-five, was being courted again. A woman with strong sexual appetites, she was able to suppress those feelings during the years when A.B. could no longer satisfy her by flinging herself passionately into her projects. Now suppression was no longer necessary.

Her suitor was Alexander P. Moore, former American ambassador to Spain, who was in Paris that summer on a mission to invite prominent Europeans to the Sesquicentennial Exposition in Philadelphia the following fall. The fifty-seven-year-old diplomat was handsome, charming and most attentive. What attracted him to Alma initially was her resemblance to his late wife, Lillian Russell. In the decade of the flapper, when the Ideal Woman starved and flattened herself to look like the Ideal Boy, Alma's voluptuous curves recalled the era made popular by the famous actress.

They shared much in common. Both were self-educated. Moore left school at age twelve to begin a newspaper career on the *Pittsburgh Telegraph* as an office boy. Soon he was elevated to reporter, then city editor, then managing editor and, finally, publisher. By the time he was thirty-seven, he was part-owner not only of the *Telegraph*, but also of the *Pittsburgh Chronicle* and the *Pittsburgh Press*, and editor-in-chief of the *Pittsburgh Leader*.

Like Alma, Moore was a staunch Republican. He left the newspaper business in 1923 when President Harding, whose campaign his newspapers supported, appointed him ambassador to Spain. Outspoken as Alma, Moore's parting remarks to reporters as he left to take his post were, "For forty-two years as a newspaper man, I have been saying what I pleased. Now I can't. I'm a diplomat, and they've put a muzzle on me. Diplomats cannot talk, you know." Nevertheless, Moore acquitted himself well as a diplomat. He did

Alma's brother Gustav de Bretteville, wearing the Olympic Club insignia, with his nephew Adolph Spreckels II at the beach in Deauville, France, 1926. (Courtesy Archives, San Francisco Public Library)

much to improve America's business interests in Spain. When he left two years later, resigning to return to America, King Alfonso, whose friend he had quickly become, paid him a warm tribute.

Much as Alma loved Moore's attentions, she was wary of them. This was different than when A.B. courted her. He had been the one with the money. Now she had it. Suppose her money was all Moore was after, she worried. Some of her jealous women friends encouraged that belief. She would make no firm commitment.

It is possible that Moore never asked her to make one. Her uninhibited behavior didn't exactly qualify her for the ideal wife of a diplomat. He seemed to be overwhelmed by the force of her personality and her financial independence. When Moore entered the American Hospital in Paris for treatment for sciatica, reporters interviewed him there and asked if rumors that he and Alma were engaged were true. He replied: "Mrs. Spreckels is most intelligent, most charming and very rich, but I consider her too smart to desire to marry anyone, especially me."[5]

Alma was happy to remain in Paris in her new chateau, continue to see Moore and enjoy her new independence. Her children had other ideas. They demanded to go home.

Meanwhile, Loie, who had been working on her idea of turning Sam Hill's mansion into an "international museum of good will," was at last about to see her wish come true. Having secured Sam's cooperation, she finally convinced Queen Marie to journey to America to dedicate it. No other woman sitting on a throne in Europe at that time could boast of more royal lineage. Marie was born into a world in which her grandmother, Queen Victoria, ruled over the British Empire, and her grandfather, Czar Alexander II, reigned over all of Russia. She was given in marriage to King Ferdinand, a member of the Hohenzollerns, rulers of the German empire and Romania. Her looks inspired such hyperbole that one writer said of her that every man of her generation was in love with her, every artist inspired by her and every woman wished to look like her.

Loie was full of plans for Marie's trip, the first visit by the beautiful and popular queen to the United States. Alma was determined to be part of it. The visit was scheduled to begin in New York in October, continue across America and climax with the dedication of the museum at Maryhill, Washington, on November 3, 1926.

With great reluctance, Alma yielded to her children's demands. She returned with them to California after installing her cousin Pierre and his wife in the chateau. They were delighted to move from their modest apartment into the luxurious town house.

Once home, Alma plunged headlong into plans for the western

segment of Marie's trip. Sam Hill appointed her his official hostess for the queen's visit to the West Coast and for the reception in Seattle. After that, Alma wanted the queen to come to California and dedicate the Romanian Room in the Legion of Honor. She immediately arranged to rent her own private railroad car to meet the queen's train midway across the United States and hook up with it in St. Paul, Minnesota. Then she invited friends and relatives to fill her car. Together with her maids, they made a party of sixty-five, just twenty less than the entire party on the *Royal Romanian.*

Alma thought she could rely on Loie to see that her car would make the trip west as part of the royal train. But Loie had lost her power. The little dancer, who had organized a group of wealthy and prominent people to sponsor the tour, had been dismissed by her own committee. They felt more qualified than Loie to work with society leaders, chambers of commerce, American mayors and charitable organizations. Her tearful entreaties to Bucharest did little good. The tour was completely out of her hands.

It was just as well. The one aspect in which Loie had a part, the performances (in Philadelphia at the Sesquicentennial and in New York, of the queen's ballet, *Le Lys de la Vie,* filmed by Loie in Paris in 1920), was a complete flop. The arrangements were so poor that no one saw the queen. Her box was placed with her back to the audience. In New York, the performance brought the queen's visit to that city to an awkward conclusion. Allegedly it was given to raise money for a "Mothers' Memorial Foundation," but only Loie made money from it. "Innocently or not, the two [Loie and Queen Marie] were involved in one of the more genteel rackets of the decade. It had little to do with personal publicity or prestige, as such. It was a simple device for obtaining easy money," wrote dance historian Clara de Morinni.[6]

By the time the scandal appeared in the newspapers, the queen, accompanied by two of her children, Prince Nicholas and Princess Ileana, was aboard the *Royal Romanian,* bound for their transcontinental tour on what the *New York Times* called "one of the most beautiful and elaborate trains ever placed on rails." The queen's offical party did not include either Sam Hill or Loie. But it did include Marie's official host Colonel J.H. Carroll, representative of the railroad companies who had agreed to give the queen free transcontinental passage. Also on board were the Romanian consul general, Ira Nelson Morris, and his wife, and the queen's personal aide, her long-time friend, Major Stanley Washburn.

In St. Paul, Alma's private car had been sitting on a siding while she waited impatiently for the arrival of the *Royal Romanian.* Her party cheered mightily as the train steamed into view. But the cheers soon ended when Major Washburn informed Alma that railroad rules forbade adding her car to their train. If she wished, Alma and her maid would be permitted to travel with the queen, but it was impossible to take all sixty-five members of her party aboard.

Alma was outraged. There it was again — another royal rejection. But this one was worse. This time it wasn't only San Francisco who would know about her humiliation. This time the whole world would laugh at her. Well, not if *she* could help it. First, Alma drew herself up to her full height, glared down at the little major and told him there was no way she was going to leave her party. She and her friends would meet the queen's train when it got to Spokane, Washington. Then she demanded a word with Marie. Alma was determined to get favorable publicity out of this. The queen had promised to bring with her more gifts for Alma's Romanian Room. Not exactly gifts, Alma thought; she had paid plenty for them.[7]

Fortunately, Marie had brought the gifts. After making a hurried inventory, Alma dispatched an airmail letter back to the San Francisco newspapers, enthusing over the wonderful objects her friend Queen Marie was bringing with her to be installed in the Romanian Room of the Legion. And the queen promised to send her workmen to duplicate exactly the walls and ceilings of her Sinaia palace.

Each gift was accompanied by a note in the queen's own hand. Some of them read: "Crochet hook with which I have crocheted thousands and thousands of woolen caps for poor children...Little gold brooch given to me as quite a small child by my father whilst he was Commander-in-Chief of the Mediterranean Fleet...Old purse which Queen Carmen Sylvia, my mother-in-law, always carried about in her pocket and in which she kept her tatting instruments..."[8]

There was also a model of the queen's crown of gold set with amethysts, moonstones and turquoise, and a mantle of solid gold cloth studded with semiprecious stones. Alma wrote she expected to have the queen come to California and install these gifts personally in her room. She ignored the telegram sent by Washburn to the mayors of San Francisco and Los Angeles canceling the queen's visit to California. Somewhat mollified by the gifts, Alma returned to her own party accompanied by the sorrowful Loie, whom Alma had invited to meet them in St. Paul, and returned with her group to await Marie's arrival in the Northwest.

While Marie's train continued across the country, with the queen stopping to charm farmers, cowboys and Indians (the Sioux made her Chief Lady Who Was Waited For), Sam Hill was working frantically to get his neglected, incomplete mansion in some sort of

Top: Queen Marie and Sam Hill at Maryhill, November 1926.
Below: Queen Marie releases doves at the dedication of the museum which
would remain unfinished and closed to the public for fourteen years.
(Courtesy Maryhill Museum)

shape for the queen to dedicate. He had abandoned work on it nine years before and neither the exterior nor the interior had been finished. No doors, no windows were in place. In fact, one of Sam's "good roads" ran right through the ground floor of the building.

Also toiling feverishly were the society matrons of Portland, setting up an elaborate program of welcome for the queen. Maryhill, on the Washington state border, was about equally distant from Portland and Seattle. The itinerary called for the train to go from Spokane, Washington, to Maryhill. Then, after the dedication, the party would motor to Portland for an overnight visit, and then up to Seattle. Portlanders, in a city which boasted its own symphony orchestra and which was, at the very moment of the queen's arrival, the site of the National Livestock Exposition and Horse Show, didn't feel they needed any outside help — especially that of Mrs. Spreckels from California — to entertain Her Majesty.

The staff of the Multnomah Hotel, Portland's finest hostelry, which had played host to President Harding and the Marshals Foch and Joffre when they visited that city, was busily polishing the gold service and making elaborate preparations to perfect the "typical Oregon" menu for the private dinner to be given there following the Wednesday dedication. The suite the queen would occupy was being completely redecorated and would be filled with the finest flowers the "City of Roses" could provide. After dinner, the queen was to go on to the specially built royal box at the horse show.

When the train reached Spokane on Monday night, Sam, dressed in a tweed suit with a cowboy hat atop his smiling Santa Claus face, came to greet Marie at a formal reception in that city. With him was a regally attired Alma, and Loie, whom reporters described as a "little, stooped, gray-haired lady."

As the train proceeded to Maryhill, Sam, now that Marie was in his world, assumed the manner of the gracious host, an attitude not appreciated by Colonel Carroll and Major Washburn. Alma, undaunted that the official itinerary did not include a trip to California, got the queen's consent to come (at Alma's expense) if she were personally invited by California governor Richardson.

On the morning of November 3, two thousand guests and scores of reporters and photographers stood outside the unfinished building and watched as Queen Marie did the impossible — she made a triumph out of a disaster. Through her brave words the people assembled in the gaudily decorated building saw not the grotesque structure that surrounded them, but what Sam had intended it some day to be, an international monument for good will.

"As I stand before you today in this curious and interesting building," said the queen, "I would like to explain why I came. There is much more than concrete in this structure. There is a dream built into this place — a dream for today and especially for tomorrow...Samuel Hill is my friend. He is not only a dreamer but a worker. Samuel Hill once gave me his hand and said if there was anything on earth I needed I had only to ask. Some may only scoff, for they do not understand. So when Samuel Hill asked me to come overseas to this house built in the wilderness, I came with love and understanding..."[9]

She also defended her loyalty to Loie, who had caused so much embarrassment that the Romanian government removed her from the official party. Marie asserted that "some may have wondered at the friendship of a Queen for a woman whom some would call 'lowly,' but in this democracy there should be no gap between the high and the lowly."[10]

After enumerating the gifts she brought with her, she declared in a voice ringing with sincerity that Maryhill represented a great ideal both she and her friend Mr. Hill stood for: the ideal of beauty. She hoped that after she was gone, this ideal could live on and that the finished project would be a joy to many.

About her other friend, Alma Spreckels, the woman who would later be the one most responsible for finishing that project, Marie said nothing.

Then Marie stepped to the edge of the platform and ended her speech by extending her hand dramatically, saying, "Mr. Hill, I would very much like to shake your hand."

Neither Alma nor Loie was present to hear Marie's words. When Loie heard later of Marie's tribute to her, she sobbed, "I never dreamed she'd do anything like that." Both women remained behind in Alma's railroad car, Loie fearful of embarrassing the queen, and Alma annoyed at the cold reception she got from the Portland society women. They were interviewed by a reporter looking for another angle to the story. Loie obliged him, stating that she was the inspiration for Sam's museum. "The isolation, the loneliness of this monument was so wonderful to me that I wondered why it could not be organized into a museum for good will..."[11]

The good will began to dissolve rapidly after the dedication, when the party returned to the train for lunch and crossed the railroad bridge into Oregon. There they were met by Oregon's Governor Pierce and a procession of some thirty Lincoln automobiles for the drive to Portland along the Columbia River Highway. Sam rode with the queen, the governor and Washburn in one car. The mayor of Portland was in another car further back. The rest of the motorcade

Looking a little like Lady Macbeth, Alma contemplates the crown (a replica)
which Queen Marie sent her for her museum. The center finial had broken off
and had to be stuck on with chewing gum for the photographers. Queen Marie,
who designed and helped to make her royal paraphernalia, apparently
believed that any object that had touched her royal person was worthy
of display, if not veneration. One can only wonder whether Alma,
in the privacy of her own bedroom, tried on the crown for size.
(Courtesy Archives, San Francisco Public Library)

bumped fenders jockeying for positions closer to the queen. Alma, in a car far down in the lineup, was fuming.

A detective hired to protect Marie was seated several cars away from the queen; he asked to be placed in the car with Her Royal Highness. The governor obliged by changing seats with him. Sam was furious. He told Washburn that he had insulted the governor of Oregon by removing him from Marie and slamming the door in his face. When Washburn denied this, a minor fracas ensued. That was just the beginning. The fight would erupt all over again later that night at the horse show, and would climax with Hill's car being uncoupled from the *Royal Romanian* the next day.

Alma, who had been ignored by the Portland ladies — they were about as warm to her as the San Francisco socialites — found out on her arrival at the Multnomah Hotel that she was not included in the private dinner being given there before the horse show. She felt highly insulted, and she knew she could probably expect no better treatment from the Seattle ladies when the party reached there. Alma decided not only to skip the horse show, but to skip the rest of the trip. She caught the midnight train from Portland to San Francisco. She didn't bother with goodbyes.

So thoroughly was Alma ignored that it wasn't until the banquet in Seattle the next night that she was missed. On Friday, reporters flocked to Washington Street to hear Alma's story.

"I had the most ordinary reasons for wanting to come home," she asserted. "I had a touch of tonsilitis, I dislike riding on trains, my brother Alexander was urging me to return and I felt it might be wise to have the Romanian Room at the Legion of Honor ready in the event that Queen Marie should arrange to visit California. I left without telling anybody goodbye because goodbyes would have entailed endless explanations."

Of all the illnesses that could have befallen Alma, a sore throat was the least likely. And the possibility that the queen would be receiving an invitation from Governor Richardson to come to California was equally unlikely. When Richardson heard of Alma's statement, after he had been informed by Colonel Washburn that the queen was not coming, he retorted angrily, "I will not discuss it."[12]

The Italian Room of 2080 Washington, where Alma received reporters, was completely furnished with the Romanian Room pieces given Alma by the queen which had been on exhibit at the Legion of Honor when it opened two years previously. Added to them was the model of Marie's gold crown, which she had presented to Alma during the trip. A photographer wanted to take a picture of the crown, but a top ornament had broken loose from it. Someone came up with a piece of chewing gum and stuck it back together. Alma placed the crown carefully on a red pillow and held it aloft while the picture was snapped.

Then, dropping wearily onto the queen's throne and summoning Gertrude, her maid, for a handkerchief to dry her eyes, Alma continued her story.

"It is not true that I came home because the women of the Northwest did not want a San Francisco woman as hostess. I am of the same opinion myself. I think a Seattle woman should be hostess in Seattle, a Portland woman in Portland and so forth. Mr. Hill did ask me to act as hostess to the queen at his dinner in Seattle. I gave him no direct answer..."

Experienced as she was at getting royal rejections, Alma did not let her wrath extend to the queen. She loved Marie. It was the people around her who were to blame.

"It's a shame after the ten thousand miles I have traveled and the time I've spent trying to do something for the people of California by bringing here the rarest collection of Romanian souvenirs in the world outside of Romania, that these ugly rumors of dissension in the queen's party have to spoil everything."

Alma gave the wet handkerchief to Gertrude and exchanged it for a dry one. Then she coughed loudly and, remembering her "tonsilitis," put a lozenge in her mouth. With a weak wave, she dismissed the reporters and returned to her bedroom. The interview — and the incident — was over.

There was dissension of another sort, this time in Alma's family, a few months later. Little Alma, shortly before she turned eighteen, eloped with Jack Rosekrans to Martinez in July of 1926. Accompanied by her friend Lutie Ireland and Jack's friend George Mahoney as witnesses, they were married in the parsonage of the Methodist Episcopal Church by the pastor and then returned to San Francisco.

Alma refused to believe the news when reporters told her. Then she hurriedly packed a bag and ran after the newlyweds, who were on their honeymoon in Del Monte.

Chapter Notes:

1. *San Francisco Examiner,* July 21, 1925, p.1.
2. Edward Kallgren interview.
3. Dorothy Munn interview.
4. *San Francisco Chronicle,* February 12, 1926, p.5.
5. *San Francisco Chronicle,* August 24, 1926.
6. de Morinni, op. cit.
7. "Mrs. Spreckels contributed $10,000 to the sum which is paying for Queen Marie's tour," *Morning Oregonian,* November 5, 1926, p.7.
8. *San Francisco Examiner,* October 26, 1926, p.4.
9. Dr. John Tuhy, *Sam Hill: The Prince of Castle Nowhere,* Timber Press, Oregon, 1983, p.249.
10. Ibid.
11. *The Morning Oregonian,* November 4, 1926, p.1.
12. *San Francisco Examiner,* November 6, 1926, p.3.

In 1927, Alma's hair was fashionably bobbed, and her beauty at age 46 was undiminished, as shown in this picture from the society pages of the San Francisco Call. *(Courtesy Archives, San Francisco Public Library)*

Alma on the Prowl

ALMA'S PURPOSE IN PURSUING the honeymooners was to convince them to come back and be married properly at a ceremony and reception at 2080 Washington. Until they did so, she felt it was indecent for her daughter to be sleeping with young Rosekrans.

Jack, who wasn't much older than Little Alma, was the son of Newton and Florence Rosekrans, respected members of the Pacific Heights set. Rosekrans, although hardly in the same class financially as the Spreckelses, was in real estate and insurance. Jack worked in his father's business.

Elopement might have been all right for Big Alma — indeed, it was the only way her union could have been legitimized — but it was unthinkable for her daughter. "She's a villain, that Alma of mine, to do this," Alma complained to Florence Rosekrans. "I insist upon a wedding."

Although it was impossible to change her daughter's mind, Alma had better luck with her son-in-law, an easygoing young man who was eager to do the right thing and have everyone share in his newfound happiness.

A week later, before fifty family members and close friends, Little Alma, clad in a dainty white-and-silver wedding gown, repeated her vows. The wedding took place in the drawing room before an altar graced by her mother's gold candelabra from the palace of Louis XVI. White lilies, shading into gold, formed a brilliant background. The Reverend Fredrick Clampert, of Trinity Episcopal Church, presided. Alma, who had no love for flowers herself ("They just die, and they cost money"), saw to it that they were everywhere. This was a wedding, and, by God, she intended to make it look like one! On the

165

bride's table in the dining room, white gardenias and lilies of the valley blended with great golden begonias. White and gold lilies in clusters cascaded through the halls and into the ballroom, where the party overflowed for dancing after the wedding supper.

But even this ceremony was not enough for Alma. After the young couple returned from a second (unescorted) honeymoon at del Coronado, she gave an informal reception at Alma Villa.

"Alma ordered another wedding cake for this affair and asked us to bring it up to the ranch," recalled Florence Rosekrans. "We also brought her brother Gus and his wife up with us. No one had met them before. I had a new outfit — hat and everything — because we were going from there to another wedding back in the city. But Alma took my outfit and hid it. She wouldn't let us leave to go to the other wedding. She wanted us to stay at the ranch for an extended visit with her."[1]

A few days later, Alma requested another visitor to remain. He was a peddler.

"The bell rang," Mrs. Rosekrans remembered, "and Alma said to me, 'You open the door.' A fellow in his forties stood there. I said, 'Yes?'

" 'Find out what he wants,' Alma yelled.

" 'Is this Mrs. Spreckels's house? I want to see Mrs. Spreckels. Tell her it's most important. I have things for her. Tell her I have pins and needles and safety pins and garters and underwear.'

"Alma got up, put a robe around herself and yelled, 'Who the hell brought that fellow here? Kick him out, Florence!'

"The peddler yelled right back, 'Tell that woman I'm not gonna be kicked out. Nobody ever kicked me out of their house before.'

" 'Shut the door in his face, Florence,' Alma hollered. Then she changed her mind. 'Well, wait a minute, maybe I do need something.'

"By the time she got through with the pins and needles, she practically bought him out," recalled Mrs. Rosekrans. "At the end of the conversation she told him to go home and get his clothes and she invited him to spend a week.

"My husband, who was somewhere around, said, 'For God's sake, does she know what she's doing?' I said, 'Don't ask me. I'm obeying orders. I don't know. We're going to be going home anyway.'

"Well, it didn't take much urging for the peddler to accept. He said, 'I forgot to tell you, I have a wife.' She said, 'Bring her, too.'

"He stayed there three months, and then left after a row. She called him every name under the sun."

Pointing to another example of Alma's impetuousness ("She'd do anything that came into her head"), Mrs. Rosekrans talked about the incident of the prize chickens.

"Once, after we were guests another time at Alma Villa, my husband, Newton, wanted to do something nice for her. She was commencing to raise fine chickens, so we went to the state fair at Sacramento and he ordered two chickens at $25 apiece so she could have some nice breeders. That was on Saturday. We were all back there on Sunday, and Sunday night on the table, here come the two chickens — cooked! She said she couldn't find anything to serve that night so she had them cooked. My husband never got over that."

As the summer of 1927 came to a close, and with her daughter now properly married, Alma turned back to the romance in her own life. Alexander Moore was now in Italy seeing a great deal of the widow of Enrico Caruso, the former Dorothy Benjamin, a New York socialite. Loie kept her abreast of the news and offered to act as a go-between and break up this new alliance. All she needed was Alma's consent — and the money to get to Italy.

"But you either do not love him well enough, or trust me enough to rely upon my judgment and my love for you," wrote Loie from Paris. "I am sure that if I had the money, you would have approved of my going, and I really think it was that which stopped you... But it has always been the same with you and me whenever a sum of money is involved. You have always had some feeling within you that resented it... My instinct was to save him and thereby save your happiness and your future good, because you will find no man like him, at least not for you."[2]

Alma, in an attempt to thwart Loie's desire to act as Cupid's helper, wrote to her friend that she was now interested in someone in California. Three days later, Loie responded: "It must be that there is something better in store for you — but I beg of you, don't marry hurriedly out there. It is so difficult to undo and so easy to have done....

"You know, Alma, your whole life points to a woman of great destiny, and it was my destiny to be the instrument by which it was to be done — and it is not finished. Everything you do — even though it seems to be wrong, is a part of what you have got to do to carry out the destiny for which you were born. And I think, under the circumstances, that you owe it to yourself to see me first before you take such an important step as to marry again..."

Loie, commenting on the pictures of Alma's children she enclosed in her letter, noted: "Certainly your son is a very handsome boy and you must be very proud of him. He will be a wonderful man bye-and-bye." Then she went on to tell Alma about what she was doing to help Sam Hill with his uncompleted museum and how that fit in with Alma's "destiny."

"You, Alma, must become a part of that work with me for the benefit of our country. The West is your country! Already they know you there for what you did in the war, and you will let them see how much your love is there now. The Queen [Marie] will help you, because she too wants her visit out there to be justified. And she believes in the Museum as a great future monument to civilization."

Maryhill Museum was the farthest thing from Alma's mind now. The "woman of great destiny" certainly had no love for the people of the Northwest. Contempt was more like it. She still smarted from their rebuke.

If destiny called Alma anyplace, it was to New York. She had to get out of San Francisco. She had persuaded Little Alma and her husband, who now worked for the Spreckels Sugar Company, to move into the Washington Street mansion with her, but living in the same house with her married daughter, large as the house was, just wasn't working out any more than it did when Little Alma was single. "Screaming, screaming! You could hear them blocks away," recalled Florence Rosekrans.

Dorothy, who had just completed her first year of high school at the second-rated Miss Hamlin's, was also eager to leave. Alma enrolled her at Miss Dow's girls' school at Briarcliff Manor, a prestigious New York boarding school, where she was readily accepted. Adolph was still attending Potter's Boys School, a block away from 2080. He was left unsupervised at home with the newlyweds when Alma and Dorothy took the train for New York in September 1927.

There was lots of excitement in the Big City that fall and winter. Mae West was heating up Broadway in her play *Diamond Lil*, while fifty-five of the actors in another play she wrote, *Pleasure Man*, were arrested along with the author. Politics was the other hot topic of conversation at cocktail parties. Al Smith, the popular New York governor, had just been nominated as the Democratic candidate for presidency against Republican Herbert Hoover, the engineer from California.

There was a new trend in advertising. Well-born women were pictured not only on the society pages but — of all places — in the advertising columns. People like Mrs. William H. Vanderbilt personally swore that Old Gold cigarettes were so mild she smoked them even with a sore throat! With smoking made respectable by women like Mrs. Vanderbilt, Alma soon took up the habit, too. For the rest of her life she would be remembered as having a lighted cigarette in one hand and an unlighted one in the other, waiting to replace it.

Alma took a suite at the Ritz-Carlton, where her brother-in-law Rudolph was living. She liked Adolph's youngest brother. He was fun, he liked a good time and he had a wide circle of friends in New York. It was his wife whom Alma couldn't abide. Fortunately, Eleanor had remained in California. Very fortunately, because Rudolph's mistress had moved in with him.

Alma readily accepted Rudolph's inamorata. Alma hadn't turned into a snob just because she was now A.B.'s widow. Besides, she wasn't any more puritanical than Rudy's young woman. She relished her new independence. She loved the idea that she was just as free as Rudy to have her affairs.

One of her first romances in New York was with Elwood Rice, known as "the man who brought the bright lights to Broadway." His famous chariot race sign in which wheels revolved and the horses appeared to be galloping was the first animated electric sign erected in New York.

Rice, a wealthy advertising executive who was originally from Dayton, remembered Alma from the time he was among the hundreds of guests who had enjoyed her hospitality during the 1915 Exposition. As president of Rice Leaders of the World Association, an organization of manufacturers idealistically organized to raise the standards of business to a higher plane, Rice displayed the group's electrical emblem at the Exposition. Alma didn't remember him, probably because he was married at the time. Now Rice was divorced, and she found this "salesman of ideas," who had received two honorary Doctor of Laws degrees for his efforts, a man worthy of her attention. Rice, in turn, found the bright, outspoken widow with her own brand of idealism a fascinating companion. He was soon squiring her around town to the better speakeasies, fancy restaurants and intimate dinner parties.

No matter where she was, Alma's thoughts were constantly on her museum and how she could attract benefactors to donate collections. She was acutely aware that the museum, now that the Louvre's loan collection was returned, needed a great deal more than the Rodins and the other things she had contributed.

In New York, she made it a point to be close to Archer Huntington, adopted son of Collis P. Huntington, one of the "Big Four" who had built the first transcontinental railroad. Huntington had already made a magnificent gift to the California Palace of the Legion of Honor the year before when his mother, Arabella, died, leaving behind her New York mansion filled with priceless possessions. Using the fact that they were distantly related via Edith Huntington, who had married J.D.'s son, Alma had persuaded Archer to give a choice group of French decorative pieces from his mother's home to fill the Collis Potter Huntington Memorial Room. Archer's wife was the renowned sculptor Anna Hyatt Huntington. He had also donated Anna's huge statue of Joan of Arc, outside the entrance to the museum, and Alma was sure that with her prodding there would be much more to come.

In San Francisco, her brother Alex tended to her finances, telling her how much to donate to the museum. He wrote that she could give fourteen Putnams in December 1927 because "your income on which you have to pay taxes this year is $80,000 and as you are allowed to deduct out 15%, I propose to give objects of art slightly in excess of that amount, reserving the balance of the collection for next year when you may have a very large income tax to pay."[3]

On New Year's Day 1928 Alma received a telegram from Paris informing her that Loie had died of pneumonia. Although the dancer had been in declining health for some time, the news came as a shock. The French press mourned her demise with such tender words as "a butterfly has folded its wings," and "a magician is dead." Alma did not attend the funeral. Although she showed little grief at the time for the woman who had so influenced her life, Alma's gratitude to Loie and the guilt she harbored for not recognizing her publicly would haunt her for the rest of her life.

A month later, Alma quit the Ritz-Carlton suite for an apartment on Fifth Avenue. She bought the entire seventh floor of a cooperative building at the corner of Eighty-third Street. It consisted of fourteen rooms and five baths. The living room was forty by twenty feet with a thirteen-foot ceiling. Her neighbors included Justice Charles Evans Hughes; Franklin Hutton (he owned two duplexes, one for himself and his new wife, and the other, consisting of twenty-six rooms, for his daughter, fourteen-year-old Barbara Hutton); opera prima donna Mme. Amelita Galli Curci; Princess Ruspoli; Major Lorillard Spencer, tobacco tycoon; and Edgar S. Bloom, president of Western Electric Company.[4]

But the most interesting neighbor — probably the one who attracted her to the building primarily — was the owner of the penthouse, which was filled with a fabulous art collection: Samuel Kress, of the dime-store chain. Alma quickly cultivated his friendship. While it wasn't until after his death that the Kress Foundation made a major donation in 1961 to Alma's museum, he did lend a splendid collection of French impressionists when the Legion had an exhibition of European master paintings in 1934.

Because she needed to have someone around to offer approval

and admiration, Alma sent for her only niece, Edith de Bretteville, Walter's daughter, to be her companion.

"I was living at her chateau at Neuilly with Uncle Pierre at the time," recalled Edith. "I was delighted to come back because Aunt Alma had always been good to me."[5]

Edith recalled the poker games Alma held at the apartment with Rudolph and his friends in which "as much as $5,000 would change hands in one evening."

She also remembered Alma's beaux. "In addition to Mr. Rice, there was Foxhall Keene, a well-known polo player from Long Island. Aunt Alma loved the sight of a man on horseback. We'd often go out to watch Foxy play, and he'd come back to the apartment afterwards to celebrate. And there was Alexander Moore."

Moore, without Loie's interference, had left Italy and the arms of Dorothy Caruso and returned to the United States. Although he did see Alma again, nothing further came of their affair. "Uncle Rudolph didn't like him for some reason. Maybe because he had been married to an actress and he didn't think he was good enough for Aunt Alma," said Edith.

The following year, President Coolidge appointed Moore as ambassador to Peru and he sailed out of Alma's life. He never remarried. He died in 1930, shortly after President Hoover named him the first U.S. ambassador to Poland.

Dorothy was not too thrilled with her mother's friends. "My mother used to visit me at boarding school, driving up in a limousine with Mr. Rice or another of her beaux. Nobody else's mother had beaux. It was very embarrassing," said Dorothy.

When the school year ended, Alma returned with Dorothy to San Francisco. Although she could now claim to be a resident of Manhattan, and although she was well-known there, Alma knew she was just as much an outsider in New York as she was in San Francisco. Without Adolph's support, her loneliness and anxieties went with her wherever she lived.

She left New York with the knowledge that Archer Huntington had sent a check for $100,000 to Legion director Cornelia Quinton with instructions to buy whatever paintings were needed to finish the Collis Huntington Room. And more than that, at the very moment Alma was going West, Dr. Quinton was leaving for the East to meet with Huntington about a gigantic sculpture exhibition, "the greatest exhibition of contemporary sculpture ever held," which Huntington was underwriting to the tune of another $100,000, for the spring of 1929 at the California Palace of the Legion of Honor.

When Alma returned, she stopped long enough at Washington

Dorothy's debut in December 1930 was the most lavish ever staged in San Francisco; Time magazine compared it to Barbara Hutton's in New York and Elsa Armour's in Chicago. (Courtesy Dorothy Spreckels Munn)

Street to catch a glimpse of her first grandchild, John Rosekrans Jr., born to Little Alma in March. Then she sailed immediately with Dorothy and Adolph Jr. to Hawaii. There she gave a dinner dance at the Waialea Golf Club honoring Princess Kawananokoa. With the same enthusiasm with which she used to plan Adolph's birthday parties and the family's Christmas parties, she had the club decorated with a "Ten Thousand Leagues Under the Sea" theme. Huge coral shells, a giant fish formed of flowers, and a bejeweled mermaid floating in a sea of blue and green tulle were used to create the proper ambience.

Perhaps it was the presence of the Hawaiian royalty, or perhaps it was loneliness, that inspired Alma to write a long letter to her friend Queen Marie, inviting her to come for a visit at Alma's expense. There was no immediate reply.

Following the Hawaiian sojourn, Alma returned to San Francisco and to entertaining at the palatial Napa ranch. The fifty-seven-room country estate was filled each weekend with artists, writers, visiting Europeans, family members and others who enjoyed Alma's lavish hospitality. Despite federal agents' efforts to enforce Prohibition, liquor flowed freely. A dozen employees, housed in a separate building on the ranch, worked with the efficiency of a hotel staff. Then, in the middle of October, in a blazing finale, the partying at Alma Villa was over.

The fire erupted shortly before 2 a.m., Wednesday, October 17, 1928. Little Alma, all alone in the mansion with the baby, his nurse and his governess, was enjoying some mid-week quiet at the ranch. Jack Rosekrans, along with Big Alma, had returned to San Francisco to arrange for another lavish party the following weekend. When the center wing, in which the occupants were sleeping, erupted, they were dangerously cut off by flames from two sides. The nurse was the first to discover the fire. Her quick action saved them all from death. She grabbed the baby from its crib, pulled Little Alma from her bed, yelled for the governess to follow them and raced for the nearest window. The governess jumped through the window to the lawn below, and the nurse handed the baby down to her while instructing the distraught mother to jump.

When Big Alma and Jack were notified, they raced up to Napa so quickly that the house was still burning when they got there. Despite the efforts of the Napa Valley Fire Department plus a full component of volunteer firemen, the fire, which lasted more than two hours, totally destroyed the beautiful mansion. With it went all of A.B.'s treasures amassed over a period of thirty years, plus Alma's collections of European paintings, Galle glass and other irreplaceable works of art. Arson was not only suspected, it appeared to be a fact, since the fire erupted simultaneously in two separate wings of the house. Prime suspects were two employees fired after trouble with Walter de Bretteville, who supervised the ranch. They were never caught. The mansion, centerpiece of the famed Napa stock farm which A.B. had fondly hoped his son would one day take over, was never rebuilt.

A week later, still depressed over the Napa fire, Alma received an answer to her letter inviting Queen Marie to visit her. The letter was one long list of complaints by Marie about how "my poor have been cheated." The queen wanted Alma's help to set things right. Since Loie's death, Marie had had time to reflect on the bizarre trip to America ("One is like a torn-up flower upon a swollen river — no standing against the rushing force which takes you along") and how she, Marie, had been the victim of the dancer's poor business practices.

"Loie had brought me several Rodins...and finally, when at Paris, she took me to a far-off quarter to see a large life-sized figure of one of the three guardians of the Gates of Hell, I think it is called...I gave 200,000 francs for this to be able to secure it...As much as I know, these statues were brought to Maryhill when we went, but of this I cannot be sure. Loie was upset and confused and could not give me any clear explanations...I do feel that it is very hard that my poor [Romanians] should have lost 200,000 francs besides which, in my position today, means to me a great loss. I thought that you understand these things, you would speak to Mr. Hill about the loss...I know that our faithful Loie, who always wanted to help me with my poor, knowing the colossal demands put upon me, would be desperate if she thought that because of her death I had lost all that money...Being a trusted friend, I, of course, did not ask a paper from her...Now, where she is, she no doubt sees 'through a glass darkly' but alas she can send me no message."[6]

Then, Marie complained about the money her poor had never received as a result of the Romanian furniture collection sent to Alma for the museum's Romanian Room. The queen acknowledged that the furniture was sent as a gift in return for Alma's war work for the stricken country. But the money for which Marie, in her discreet royal way, was dunning her, was the sum Alma had agreed to pay to have Romanian craftsmen create a frescoed background — walls, ceiling, windows and doors — to complete the room under the queen's personal supervision. Alma was to send monthly checks in the queen's name, in accordance with a telegraphed request by Loie in November 1922, shortly after the furniture arrived, with the "greatest expenditure forty thousand dollars for the gold for gilding the walls."[7] The queen had agreed not to cash the checks until the work was done. Six years later, the work still had not been done, and the queen was left holding a fortune in uncashed checks.

"You know those carved golden furniture Loie carried away are *unique* and I could *never* have them done again," Marie wrote. "The gilding alone would cost me more than I could pay, and the carving is magnificent. We no more produce the workmen who can carve such treasures...I was to make the background to the room, but something was to remain for my poor for having given up all my precious furniture and still more precious personal souvenirs...

"Everything was taken from me on sentimental grounds but none of what was to come to me ever came and I still have those many useless cheques in my possession. You understand that I am discouraged. I have given but not received."

What the queen wanted to receive was the money for those uncashed checks. "The fair thing would be that I should use half the money for the room and half should remain with me for my poor," wrote Her Royal Highness. "If this cannot be, I shall send back all the cheques and then give up working under circumstances which are too difficult and which I do not understand. I am an artist, I have taste and knowledge, but I am not a millionaire. Loie comes and sweeps my house of memorable treasures but my poor get nothing.

"But if we are really to continue to work together I must be able to see clearly or I lose both money and possessions as well as my precious energy so necessary to the country. Forgive my being so outspoken..."

Marie concluded her lengthy letter with, "I would love to visit Honolulu and also your beautiful place in San Francisco. But I shall never come back to America...I hope that in spite of difficulties and disappointments we shall remain in touch with each other."

They did remain in touch; Alma kept Marie's autographed photo in a prominent place at Washington Street, and she also kept the queen's letter. Alma never cheated anyone in her life, even when she was poor. She was no businesswoman, but she didn't need anyone to tell her that you don't pay for something you have never received. Some time later, she gave the letter to her brother Alex, with this note: "Please file this letter of the Queen of Romania. She has no claim (financial) on me as she was to do a ceiling and walls for me and she never did them!

"I don't think she will ever claim anything, but still you never know, I might die and you can never tell — This can prove my contention. She never lived up to her agreement and she was more than paid for her furniture. She has some checks that I stopped years ago in Anglo-London and Paris Bank and which she promised never to cash."[8] The matter ended there. The queen made no further claims, and Alma outlived her by thirty years.

With the queen's declining the invitation to visit San Francisco, Alma returned to her Manhattan apartment in the fall, and Dorothy returned for her second year at Briarcliff. By winter, Alma was ready for the balmy weather of the Riviera and the warm reception she always received in Paris. Elwood Rice gave her a lavish bon voyage party for forty people at the Ritz, and Alma set sail once again for six glorious days on the *Ile de France.*

Arriving at her mansion at Neuilly, Alma found that Pierre and Yvonne had a houseguest, Ulla de Bretteville, the young Danish daughter of Kaj, who was going to school in Paris to perfect her French. Alma immediately invited the girl to come live with her in the United States. But Ulla, only sixteen at the time, politely refused.

Then Alma turned her attention to the Williamses and the Gulbenkians, two couples whose friendship she had been actively cultivating. Both couples met Alma's exacting criteria for people worth pursuing: they were very wealthy, they spent a lot of their money to build art collections, and they had no children to leave those collections to.

Calouste Sarkis Gulbenkian, reputed to be the richest man in the world, made his billions in oil pipelines. He was being courted by many European governments who were promising to build special wings in their museums to house his treasures. Although Alma fought valiantly for the next twenty-five years to get the Gulbenkian collection for the Legion of Honor, she lost out to Portugal. She couldn't match its offer. Portugal agreed to build an entire museum, in Lisbon, to be called the Calouste Sarkis Gulbenkian Museum.

Alma had much better luck with Millie and Harry Williams. Harry inherited a fortune from his father, who had made his money in lumber and White Rock Mineral Water. Alma and Millie had much in common. They were both very earthy, straightforward people without any pretensions. Millie was born in San Mateo to a family as poor as Alma's; both began their road to riches as mistresses of wealthy men. Millie's paramour was Henry Clay Frick, the coke and steel pioneer, whose eye she caught when she went to New York as a young girl. From her aged lover Millie learned not only about the good life, but about good art. When Frick died in 1919, he remembered Millie in his will, but not to the tune of $500,000 as he had promised. Instead, much to the irritation of the widow, but to the delight of Millie, she inherited $5 million. Millie promptly bought herself a house on Long Island and a Rolls-Royce, and began a search for the only thing she didn't have — a husband.

"Harry Williams had an eye for the girls, but he was a very elusive bachelor," said Tom Howe, who as director of the Legion would later get to know both of them well. "One day Harry was lunching on Long Island and Millie arranged to have her car break down on a dusty road where she knew Harry was going to be driving by on his way home. He stopped to help her, and not too long after, she became Mrs. Williams. She was a jolly number, and they had a wonderful life together."9

At their Avenue Foch home, where she was a frequent visitor, Alma, never one to mince words, came right to the point. She repeated the conversation to Tommy Howe later. "Harry, " she rasped, "you and Millie don't have any children. Why don't you leave your collection to the museum?"

Their collection was superb. It contained landscapes, genre paintings and portraits from the seventeenth-century Dutch and Flemish schools and the eighteenth-century English and French schools. Many of the subjects, in accordance with the earthy tastes of Millie, were of voluptuous nudes, or ladies in court gowns with one breast coquettishly bared. They bore titles like *Sleeping Venus Surprised by Cupid*, by Eustache Le Seur, and *The Triumph of Chastity*, of the School of Fontainebleau.

Harry was very receptive to Alma's request, and Millie enthusiastically agreed. The Williamses not only deeded their collection to the Legion of Honor museum, but they endowed it with a million dollars for future acquisitions. Harry made only one stipulation. After he died, he wanted Millie to retain the collection for her lifetime.

"Since she was fifteen years younger than Harry it never occurred to anyone that she would go first," continued Howe. "Then, in the summer of 1939, Mr. and Mrs. Williams came over to America and stopped in Los Angeles before coming to San Francisco. While lunching down there, Millie met with a grotesque and, sad to say, fatal accident. She choked to death on a chicken bone.

"Although he was grief-stricken, Mr. Williams came up to San Francisco and insisted the collection be brought over at once. We called an emergency board meeting.

" 'I think there will be a full-scale war in Europe,' he told the board. 'A lot of it will be fought on French soil, and it will last a long time.'

"One of the trustees, Mr. O.K. Cushing, Mrs. Spreckels's lawyer — she liked him well enough but she thought he charged her too

Alma had friends in all walks of life, from royal personages to San Francisco Fire Chief Charles Brennan, with whom she took a ride in April, 1931. (Courtesy Archives, San Francisco Public Library)

much for estate taxes — said: 'Mr. Williams, I think it would be prudent to have the contents of your house on Avenue Foch taken to a remote part of France — say Normandy or Brittany — and stored in a suitable warehouse until the war is over.'

"Thank God Mr. Williams didn't agree. He said, 'No, I want those things brought over now.'

"So then Herbert Fleishhacker used his connections with the steamship lines. All the things were packed in an emergency manner in Paris and were put on the last ship out of Marseilles before the war in the autumn of 1939."

That spring in 1929 when the Williamses agreed to leave their collection to Alma's museum, Alma remained in France when the sculpture exhibit, underwritten by Archer Huntington (called the "greatest exhibition of American sculpture ever held anywhere") opened as scheduled at the California Palace of the Legion of Honor, on April 28, 1929. It remained, to the delight of art lovers, for the next six months.

It was just the kind of an opening that Alma would have relished, with the president of the National Sculpture Society coming from New York to officiate. There was to be a gala preview with a magnificent buffet dinner the night before, and lots of dignitaries to deliver the flowery speeches interspersed with vocal and instrumental music — all the ingredients Alma loved. Among the three hundred American sculptors whose works were exhibited were San Francisco artists including young Jacques Schneir and Alma's old friends Earl Cummings, Edgar Walters and Haig Patigian, as well as her former teacher who had used her as a model, Robert Aitken. But Alma made no plans to attend.

Possibly Alma's absence had to do with the wedding of Rudolph's daughter, Claudine. Ten days before the exhibit opened, Claudine was married in an elaborate ceremony to George Montgomery at the Burlingame home of Rudolph and Eleanor. Despite her close friendship with Rudolph, Alma was not invited. She was still a social pariah. Her name was carefully excised from the list of relatives of the two "notable families" united by the marriage.

Alma returned to San Francisco the next fall and brought Dorothy with her. The young girl, who would later make the best-dressed lists on two continents, was growing bored with wearing school uniforms day and night at the New York boarding school. She hated the strict rules and wanted to come back to San Francisco and, specifically, to go to Miss Burke's.

Unhampered by any notions of pride, Alma refused to be stopped by the fact that the door to that school had once been slammed in her face. If that's where Dorothy wanted to go, then by God, she would see that she got in.

"Mother took me by the hand, marched me into Miss Burke's office and demanded, 'Isn't it about time you accepted my daughter?' " she recalled.

Dorothy, a quiet, shy student who had none of her mother's abrasive qualities, was finally admitted.

"They skipped me a year — my marks were pretty good — and I entered as a senior, when I was sixteen."

Dorothy began cultivating friendships with the daughters of the Burlingame set and looked forward to the day when she would make her debut. The idea of a debut was fine with Alma, who promptly set about planning the event. Although Dorothy's eighteenth birthday was not until March 1931, Alma decided to hold it during Alma's favorite time of the year, the Christmas season, three months before that date.

Dorothy's debut was not Alma's only involvement at that time. With her usual gusto, she was immersed in two other projects. One was the city's "little theater" movement, headed by Reginald Travers. Alma's interest in the theater evolved because Dorothy, a lovely-looking girl with a tall, willowy figure, had tentative aspirations toward a stage career after high school. When Dorothy was invited to appear before Travers's group in a private recital, Alma, with almost the same fervor she had shown for Rodin, took it upon herself to make Travers famous. She ignored the fact that the Travers Theater in the Fairmont Hotel had been well-known for the past twenty years.

Alma sponsored a poster design contest in which she offered two prizes to students of the California School of Design for the best posters advertising the Travers Theater. She held a large reception, with all of the submissions on display, in the foyer of the theater. Her guests included the board of directors, the cast of the theater's current production, *Lysistrata,* and, of course, the press. Alma herself was one of the judges along with Travers and Edgar Walters, now on the faculty of the California School of Fine Arts.

The poster contest was followed by a tea some weeks later at Washington Street in honor of Travers. Alma invited her many guests to share her enthusiasm for the little theater movement. Balalaika music, played by a Russian orchestra in full costume, entertained the more than one hundred guests.

Then, a few weeks before Dorothy's debut, Alma held a party at the Travis Theater in which she brought together an eclectic mix of people she so enjoyed presiding over. "As interesting and as representative a body of San Franciscans as has ever been brought together," the *Chronicle* reported.[10] The play, a puppet presentation of Eugene O'Neill's *Emperor Jones,* was just as unusual as the guest list, which included author Gertrude Atherton; tennis champion Helen Wills Moody; actress Virginia Phelps, appearing in the local production of *Salome;* Senator Sam Shortridge; a British authoress from London; drama critic Alex Fried; society editor Marie Hicks Davidson of the *San Francisco Call-Bulletin;* plus a number of foreign consuls, musicians and painters.

With her customary bluntness, Alma told reporters, "Everybody here has done something. It's more fun to get them together than a new pearl necklace."[11]

Another project very much on Alma's mind was waging a local war against hunger. With the country in the throes of the worst depression in its history, Alma, who always was beset by fears that at any moment she would return to being poor again, felt a great empathy for the hordes of newly created poverty victims. She began working on an idea for raising money. As with her Tombola, she decided the way to do it was to collect things, instead of money — things like used clothing and household goods. Then she planned to hold rummage sales. "There's money to be made in salvage," she proclaimed sententiously. She set about organizing a Salvage Shop, moving the limousines out onto the driveway and turning her huge garage into a rummage depot.

Despite the Depression, Alma saw no reason to curtail her own spending on the historic occasion of her daughter's coming out. On the contrary, she reasoned that her elaborate plans would provide work for countless unemployed people. And it did. The debut, which was spread over a weekend, began on Friday with an elaborate tea. It was followed the next night with a dinner dance for five hundred guests which lasted well into Sunday morning. Platoons of carpenters, electricians, florists, caterers, waitresses, barmen and musicians were given work, as were the dressmakers, hairdressers, jewelers and others whose services were necessary to prepare the guests for the two affairs.

"Because I hardly knew anyone in San Francisco," recalled Dorothy, "my mother asked a friend of hers, Lansing Tevis, who knew all the right people, to draw up a guest list. And they all came!"

In all the excitement of the preparations, the birth of Alma's second grandchild, on December 10, Adolph Spreckels Rosekrans, nearly went unnoticed by his grandmother.

The decorations for the Friday afternoon tea were in evidence before guests even entered 2080 Washington Street. The marble steps were covered with a red velvet carpet, and guests walked up under a canopy hung with antique Spanish brocades of royal red.

The entire house was thrown open for the party, and each room was decorated in red and silver with silver wreaths joined by garlands of silver. In corners of the various rooms were large Christmas trees trimmed with gold and silver ornaments and blazing with colored lights. A Spanish orchestra played during the reception. Enough food to care for San Francisco's hungry for a month filled the enormous "tea" table in the Louis XVI ballroom.

Alma and her daughter received their guests in the circular Pompeiian Room, under a bower of white orchids. The debutante wore an "enchanting gown" of white tulle trimmed with silver lace, while Alma, hovering over her shy daughter, wore a "stunning frock of silver and black brocade."[12]

Alma, true to her promise to her very proper daughter, did little to embarrass the debutante. Although butlers kept refilling her martini glass as she had instructed them before the party, she never lost her dignity. She did kick off her pumps before the last of the guests passed through the receiving line. When people commented, she responded honestly and loudly, "For Christ sake, my feet hurt. Whattya expect me to do?"

The following night, more than five hundred people walked across the red carpet to an even more elaborate setting. The ball was given primarily for the "younger set." Guests were startled when they were greeted at the door by a pair of pages dressed as Nubian slaves in loincloths, resembling, right down to their rhinestone collars, the statues chained to the fireplace in the Italian Room. The grounds around the house were illuminated like a veritable fairyland, with hundreds of twinkling colored lights arranged in the hedges and trees in the gardens, with fountains splashing over colored globes.

"The party took up a whole square block, with a big tent over the driveway," reminisced Florence Rosekrans. "It was so big and so wonderful I thought I was in a queen's palace."[13]

Guests walked from the house to the pavilion in the garden along a covered corridor done in blue, silver and gold. In the tent, they sat at small tables decorated with wrought-iron Christmas trees and modernistic reindeer. They feasted on caviar washed down with champagne and scores of other delicacies. Following the epicurean seven-course dinner, there were cabaret acts and dancing until dawn.

The rich food held little appeal for the girl who was being honored. Some time around midnight, Dorothy slipped out for a hamburger with a young man from a pioneer Oakland family, Andrew McCarthy, who would later become her second husband.

So elaborate was the affair that it received mention in *Time* magazine, along with the two other outstanding debuts that week, Barbara Hutton's in New York and Elsa Armour's in Chicago. Alma was delighted. Nobody's daughter in the Burlingame crowd ever got that kind of notice!

Once the debut was over, Alma, who, despite her outrageous extravagances, could also be very frugal, packed up all the yards and yards of Christmas tree lights, wrought-iron trees and the reindeer and put them away for future use. They came in handy after she met Jean Frickelton and became involved in her Outdoor Christmas Tree Association.

Chapter Notes:

1. Florence Rosekrans interview, Dodie Rosekrans tapes.
2. Loie to Alma, Sept 2, 1927, Loie Fuller Papers, Lincoln Center Dance Library.
3. Alexander de Bretteville to Alma, December 17, 1927, John Rosekrans papers.
4. *New York Times,* February 28, 1928, p.44.
5. Edith Walsh interview.
6. John Rosekrans papers.
7. Ibid.
8. Alma to Alex, September 3, 1931, John Rosekrans papers.
9. Thomas Carr Howe interview.
10. *San Francisco Chronicle,* November 17, 1930, p.6.
11. Ibid.
12. *San Francisco Chronicle,* December 20, 1930, p.6.
13. Florence Rosekrans interview, Dodie Rosekrans tapes

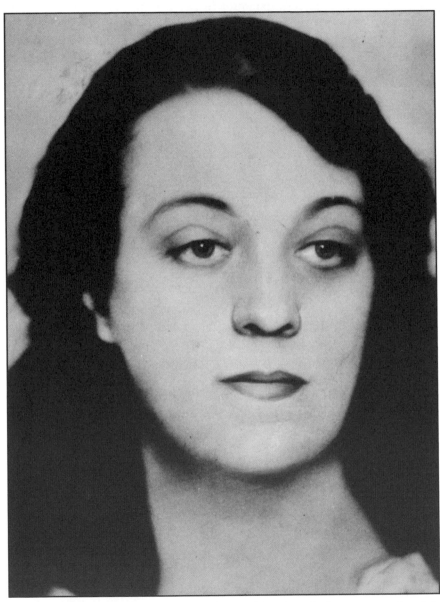

Alma's campaign for the Outdoor Christmas Tree Association was spearheaded by Jean Frickelton, her devoted public relations expert, who had this portrait retouched for newspapers. (Courtesy San Francisco Chronicle)

CHAPTER ELEVEN

The Honorary President
of the Board

 "MOUSY" IS THE WAY Tom Howe described Jean Scott Frickelton. Others called the tiny spinster who lived with her mother "a person of gentle demeanor, soft-spoken, almost diffident." The first woman to start an advertising agency in San Francisco if not the West, she was also described as "more like the headmistress of an exclusive girls' school than the victor in a score of advertising battles."[1]

Frickelton was the opposite of Alma in every way. Well educated, she was a Stanford graduate with a degree in journalism, a fact which Alma always pointed out when introducing Jean or writing about her to anyone. Jean was to remain her closest friend for the rest of Alma's life — and beyond. "My devotion to Gangy [the name given Alma by her first grandchild, John Rosekrans, which was readily adopted by the rest of the family] goes beyond the grave," Frickelton told John many years later. She proved her devotion by destroying all the papers, letters and other material Alma had given her over the years to save for the biography she wanted Jean to write, because "they were too personal." Frickelton added, "Gangy had great confidence in me and I will never do anything that would ever discredit her in any way."[2]

"Jean Frickelton was in love with my mother," Dorothy Munn stated flatly.

While there is nothing to suggest a lesbian relationship between Jean and Alma, it is clear that Frickelton idolized her from the first moment they met, on December 2, 1930.

The meeting occurred as a result of the Outdoor Christmas Tree Association. One of Jean's advertising accounts was the Northern California Electrical Bureau. The Outdoor Christmas Tree Association was formed ostensibly to save live trees from being cut down. It was really a gimmick to stimulate the use of more electricity by promoting the idea of lighting outdoor trees and other holiday decorations. The luncheon that day at the Palace Hotel was the kickoff of the annual campaign.

"One of the newspapers wanted to have a contest for best outdoor lighting and they asked me to get some San Francisco women to act as judges," Jean said, in the often repeated story she loved to tell. "They wanted an assortment: a clubwoman, a housewife, a teacher and a socialite — a term Gangy would not like herself because she was such a democratic person. I was right near deadline, and in desperation I went to Marie Hicks Davidson, society editor of the *Call Bulletin,* and asked her, 'What am I going to do for a socialite?'

" 'That's easy,' she said. 'Right over there is Mrs. Spreckels with her sister-in-law. Why don't you go up and ask her?'

"I said, 'I wouldn't do that for anything. The great woman who built the California Palace of the Legion of Honor! I'd be scared to death!' I almost fainted at the idea."

"She said, 'She's a very nice person. Go over and ask her!'

"So, with teeth chattering and knees trembling, I walked over and said, 'Pardon me, Mrs. Spreckels.' And I told her my story. She turned around, gave me a big smile, and said, 'I'd be glad to be a judge.' "[3]

It wasn't just flattery that made Alma accept so readily. She had a little quid pro quo in mind. She needed someone with public relations experience to help her launch her Salvage Shop idea. When Alma invited Jean to her home "because I have a project I'd like to discuss with you," Jean knew she was about to be used.

> I told the girl I was working with that I wasn't going to go. I had started my own agency just two years before and I was having quite a struggle. And I bought a house with a huge mortgage in '29 and I had to support my invalid mother and myself. I had no one in the world to do anything for me and I couldn't afford the time. Most of those rich people will take your time and give you nothing for it.
>
> My friend said, "Please go, just this once because if you don't go then I can't go." So I went to please her.
>
> Mrs. Spreckels said she wanted to start a Salvage Shop to benefit the poor. Well, I don't think anyone ever said no to her. I don't think they could, because she was so persuasive and had such a personality and such a presence. She was so fascinating to listen to her talking that I completely succumbed. I thought,

well, I'll manage it some way.

I did. I worked with her about six or seven months until she went to Europe and turned the shop over to the Salvation Army. We got along very nicely. She paid me $75 a month. I must say that was the last money she ever paid me. After that, I volunteered everything I did with her.

One reason I volunteered was that she really became my friend and I hated to take money from a friend. And another reason was that I saw these vultures hanging around and I got so fed up and disgusted with them that I wanted to have her know that there was one person in her collection of people who was not after her money or her influence. As a result, I saw people come and go and get thrown out and only two people seemed to last with her. One was Lita Clerfayt and the other was me.

That is not the way Tom Howe saw it. He entered Alma's life very shortly after Frickelton did, when he went to work for the museum.

"The Frickelton relationship was a very sycophantic thing," he said. "She fed Mrs. Spreckels's ego. Mrs. Spreckels was usually pretty sharp about people who were sucking up to her. But not with Frickelton. She had some sort of recipe for appealing to Mrs. Spreckels's vanity and I think Mrs. Spreckels treated her awfully well."[4]

If Frickelton had any "recipe" it was her sincere admiration for what she regarded as a fascinating woman of great accomplishment. Almost young enough to be her daughter (Jean was seventeen years younger than Alma), Frickelton gave Alma something she never got from her own children. She gave her respect. Unlike Alma's children, Jean bore her no resentment for past neglect; she was never embarrassed by Alma's behavior. Alma, the high school drop-out with a tremendous admiration for educated career women, could hardly regard Jean as a sycophant. A more apt term for their relationships would be "symbiotic." Jean needed Alma to brighten her colorless life, and Alma needed Jean to validate hers.

Frickelton earned every penny of the money Alma paid her to publicize the idea of a Salvage Shop. First, she designed the stationery for the new organization. Across the bottom of the page was the motto "Phone And We'll Send for Your Goods." Because Alma wanted a picture of Rodin's *Thinker* somewhere on the letterhead, Jean obliged by firmly implanting him (sans a phone) in the midst of the organization's name, The San Francisco Salvage Shop. And, as in the days of Alma's Belgium Relief Society, an imposing list of sponsors graced the left-hand column.

Jean got her the platforms from which to deliver her pitch. Sport-

Dorothy and Alma attend a fete for the Outdoor Christmas Tree Association in 1931. Dorothy, a tall, slender beauty, was trying for a career as an actress in local productions. (Courtesy San Francisco Chronicle*)*

ing her new title, President of the San Francisco Salvage Shop, Alma spoke first before the county council of the American Legion. The newspapers duly reported her message that "We are not asking for funds but we want used clothing, bric-a-brac and furniture. We will give employment to the unemployed in the reconditioning of these things." And while she had the floor, she also "reviewed the purpose in presenting the Palace of the Legion of Honor to San Francisco."[5]

The idea of the Salvage Shop caught on, and by June, Alma was being honored by various organizations. A men's group was the first to jump on the bandwagon, as the Indoor Yacht Club had been the first to honor her nearly two decades before. This time it was the Masons. For the first time in their history, the Masters and Warden's association paid tribute to a woman when Alma was honored at a banquet at the Palace Hotel, June 13, for her "outstanding civic and charitable work."

She was surrounded at the speakers' table by her brothers Walter and Alex and her son, now a young man nearly twenty. Adolph, once finished with high school, had no intention of putting in any more time on education. A lifestyle of hedonism was more to his liking.

Meanwhile, Alma was following very closely the employment problems at the Palace of the Legion of Honor. While Alma had been living in New York, her friend Cornelia Quinton, the museum's efficient director, had become addicted to cocaine. In time it got so bad that Quinton's secretary would take the mail to her house because she couldn't make it to the museum. In 1929, she was replaced by Lloyd Rawlins, a Harvard graduate who came from Cambridge to take over the direction of the Legion of Honor.

Then shortly after Rawlins's arrival there was trouble at the de Young Museum. Its director, George Barron, took to drink and was relieved of his duties. Herbert Fleishhacker, as head of the Park Commission, was an ex officio member of the park's two museums. He was president of the Legion's board and ran the boards of both museums, having shaped them in Alma's absence to suit himself. Fleishhacker sent Rawlins, who was doing an excellent job at the Legion of Honor, over to the de Young to clean up the mess there. Rawlins had personal problems of his own which, fortunately, didn't surface until later. A homosexual, he had difficulties keeping his amorous adventures discreet.

When it became apparent that Rawlins needed an assistant to take over at the Legion because so much of his time was spent at the de Young, Rawlins appealed to his alma mater, Harvard, who sent out Thomas Carr Howe.

Howe was then a young student working on his doctorate in

*Thomas Carr Howe, who served the Legion of Honor Museum for 37 years, 29
of them as director, guided the acquisition of important collections, such as the
Williams, Sachs, and Wentworth collections, as well as many individual works
such as Rembrandt's* Portrait of a Rabbi, *Manet's* The Milliner, *and Renoir's*
L'Algerienne. *Alma's demands on him were frequent and sometimes bizarre; he
met them with a sense of humor and great style. Mr. Howe retired in 1968, the
year of Alma's death. (Courtesy Fine Arts Museums of San Francisco)*

eighteenth- and nineteenth-century European painting. He arrived the first of April 1931, and shortly after that he was summoned to tea at Washington Street to meet the woman he would always refer to as "Mrs. A.B." A tall, handsome young man with courtly manners who had been raised in Indiana, Howe was overwhelmed by the surroundings on Washington Street.

"The butler ushered me into the drawing room, which occupied the entire west end of the house. It was very elegant. Louis XVI furnishings. There was even a sedan chair, which is in the museum today, with panels on each side by Antoine Coytel, the eighteenth-century painter. In true Elsie de Wolfe fashion, Mrs. A.B. had a telephone installed in it!

"Helping at the tea table was Mrs. Ashton Potter, who acted as a sort of social advisor to Mrs. A.B. except that she never took anybody's advice, as I was to find out later. Mayme Potter had great connections and was a marvelous hostess, in a limited way, because she didn't have much money. Mrs. A.B. turned to Mayme as a kind of social guide, but then it was too damn much trouble. She didn't care that much.

"Mrs. A.B. swept in, making quite an entrance. She couldn't have been nicer to me. She disliked Lloyd Rawlins because she felt he spent too much time at the de Young, so she decided to be particularly nice to me to irritate the hell out of him."[6]

There were other reasons Alma was "particularly nice" to Howe. As with Frickelton, she was impressed with his scholarly credentials — Harvard University and his stint at the Fogg Museum. And, as with Frickelton, she sensed his respect for her own knowledge. ("She had an instinctive taste in the finest of eighteenth-century French furnishings. It was a sixth sense. And she was also very, very much drawn to fine sculpture," said Howe.)

But at the same time she was being "particularly nice" to him, Howe found she could also be particularly embarrassing, as she was one afternoon soon after their initial meeting.

"Mrs. A.B. invited me to drive with her to the home of Mrs. Lenore Woolums, in Marin. Mrs. Woolums was a fine pianist. We were going over to lunch with her at noon. We drove in Mrs. Spreckels's Rolls-Royce with a chinchilla lap robe despite the fact that it was a lovely May day. She was blazing with red and green jewels enlivened with diamonds, and I felt, with all this luxury, as if I was in the mysterious East. I said, 'What beautiful jade!' She looked at the jewelry as though seeing for the first time, and roared, 'My God, Mr. Howe, those are emeralds!' "

When they arrived at the Woolums's, Howe found that one of

the luncheon guests was the new conductor of the San Francisco Symphony, Pierre Monteux.

"Over coffee, Mrs. A.B. said — to my absolute horror — 'Oh, Mr. Howe, you play the piano. I'm sure Mr. Monteux would love to hear you play.'

"I wanted to go right through the floor. I had to sit down and play a Chopin waltz and I have no more sense of time than a rabbit. It turned out to be the basis for a wonderful friendship between me and Mr. Monteux because he understood perfectly my embarrassment."

There were other things that embarrassed the new assistant director of the Legion. Like being summoned to do museum business in Alma's boudoir as she issued orders from her green velvet canopied bed with the gold swans.

"She'd call and say, 'Mr. Howe, could you and Mr. Rambo come by on Wednesday for breakfast?' That meant being out there at 6:45. Jim Rambo was the brilliant curator of decorative arts. He hated getting up in the morning more than anything else in the world, but we always went. Other times she'd ask us to stop by on our way home. Usually, all she wanted was to talk and to have us mail her letters for her. And we'd say, sure. We got our old-fashioneds and she got her pitcher of martinis. We never knew what mood we'd find her in. Sometimes she was depressed, or she was excited over some new idea, or she was terribly angry or she was just lonely and wanted company. The only thing that was constant about her was that she was always variable."

Alma's complete lack of self-consciousness could be very disconcerting to Howe. Once he arrived a few minutes early for an appointment. She received him as usual in her bedroom. Having just returned from a shopping trip, Alma tossed her large flowered hat onto one of the bed's swan headposts and continued to disrobe, wiggling out of her girdle and stockings in front of the very red-faced young man.

Alma's remarks were often a cause for acute discomfort for Howe. There was the time he brought the newly elected president of the Legion's board of directors, Harold Zellerbach, to meet her. Zellerbach, president of one of the country's largest paper manufacturing companies, came in with the city's leading banker, A.P. Giannini, whose support for the museum Zellerbach hoped to get. Neither one of them had ever met Alma before. Even before Howe could make the introductions, Alma opened the proceedings with a startling bit of news. "Guess what? I just found my cook in bed with the butler!"

Then there was the evening Howe sat next to her at a museum function when the speeches were long and the speakers were dull. She leaned over to him and whispered in his ear. "Mr. Howe, do you know how to speak Danish?"

"When I replied I didn't, she said, 'Well, I'll teach you something. It's what I'd like to do to that fella up there now,' and she muttered a string of words.

" 'You know what that means?' She had a way of drawing out her vowels when she spoke, and in a voice that you could hear all over the room, she replied, 'Light a fiire up your aass!' "

Alma's ideas about the value of art objects always puzzled Howe.

"I brought back from Holland in 1951 a Van Gogh painting, a still life with two blue gloves. A very elegant picture. It belonged to a Dutch family I knew pretty well. It was selling for $50,000 — a fraction of its value today. The museum had the money to buy it. I showed it to Mrs. A.B. For some reason, it didn't draw blood. She said, 'Frankly, I don't think it's worth all that money.'

"Once she asked me to evaluate for tax purposes some things she wanted to give to the museum. Well, I couldn't do that, working for the museum. The government wouldn't accept it. So she got Haig Patigian, a local sculptor, to appraise them. Two Rodins — *St. John the Baptist,* and *Walking Man.* And he evaluated them at $4,000 apiece! And she accepted that! I think the last sale of *St. John* was either $90,000 or $120,000."

She was also capricious about her generosity. She could be downright stingy when asked for money. Tom Howe found that out when the staff of the Legion was organizing a baseball team and needed $50 for uniforms. Knowing Alma was a baseball fan, and noting that the team intended to call itself the Adolph B. Spreckels Memorial Baseball Team, he dared to bring the matter up at a breakfast meeting. Would Mrs. A.B. care to donate the money for the uniforms?

Infuriated, Alma dumped the contents of her purse on the table next to her bed. Out poured a lipstick, cigarettes, matches, an emery board, a handkerchief and a few coins.

"Where do you expect me to get fifty dollars?" she thundered. "My God, you people have got my skin. Now you want my guts!"

On the other hand, there was the day she asked her son-in-law, Jack Rosekrans, to drop by on his way home from work.

"Gangy," he said, "is it really important? It's been an awfully bad day for me."

"Yes, it is," she replied, "very important."

So Rosekrans went, and he got his drink and they talked. She said nothing of interest at all, and then she said — as he knew she would — "Here are some letters. Will you mail them please, but not this one. Wait until you get home to open it. It's important."

"It *was* important," related Howe. "It contained a check for $175,000! She gave it to Jack for no particular reason. Probably because she wondered how he could stand being married to her daughter!"

Howe also learned that Alma considered herself to be above the rules that pertained to other people. The Legion of Honor's closing hour was four o'clock in the afternoon. But not for her. Shortly after Howe's arrival, he was informed that "Mrs. Spreckels's secretary called and wishes that arrangements be made to illuminate the outside of the building at 9:30 on the evening of Tuesday, September 1, 1931. She expects to bring out some guests. This is an arrangement which Mrs. Spreckels makes quite frequently and it is necessary to have someone open and close doors and to see to turning on and shutting off lights." Mr. Howe got the message.

"No Smoking" signs were anathema to Alma. "When she came out to the museum, she'd say, 'Mr. Howe, I want a cigarette.' And I'd say, 'You know, Mrs. A.B., the only reason you want a cigarette is because you know you're not supposed to smoke in here. But I'm not going to tell you that you can't smoke in here.'

"So we'd sit down in the garden court and she'd smoke away and love it when people looked in and saw somebody smoking with all the 'No Smoking' signs."

A moving van from Stringer's Van and Storage was an almost daily occurrence outside the museum when Alma was in town. At first, Howe thought the van signaled some new gift from its principal benefactor. But he soon learned that Alma was either taking out or putting back some of the Rodins that she had loaned. Sometimes she took them out because she was entertaining important guests. Sometimes she just got lonesome for her "children" and wanted them home for a while.

Feeling she was above the rules that applied to other people was one of the reasons she never was accepted by San Francisco society, Howe surmised. "If she'd just cared more about conforming, she'd have had it made. But she loved to put her feet up on the coffee table and have a glass of beer with the local tradesmen. She made no effort to put on airs. She was a perfectly natural human being," said Howe.

It was perfectly natural, to Alma's way of thinking, for her to sue her children in 1931 for an income change which ultimately cost them $1,700,000. That was the total amount that Alma had drawn in monthly advances against the estate since A.B.'s death. The first four years she received $25,000 a month, on which she learned to live quite nicely. She thought she was being very magnanimous when she consented to cut that amount in half in 1929. She had been scraping by on $12,500 a month ever since. If she were big enough to do that, she felt, then her children, who were going to inherit the whole estate after her death, could also do with a little less.

While the children's lawyers fought that out in court with Alma's lawyers (the legal fees alone took more than $330,000 from the estate), Alma left town. Now that she had her San Francisco Salvage Shop well organized, and she had milked from it all the publicity she could get, Alma turned it over to the Salvation Army. She went on an extended trip to Europe with Dorothy.

Dorothy was ready to go. Her brief fling as an actress had climaxed with her first professional appearance in a comedy called *The Marriage Lease,* which ran for three nights at the Western Women's Club at Sutter and Mason. While the play did not go on to become a Broadway hit, Dorothy received favorable notices. Wrote the *Chronicle,* "Dorothy Spreckels...showed herself an attractive and poised young actress."[7] But the young ingenue had one ineluctable drawback: she was close to six feet tall, and it was difficult finding leading men who were not dwarfed by her. The beautiful post-deb wasn't going to sit around waiting for actors to grow up.

"Mother was fun to travel with — most of the time," said Dorothy. "She had swing moods. She could get terribly depressed, a regular Danish Hamlet. She loved to travel. During that 1931 trip, we sailed on the *Kungsholm* to Russia. We were among the very first Americans to visit there after the Communists allowed tourists in. Mother couldn't wait to visit the Hermitage. She got very angry when the Russians refused to allow a Jewish man off the ship.

"Ely Culbertson was also one of the passengers. Contract bridge was just coming into vogue, and Mother made me learn how to play. I thought it was very boring at the time."

They stopped in Denmark where Alma visited her relations. She learned that Kaj de Bretteville had died and she urged his wife to send their daughter, Ulla, now nearly twenty, to come and live with her. Ulla again refused.

On their way motoring across the Riviera to Italy, where they were to rendezvous with Adolph, Alma stopped in Monaco to visit the Oceanographic Museum there. She was thinking in terms of another museum. She expressed her desire in a letter to Jean Frickelton. "Who knows, perhaps our dream of an oceanographic museum for San Francisco may be realized some day. Truth is stranger than fiction."[8]

Alma's words were prophetic. Truth was, little more than two decades later, San Francisco would have such a museum. But one of the great sorrows of Alma's life was that she would never be given the credit she felt she deserved for establishing it.

In Italy, they were the guests in Florence of the Count and Countess Fabricotti, where Adolph met them. Alma's son, a startlingly handsome young man, pursued a life of pleasure. Nothing held his interest for very long. He made friends easily; keeping them was another matter. People were drawn to him because of his charm and his generosity. They were repelled by his temper when he didn't get his way. His behavior was particularly obnoxious when he had too much to drink. Alma alternately adored her only son and heaped abuse on him.

Shortly after their reunion, mother and son were screaming at each other. Alma implored him to make something of his life, to take an interest in the sugar business or horse breeding. Adolph wanted only one thing: to be rid of his mother's domination. He was counting the days until his twenty-first birthday when he would come into his inheritance.

The two parted company quickly. Adolph went to Mexico, where he developed a fondness for marijuana. From Mexico, he went to Cuba, where he was arrested for trying to smuggle the weed into that country. It took the intervention of the American consulate and the payment of a large fine to get him out of the Havana jail.[9] When he came home, he fell in love and got married. He didn't bother to wait until he was twenty-one.

When Alma, still in Europe, got word of the news she flew into a rage. Bitterly, she anguished about the second of her children to marry so defiantly, so secretively. Not only had her son taken a wife, he had chosen one who had children!

Maybe it's not so bad, she thought, always willing to see the best side of whatever Adolph did. Maybe marriage is just what he needs. With responsibilities maybe he'll settle down now.

His bride, Lois Clarke de Ruyter, was just as irresponsible as he was. They met over the gaming tables in Reno. She was there getting a divorce. The daughter of the Lewis Latham Clarkes, Lois, a beautiful New York socialite, scandalized New York society when she eloped at age seventeen to Maryland with Jack de Ruyter, scion of another prominent New York family. Four years later, she shed both her husband and her two sons, who were left behind with the de Ruyter grandparents. Immediately after meeting the charismatic Adolph, some months her junior, Lois announced she would marry him as soon as her divorce was final.

They were married in San Francisco in July 1932, two months before Adolph's twenty-first birthday, at a small church wedding. They tried to keep it secret, but it was quickly reported in San Francisco papers and the *New York Times*. Little Alma, delighted that her brother was following what was becoming a family tradition of weddings without the presence of their domineering mother, gave the bridal dinner at her Woodside home. Present were Lita Clerfayt, Clarisse and Alex de Bretteville and two friends of Adolph's.

Dorothy's wedding, two years later, was more to Alma's liking. In the first place, she was not only invited, she was allowed to plan it. And second, the groom was a handsome, romantic and very rich Frenchman who was all that his ecstatic future mother-in-law could have wished for her daughter. Jean Dupuy, the son of the late French senator Paul Dupuy and heir to a huge Paris publishing fortune, met Dorothy in Europe and followed her back to New York, wooing her on the transatlantic cruise. She turned him down, but the smitten young man was persistent. When he took the ship back, he continued his suit from the middle of the North Atlantic. Intrigued, Dorothy said yes, thereby gaining the distinction of being the first woman to accept a proposal by ship-to-shore phone.

The marriage ceremony, despite the fact that it merged two extremely wealthy families, was comparatively modest. Not by Alma's choice. Given her wishes, she would have staged another spectacular, equal to Dorothy's debut. But perhaps it was the groom's family's idea to keep it low-keyed. Jean Dupuy was twenty-four; Dorothy was barely twenty-one.

The wedding took place April 28, 1934, in Alma's New York apartment at the Hotel Pierre, before two dozen guests. (In an "economy" move, in response to Alex's pleas, Alma had sold her Fifth Avenue co-op and had moved into the Pierre.) Little Alma, pregnant with her third son, Charles, came from San Francisco to be her sister's only attendant. Uncle Rudolph Spreckels, whose financial empire had collapsed along with the stock market, gave the bride away. It was about all he had left to give away. Adolph was not among the guests, although his in-laws, the Lewis Latham Clarkes, were. Alma liked Lewis Clarke, who was president of the National Institute of Social Sciences, an organization which accepted for membership only people who had done worthwhile things. She was quick to join after she persuaded Clarke to sponsor her.

Also present at the wedding were members of the groom's distinguished family, including his sister and brother-in-law, Prince and Princess Guy de Polignac, Count Louis de Polignac and other relatives. Following the wedding, the young couple went to Paris, where they made their home in Dupuy's sumptuous town house and Dorothy quickly established herself as the darling of the international set.

Six months later, when the newlyweds visited San Francisco, Alma gave an elaborate dinner dance at the Mark Hopkins to introduce her son-in-law to several hundred people. All of Dorothy's classmates from Miss Burke's were there, even the daughters of the de Young sisters, who were among her closest friends. San Francisco society, while not exactly taking Alma to its bosom, was now at last, in deference to Dorothy, tolerating her.

With her children all married, Alma was ready to throw her considerable energy into other projects. The idea for a maritime museum was uppermost in her mind when she was asked to address the San Francisco Beautiful Committee. The committee of women was formed to plan ways to spruce up the city three years hence, when, in 1937, with the completion of the two bay bridges, San Francisco would once again play host to the world.

As a result of her membership in the National Institute of Social Sciences, Alma had enlarged upon her original idea of a museum just for ships. She sought a broader concept, one that could perhaps earn for her the NISS's Gold Medal Award. It was given annually to persons who had made a major contribution in the field of social sciences.

In her speech to the women, she emphasized the need for "centers to house not only maritime collections, but mining, industrial exhibits and other typically California displays in which visitors to the city would be interested." For her suggestions, which were received with much enthusiasm, she was made an honorary member of the committee.[10]

Alma's ideas for her next museum were put on hold temporarily, while she juggled two other projects. One was the remodeling of 2080 Washington Street, and the other was the renovation of Sobre Vista, Rudolph's three-thousand-acre country home in Sonoma, which she bought from him at a bargain price, just one step ahead of his creditors.

By this time, Ulla De Bretteville, now a young woman of twenty-three, finally accepted Aunt Alma's invitation to come and live with her. "It all sounded so glamorous," said the naive girl from Denmark. The fun was about to begin.

Chapter Notes:

1. Bert Goldrath, *Western Advertising,* February 1956.
2. Jean Frickelton interview, Dodie Rosekrans tapes.
3. Dodie Rosekrans tapes.
4. Thomas Carr Howe interview.
5. *San Francisco Chronicle,* March 5, 1931, p. 12.
6. Thomas Carr Howe interview.
7. *San Francisco Chronicle,* April 24, 1931.
8. Alma to Jean Frickelton, September 9, 1931, John Rosekrans papers.
9. *New York Times,* January 11, 1932, p. 15.
10. *San Francisco Chronicle,* July 4, 1935, p. 16.

Alma's famous ermine wrap served her for many seasons, as did her gowns. She had little interest in buying clothing or jewelry; society page photos (this one in 1937) show her wearing the same ensemble over and over. (Courtesy Archives, San Francisco Public Library)

CHAPTER TWELVE

Alma Takes a Husband

ALMA WASN'T THERE to greet her niece when Ulla finally arrived in San Francisco. She was too busy tearing up her house. The young woman who got off the boat was tall, slender, blonde and pretty. Or she could be, thought Alma, when Ulla rang the doorbell. God, I'll have to get her to a dentist right away and get those teeth straightened![1]

Ulla walked into a mess. The beautiful mansion she had heard so much about was undergoing extensive remodeling. Carpenters were knocking down walls, tearing out windows and plastering up openings. Her aunt, considerably heavier than she had been when Ulla had last seen her in Paris, walked around in a chenille bathrobe, screaming at the workmen.

"Five minutes after she yelled at them, Aunt Alma would be sorry, and she'd ask Swayne, her butler, to bring them all drinks. And she'd sit down and drink with them! This happened repeatedly, I was to learn."[2]

Ulla was put in the new bedroom on the parlor floor next to Alma's bedroom, in what had formerly been the ballroom. Alma explained that she needed bedrooms more than a ballroom. Between the two rooms was a bathroom, carved out of what had been the center of the ballroom. Left intact was the imposing floor-to-ceiling Louis XVI fireplace, its elegance diminished by a toilet on one side and a claw-foot bathtub on the other.

Opposite the tub was a row of cupboards. Since neither her bedroom nor her aunt's contained closets, Ulla had to hang her garments in one of the bathroom cupboards. Uninterested in clothes, Alma saw no need to waste space on them. After the luxurious bathroom and boudoir Alma had enjoyed in her quarters on the third floor, it is curious that she created such spartan surroundings for herself when she moved to the parlor floor.

But if Ulla thought the bathroom was an odd bit of remodeling, she was even more surprised at what was happening to the front entrance. "Aunt Alma had the marble steps torn down, and the front doors removed, and the whole thing cemented over. You had to come in through the porte cochere entrance, up the small elevator built for Uncle Adolph. You felt you were coming into the lobby of an apartment house."

That was Alma's idea, to transform the house into apartments so that she could rent them out — preferably to her family. Padding about in men's scuffs, the only kind of slippers she was comfortable in, she directed workmen in making two apartments off the lobby in the basement, in the area that had been the huge kitchen, the silver vaults and other storage rooms.

Alma took the parlor floor for herself. When she finished cutting it up, she had a three-bedroom, three-bath apartment. All the remodeling was done without the use of an architect and without building permits.

"What do I need an architect for? I know what needs to be done," Alma told astonished friends. And permits from the city? "Get *their* permission?" she roared. "Hell, haven't I done enough for this city?"[3]

The only one who took advantage of his mother's offer of an apartment was Adolph, who by now was divorced from Lois after three rocky years of marriage. Leaving behind a daughter, the child she had with Adolph, Lois ran off a week after the divorce to marry his best friend. Adolph moved in — briefly — with Little Lois and her governess, on the floor that had previously contained the family living quarters. Alma had remodeled A.B.'s suite into a dining room, and her former quarters into a kitchen, so the apartment was complete in itself.

"Adolph and I rearranged some furniture in the living room up there," recalled Ulla, "and the next day Aunt Alma walked in and put it back the way it was again. There was only one way, her way. She would give orders to Adolph's butler and his cook. One day soon after he moved in Adolph got fed up and moved to the Fairmont."

Ulla quickly realized that the reason her aunt had persisted in getting her to move in with her was that "she had to have someone around at all times whom she could order around. She couldn't order her children around because they just didn't take it. They fought with her continually."

She also noticed that Alma liked to run people's lives for them.

"Aunt Alma loved to take complete charge. If I had to go anywhere, she planned it all out in detail for me. She never thought I could do anything alone. She decided that I should go to secretarial school so I could become her secretary. The next thing I knew I was memorizing shorthand and learning to type.

The immigrant girl was bewildered by her eccentric aunt. "She was a remarkable woman. She could be very gracious and lovely, but you never knew what mood you were going to find her in. She could be very sweet, especially when the two of us were alone. But the next day, she would scream at me for no reason at all. You never knew from one day to the next how she was going to feel about you. Once, she tore up all my clothes. I still don't know why..."

Perhaps it was the size of those clothes that infuriated Alma. Ulla was very slim, while Alma was fighting a losing battle with her own weight. The more frustrated she got, the more she ate. The only clothes she felt comfortable in were bathrobes.

But her astounding energy never left her. At the same time that she was acting as her own architect and contractor on the remodeling, Alma was also engaged in a major project at Sobre Vista. She saw it as a replacement for the Napa ranch, and maybe someday, as A.B. had hoped, her son would want to run it.

The huge estate, in the midst of a redwood grove in the Valley of the Moon, contained a five-acre artificial lake. Several houses were set among manicured lawns and beds of beautiful flowers. The main house, atop a knoll, was a white seventeen-room mansion. Down a path to the left was the "clubhouse," as commodious and well appointed as a country club. On the right was an equally spacious bathhouse and a large outdoor swimming pool. It was all very nice, Alma conceded, but it wasn't up to her standards.

First she had to do something about the electricity. There were no modern conveniences in the buildings, which had been constructed at the turn of the century. A small portable power plant provided a limited and uncertain supply of electricity for illumination. Cooking and water heating were done with old fashioned oil-fired equipment. Alma quickly changed all that. She called the Pacific Gas and Electric Company to run in lines. Before she was through, she had installed enough electrical appliances in the residence, clubhouse, bathhouse and other buildings to equal the total load used in seventy-five average homes.[4]

She gave employment to two hundred men in Sonoma County at the depth of the Depression in 1934 when she ordered seventeen miles of fencing built along the property. Then she retained the men to pave a road next to the fence. Part of that road ran up to where her property met that of the Jack London ranch. The author and his wife, Charmian, had long been Alma's friends. He died in 1916, but his widow continued to live on the ranch.

"There were some awful hairpin turns in that road," said Ulla. "One morning, when we were up at Sobre Vista, Aunt Alma woke me at 6 a.m. to get the pickup truck so we could take a ride around it. I'd never driven a pickup. Took me half an hour to get it started. I was terribly nervous on those turns, but Aunt Alma sat there shrieking with delight. She thought it was wonderful. Every time we went to Sobre Vista we had to take a ride around the mountain because she was so happy with that road."

One of the men who worked on the fencing and paving gangs was Walter Piezzi. "She offered me the job as her superintendent after she hired and fired seven other men," he recalled. "I said, no way. Her auditor asked if I would take it just until he could find someone. I said I'd do that. I got going straightening out things and my wife did the bookkeeping, which was all mixed up at the time. After we got the books straightened out I asked the auditor, 'Did you find someone yet?' And he said, 'No, we're not going to. You're the only one who straightened out this ranch.'

"There was this shack. It was way up in the timber and Alma says, 'Move it down,' and then she says to me, 'Move in.' It was nothing but a barn with a wood stove. So we fixed it all up and made a nice, comfortable house."[5]

Alma gave several acres to her brother Alex for a summer home, and she also gave her friend Paul Verdier land on which he promptly built.

"As soon as the construction was over at Washington Street and the ranch was electrified, Aunt Alma decided she wanted to be thin again and entertain and have parties," said Ulla. "She went on diets and slimmed down and got new clothes and went into another phase."

"In the summertime she'd have fifty guests at a time at Sobre Vista," remembered Piezzi. "I'd make ten trips a day hauling garbage. There were twenty bedrooms up there, ten in the big house, five in the clubhouse and five in the bathhouse, and each one was decorated different. One was Mexican, one Italian, some French, like that. People came from all over. Then she goes and buys a golf course near by so's they could play golf. The Sonoma Golf Course, 180 acres. Cost her plenty."

Among the visitors to Sobre Vista, chauffeured there by Joe Grasso during his ten years in Alma's employ in the thirties and early forties, were Charlie Chaplin, Billie Burke, Bing Crosby, Douglas

Fairbanks and his wife, Mary Pickford, John Barrymore, Joe E. Brown and his wife, heavyweight boxing champion Gene Tunney, Leo Carillo, and A. P. Giannini, founding president of the Bank of America.[6]

"She built a chicken house, and a duck house. We had four hundred pigeons, forty rabbits and some cows," continued Piezzi. "She'd call over to my house on a Sunday morning and holler, 'I want seventy-five broilers for dinner.' We raised them and we'd fatten them on corn and milk and when they were a pound and a quarter, we'd kill them."

Alma's attitude toward her garden often confused the superintendent. "There was a large fountain in front of the main house, with flower beds around it. If she decided she wanted purple flowers in those beds, she'd have the gardener go down and buy all the purple pansies he could get. After he got them in, she yells, 'Rip them out. I want something yellow there.' The poor guy would have to run all over town to find yellow plants.

"She'd get me up at five o'clock in the morning to talk over what we were going to do," Piezzi continued. "She'd make plans to do this and do that... She was always changing, changing, changing. Remodel this, tear this down, build something else... Incredible woman!"

Once she ordered a change in the landscaping right in the middle of a luncheon. Before sitting down to eat, one of her guests, admiring the beautiful view from the veranda of the main house, remarked that it would be even more beautiful if a large tree hadn't obscured part of it. After lunch, when the party reappeared on the veranda for coffee, the tree was gone.

"She was the kind of a woman one time she'd give you the shirt off her back and the next time she'd kick your shirt and pants off," said Piezzi. " But I never paid no attention. She would call my wife up and bawl her out about something she should have talked to me about, but I was up in the mountains somewhere. So I finally went to her one night and said, 'Mrs. S, I give you half my life and I'll be God damned if I'm gonna give you the rest of it.' And by golly, that did it, and everything went fine after that. She treated me like a prince."

Not everyone gave Alma the kind of loyalty that her superintendent did. "The help up there at Sobre Vista would buy whole truckloads of booze by the case, and then the butler would sell half of it. She never knew the difference," said Piezzi.

He didn't think very much of his boss's son. "Adolph was kinda messed up. He drank a lot. Alma wanted me to keep the gates on the property all locked. I put gates on all the roads. Adolph would come along with a pistol, and bang, bang, he'd shoot the locks right off. You couldn't say nothing. Just put another lock on — and he'd come along and bang, bang again."

Just as Alma had remodeled 2080 Washington to keep her children — especially her son — close to her, so she hoped that by improving Sobre Vista she could entice Adolph into running it for her. Florence Rosekrans recalled the time she and her husband were guests at the ranch.

"We were walking around with young Adolph, and Newt said to him, 'My, you have a wonderful opportunity here, Adolph, with this place. Your mother's been fixing it and you can see all the improvements. A wonderful layout. All the things are here that you like to do.'

"He said, 'Mr. Rosekrans, if you don't mind, I do not care to discuss this.' I guess he knew he didn't want to be a farmer. He was so handsome, and if you didn't know him, a perfect gentleman."[7]

The more Alma tried to get her son interested in Sobre Vista and Sonoma Valley, the more he resisted. To endear him to the community, she hosted a huge joint birthday party attended by "practically everybody in the valley," according to the *Sonoma Times-Index.* The party honored Adolph and James B. Morris, a prominent valley rancher. It was Adolph's twenty-fifth birthday and Morris's ninety-fifth. Adolph did not attend. Hiding her disappointment, Alma presented the rancher with a gold horseshoe, "a gift from my son, who couldn't be here today. Anyone who attains his ninety-fifth year is worthy of recognition by the community."

Adolph, at age twenty-five, was already into — and almost out of — his third marriage. Shortly after his divorce from Lois, he met and married Gloria Debevoise of Baltimore. He took her to Europe on a honeymoon and before they returned home, the marriage was over. The bride's mother was appointed guardian to prosecute the divorce suit because the second Mrs. Spreckels was only eighteen years old. She charged cruel and inhuman treatment, detailing blow by blow the beatings she took.

Adolph's current bride was Geraldine Spreckels, his second cousin, daughter of John Spreckels Jr. Geraldine, a dazzling brunette, was being groomed for a movie career. When they returned after their elopement, Alma dutifully entertained for the newlyweds, hoping this latest union would succeed. It didn't. Fourteen months later, after several trial separations — during one of which the gorgeous Geraldine flew to the waiting arms of movie actor Robert Taylor for comfort — she filed for divorce. The grounds, which tore into Alma with fresh intensity each time Adolph's escapades hit the newspapers, were the latest manifestation of his "extreme cruelty."

Distraught about the way her son was wasting his life, Alma reacted by throwing herself into another project, completing the museum at Maryhill which Queen Marie had dedicated ten years before. Sam Hill died in 1931, with the building still unfinished. In his will, he left his art collection — including some important Rodins Loie persuaded him to buy — and his fortune to the museum. The art, plus all of the gifts Queen Marie brought with her in 1926, lay in unopened crates in the incompleted building. His estranged family went to court to break the will. By the time the litigation was settled, all that was left to support the museum was the revenue from the cattle ranch and peach orchard nearby. The family stated publicly that Maryhill was a joke and would never be a museum at all. That was all the challenge Alma needed.

"The reason I am taking such a personal interest in the affairs of Maryhill is because I was horrified when I heard that Mr. Samuel Hill's son called his father's museum a 'fake museum,' and I determined then that I would see that Maryhill was made the kind of Museum of which Mr. Samuel Hill would be proud if he were alive to know it," Alma wrote to the board of trustees.[8] It took her three years of hard work, during which she managed to antagonize scores of people, but she got the museum opened. How she did it deserves a chapter of its own.

Meanwhile, Alma spent the spring of 1937 in Paris, the city she loved so much. Paris now had an additional attraction for her — her daughter Dorothy. Alma was very proud of the way the soignee Mrs. Dupuy had become the toast of Paris. The very correct and proper Dorothy, who always strove to make the right impression, was quickly adopted by the international set.

Now that Alma had sold the chateau at Neuilly, she didn't bother moving into a hotel; she simply took over Dorothy's elegant home.

"It was bad enough having my mother ordering my servants about, but it was very difficult when she invited all her San Francisco friends to come over and stay with us, too," said Dorothy. "It was all terribly embarrassing."

Later that year there was much more embarrassment in store for Dorothy when Alma, in a prime example of her impetuousness — and poor business judgment — bought a white elephant hotel in Santa Barbara, which led to her meeting with the cowboy who was destined become Dorothy's stepfather.

It began when Alma, on her way back from a brief holiday at del Coronado in December 1937, stopped at Santa Barbara at the

*Alma bought Sobre Vista, north of Sonoma, from her
brother-in-law, Rudolph Spreckels, who needed cash more
than he needed 3,000 acres, a neo-classical country house, a
swimming pool, and a race track.*

Alma entertained lavishly here in the late 1930s. Charlie Chaplin, Bing Crosby, John Barrymore, Herb Caen and A.P. Giannini were just a few of those who enjoyed her hospitality. (Courtesy Sonoma League for Historic Preservation)

invitation of Mrs. William Roth. She was invited to sit in the Roth box at the horse show at which Lurline Roth, a noted horsewoman, was showing her trotters. William Roth, the owner of the Matson steamship lines, got his start in the shipping business when he worked for A.B. in the Oceanic Steamship Company. The Roths owned a magnificent estate in Woodside named Filoli. They also had a *pied à terre;* in San Francisco they were tenants of Alma's on the top floor of 2080. Since she couldn't rent it to her children, Alma felt justified in renting it to acquaintances. The arrangement worked out fine. The Roths seldom used the place and Alma seldom went upstairs to move the furniture around.

Alma was in a very expansive mood that night. She felt rested from her sojourn at del Coronado where, since she owned the place, she could order the help around with impunity. She also felt stylish again, partly because she was able to keep her weight down, and because she had allowed Dorothy, who was now a regular on the international best-dressed lists, to talk her into buying some new Paris clothes.

Alma smiled with delight at the excitement in the ring. Something about a man on a horse had always quickened her pulse. She thought about "Foxy" Keene and the Long Island polo matches. But the polo players in their hard hats and khaki breeches swinging their wooden mallets paled in comparison to these men in their colorful Western outfits galloping by her box, carrying aloft their banners and the American flag.

One man in particular caught her fancy. He rode a golden palomino unlike any of the racehorses A.B. used to breed, and when he made his horse stand straight up on its hind legs, the effect, from bottom to top, was dazzling. The stirrups gleamed with silver, the rider's heavily ornamented chaps shone against the silver saddle. His belt buckle, the corners of his shirt collar and the band around his sombrero all flashed with silver. It seemed to Alma that horse and rider were one vertical streak of silver against a golden background. The man seemed to know everyone in the stands, and they responded to his broad grin and the wave of his hat with chants of "Uncle Emo, Uncle Emo." Suddenly, Santa Barbara seemed like a wonderful place.

That night, in the Roth box, someone mentioned that Samarkand, a lavish Santa Barbara hotel that was designed as a Persian wonderland out of *A Thousand and One Nights,* was for sale at a ridiculously low price. It had been an elegant boys' boarding school when it opened in 1916. On the grounds was an artificial lake of one and a half acres containing a sculptured relief map of the world,

Over lunch at the Persian Room at the Sir Francis Drake Hotel, Alma talks business with H.B. Klingensmith, manager of the Samarkand Hotel in Santa Barbara, in May 1938. The Samarkand seemed a bargain when Alma bought it, but proved to be a massive millstone around her neck before she finally got rid of it years later. (Courtesy Archives, San Francisco Public Library)

complete with erupting volcanoes and waterfalls coming from snow on mountain peaks. The school was closed during World War I, when its director, Dr. Prynce Hopkins, an ardent pacifist, went to jail. Dr. Hopkins, who was preaching his philosophy to young men on their way to becoming cannon fodder, was jailed for hampering recruitment. When he got out, he went into self-imposed exile in Europe.

Dr. Hopkins's mother remodeled the boarding school into an ultra-exclusive hotel. She did away with the geography lesson, stripping the artificial lake of its volcanoes and mountains. She turned the lake into a reflecting pool with a colonnade of eighty white pillars. She stocked the pool with goldfish and surrounded it with a rose pergola. Inside, she decorated the hotel in Persian style with red, brown and gold colors predominating. The administrator was known as the Caliph of Samarkand. He wore a satin turban, brocade jacket and silk bloomers with curl-toed Arabian slippers. The rest of the help were similarly dressed. The grand opening was New Year's Eve 1920, when Ruth St. Denis and Ted Shawn, then America's premier dance team, performed Hindu dances.

But Samarkand received a mortal blow with the debut of the Santa Barbara Biltmore in 1928 and the stock market crash in 1929. In the following decade, the hotel alternately opened and closed with regularity. The formal gardens withered, the goldfish died in the reflecting pond and the buildings deteriorated. Skunks and rodents were the only inhabitants. Samarkand was now on the market for a paltry $55,000, including the thirty-two-acre grounds. Despite the fact that it was known as a white elephant, a jinxed, inconveniently located piece of property, Alma decided to buy it. Not surprisingly, hers was the only bid. She felt confident she could restore its former prestige, and she promised magnanimously to everyone within earshot that she was going to put Santa Barbara on the map.

Once the hotel was hers, Alma went to work immediately. Much to the horror of her brother Alex, who felt his sister had gone mad to get into something she knew absolutely nothing about, she spent more than $215,000 refurbishing Samarkand. She replaced the elliptical fish pond with a heated swimming pool. She called in gardeners to "do something about that mess out there." Then she went inside and threw out all the Persian furnishings. Racing back to San Francisco, she ordered the movers to load their trucks with a fortune in her personal *objets d'art,* including gorgeous Flemish tapestries and bales of rare Oriental rugs.

"It is my belief," she told the *Santa Barbara News Press,* "that those who can afford to collect outstanding works of art should not hide them in private collections. They should be available for the pleasure of all people; as in the California Palace of the Legion of Honor, so it will be in Santa Barbara. My interest in Samarkand as a commercial development is second only to my interest in making it a center of public art." In answer to the question of where she got her hotel experience, Alma reminded reporters that "the Spreckels interests include the del Coronado Hotel in San Diego."

Two weeks later, when Ulla was dispatched to Santa Barbara, the hotel was in the same kind of a mess 2080 Washington Street had been when the girl first arrived in San Francisco. Alma's astonished niece, now acting as her secretary, found herself typing invitations for a Christmas luncheon to be held at Samarkand, one week away, sponsored by the Outdoor Christmas Tree Association.

The OCTA, Jean Frickelton's scheme for the Pacific Gas and Electric Company to increase the use of electricity during the holiday season, was now a statewide organization, with Alma the California president. Its slogan, "An Outdoor Christmas Tree for Every California Home," was fully supported by its sponsor, the California State Chamber of Commerce. Alma lined up an impressive list of names for her board of directors, including "America's sweetheart," Mary Pickford; banker A. P. Giannini; Mrs. Felix McGinnis, wife of the president of Southern Pacific and Alma's next-door neighbor in San Francisco; Mrs. George Cameron, whose husband was now publisher of the *Chronicle;* Harry Chandler, publisher of the *Los Angeles Times;* and Alma's close friend, Mrs. Earl MacBoyle, wife of a wealthy Grass Valley mine owner, whom Alma made vice president of the organization.

Determined to carry out her duties as state president of the OCTA and get exposure for her hotel at the same time, Alma rushed into plans for the luncheon. She coaxed Mrs. MacBoyle to donate a gold cup as first prize for the best outdoor display and intimidated other friends into following suit. Soon she had twenty prizes which were displayed in the hotel lobby. She set an example for outdoor decorations by dressing up the hotel's exterior with the thousands of globes and miles of wire and silver wreaths that she had saved from Dorothy's debut.

Recalling that luncheon later, Alma said, "Inside, the hotel was terrible and I was ashamed of it. One hundred and seventy-five people came, including the mayor and his wife.[10]

Luncheon guests heard Alma's rendition of the Clarence Pratt story. Pratt was the founder of the OCTA. His story was told at all OCTA gatherings.

One year, at Christmastime, Mr. Pratt, a kindly man with no children of his own, decided to decorate the pine tree outside his home with colored lights, and every night for a week that tree spread its cheer throughout the neighborhood. Imagine his delight when he received a note in a child's scrawl from a little boy who lived an apartment house across the street.

'I am sick in bed,' the little boy wrote, 'and when I look out my window and see that beautiful tree all lit up, it really made me feel better. Thank you for sharing Christmas with me.' Mr. Pratt decided then and there that he would encourage everyone to share the glow of Christmas far and wide. That is how our organization came to be founded, and I hope that you will join with Mr. Pratt and me in bringing Christmas to all the little boys and girls in Santa Barbara.

Alma sat down to mild applause and cold expressions on the faces of her audience, particularly that of local society leader Pearl Chase. Suddenly struck by *déjà vu,* Alma felt she was back in Portland again. What she didn't know — and never made it her business to find out — was that that was exactly what Pearl Chase and the ladies of the city's prestigious Garden Club had been doing for years. They took pride in the fact that all the downtown buildings and parks and most of the private residences were decorated each Christmas, going back almost to the days when the land belonged to Spain. They didn't need Mrs. Alma Spreckels to tell them what to do! OCTA did not increase its membership in Santa Barbara and Alma received no cooperation from the residents in her attempt to put Santa Barbara on the map.

On Christmas morning, Alma came face to face with the silver-studded cowboy, Elmer Awl.

"We met over a pool table," recalled Awl. "A newspaper man took me out to meet the owner of Samarkand. She had a pool table at the hotel she wanted to give to the Rancheros. My first impression was that she was a very powerful woman. But I liked her right away. She was a very impressive person. A wonderful person, but she overdid everything."[11]

Alma quickly learned that Elmer wasn't just a cowboy. He was the manager of J. Ogden Armour's large ranching interests in Santa Barbara, headed by Armour's son-in-law, Jack Mitchell. Awl was forty-seven, nine years younger and a head shorter than Alma, even in his high-heeled cowboy boots. He was divorced and had a grown daughter. A man of modest means himself, he was right at home with wealthy people. They readily accepted him as one of their own because he was such fun. A hard-riding, hard-drinking man who loved to be the center of attention, Uncle Emo, as people affectionately called him, could always be counted on to tell a funny story, sing a cowboy ballad or send his audiences into loud guffaws when he pranced around dressed in women's clothes. He helped organize Santa Barbara's Fiesta activities in 1924 and had continued to serve as director of Old Spanish Days ever since.

"One year I rode my horse right up to the bar at the 'Barbara hotel during the parade," he told Alma later over drinks in her suite.

But the activity that Elmer was proudest of was his Rancheros. He told her how the group got started. "Back in 1929, my good friend, the artist Ed Borein, comes to me and says, 'I have a chuck wagon ... let's go out for a few days with the boys.' That's how the Rancheros Visitadores was born. Every year since we invite riders from all over — some pretty fancy fellas from back East, friends of Jack Mitchell and movie fellas from Hollywood, and my buddies Will Rogers and Leo Carillo, and we ride and make camp all over the hills. It's a hell of a lot of fun, let me tell ya."[12]

It was also a hell of a lot of fun being in Elmer's company, which Alma was often, whenever she was in Santa Barbara. He made her feel young again, and desirable, and he refused to be awed by her money. He also made a favorable impression on Ulla. To Alma's niece from Denmark, he was a hero right out of the books she had read about the American West.

That winter, after Adolph was nearly killed in a plane crash in February 1938, Alma had little time to think about Elmer. Adolph had bought himself a Lockheed twelve-passenger plane and was on a jaunt to Reno with his first wife, Lois, supposedly to get remarried. Lois had divorced Adolph's friend Clinton, with whom she had had another son. The plane crashed at the Reno airport, killing the pilot and critically injuring Adolph and Lois. Alma insisted, after they got out of the hospital, that both of them recuperate at 2080 Washington Street. They did. That time together killed any plans the two might have had for a reconciliation.

Alma didn't think about Elmer until the following summer at Sobre Vista when she held a huge party to celebrate the annual Sonoma Rodeo. The rodeo was held each June to commemorate California's becoming a republic. She watched the barrel races and the steer roping and the bucking bronco contests from her box, where her guests included San Francisco Mayor Angelo Rossi and Police Chief John Quinn. "Wouldn't that Uncle Emo fella get a kick out of this," she murmured to Ulla.

Two weeks later, Alma was watching Elmer ride during Fiesta Days in Santa Barbara. She invited him to come over to the hotel afterwards. She needed cheering up. She had just got word that

*Alma and Elmer Awl, the happy newlyweds, disembark from the plane
they chartered for an elopement to Reno in 1939. Never has the adage
"Marry in haste, repent at leisure" been more conclusively proven;
the haste was breathtaking, and the repentance dragged on
for years. Yet Alma's genuine happiness here is unmistakable.
(Courtesy Archives, San Francisco Public Library)*

Queen Marie had died. First Loie, then Sam and now Marie. All of them were lonely dreamers of great dreams like herself. All of them gone. Who appreciated them? Who appreciated her? Certainly not her children. Who else besides her father would ever call her "a blessing to all humanity"? Was she doing enough good with her life? She had to finish what Sam and Loie and Marie had started at Maryhill. She owed those three a debt. Meanwhile, she thought, looking over the rim of her martini tumbler at the good-looking cowboy next to her, I'm entitled to have a little fun.

The fun continued all summer, and peaked when Dorothy paid a suprise visit to her mother late in the fall. "I had just come home from Paris, where, as Mrs. Dupuy, my own life was very proper, very orderly. I was on my way to Coronado with my friend. We stopped to see Mother at her suite at the Samarkand. There she was in a tea gown entertaining a bunch of cowboys, sitting with their boots off, all of them drinking martinis. The whole place," continued Dorothy, used to the perfumed scent of Paris drawing rooms, "smelled of skunks. I was so embarrassed. How low can my mother sink, I wondered?"[13]

Fortunately for Dorothy, she was back in France a few months later when Alma invited Elmer to Sobre Vista for a weekend in February 1939. He had planned to come up North to attend the opening ceremonies of the California Trails Building at the Golden Gate Exposition on Treasure Island, the world's fair held to commemorate the opening of the two bridges spanning San Francisco Bay.

"Come on up to my place in the country first for the weekend," said Alma. Elmer accepted. He never made it to Treasure Island.

Sunday night, after two days in the romantic Valley of the Moon showing off her ranch to Elmer, Alma was feeling very mellow as she sat at the dining table with her guests. Present were Little Alma and her husband; Alma's friends, the MacBoyles; Paul Verdier and his mistress, opera singer Verna Osborne; and Ulla.

Midway through the elaborate meal, when she had drunk enough liquor to dissolve any lingering inhibitions, Alma bellowed out, "Elmer, why don't you leave Mitchell and come and work for me?"

"Hell, lady, you'd have to marry me first," he retorted, always loyal to his friend.

"O.K., let's go," said Alma, rising from the table as Little Alma gasped in astonishment.

Dialing United Airlines, she made arrangements to charter a plane leaving from San Francisco that night. "C'mon folks," Alma said to her guests, "we're going to a wedding — mine!"[14] Little Alma grabbed her husband's arm and stormed out of the house shouting,

"Mother, this time you've *really* lost your mind." The other guests, including the bridegroom-to-be, thinking it was a great lark, piled into cars and drove down to the airport in San Francisco. Her daughter was wrong, Alma hadn't lost her mind — not completely. She had at least enough sense to do what A.B. had done. She made her intended sign a prenuptial agreement. On the plane, Elmer agreed that should the marriage be terminated by her death or any other reason, all he'd get would be $25,000.

When they reached Reno, Alma had a chance, if she so desired, to change her mind. They found the county clerk's office was closed. The clerk had the mumps, and there was no one else who could issue a marriage license. Undaunted, Alma told the pilot to fly them to the next county seat, Minden. There they woke up the clerk and got the license. Then they returned to Reno and were married at 4 a.m. Ulla was her aunt's maid of honor. Nobody gave the bride away. It was dawn when they flew back to San Francisco, and Elmer, forty-eight, and his bride, fifty-nine, fell asleep, exhausted, in the bed in which kings had made love.

Reporting on the elopement a few days later, the weekly *Sonoma Times-Index* wrote, "The romance was a great surprise to Sonoma Valley friends, for Mrs. Spreckels had travelled all over the world and had not lost her heart to anyone. However, she described Mr. Awl as 'the most fascinating man I have ever met,' which is a fine compliment from the former wife of the sugar king, the late A.B. Spreckels, who had met many fascinating persons including royalty, artists and literary lights."[15]

In San Francisco, the news of the elopement was treated less graciously. The wire services reporter, phoning the story in to a San Francisco society editor, was asked how to spell the groom's last name. "A-W-L," he replied, "as in the tool for punching holes in old leather." The story was repeated in drawing rooms from Nob Hill to Burlingame.

So was the sing-song question, "What did Alma give Elmer when Elmer gave Alma his Awl?" And there was the wit who asked, "What did the bridegroom say when he woke up the next morning?" "My God, I'm all covered with Spreckels!" was the reply.[16]

Blissfully ignoring what other people thought, Alma was pleased with what she had done. She had been a widow for fifteen years, with no man to rely on except her brother Alex, and God knows, Alex was no fun — always telling her what she could do and couldn't do. Always criticizing her for spending too much money. Elmer thought she was wonderful. He got such a kick out of everything she did. True, he wasn't like the other men she came near marrying,

Elwood Rice or Alexander Moore. Maybe he wasn't as grand or as important as they were, but they had acted like she didn't need a husband just because she had money. Elmer treated her like she didn't have a dime. Her money didn't matter to him, one way or another. Only *she* mattered to him.

She knew her new husband would do anything she wanted him to. She could count on him. He would help her get rid of Samarkand. Once that hotel was fixed up and running properly, she would sell it and make a lot of money. Then they'd live at Sobre Vista. She would show him what a smart woman he married.

From Elmer's point of view, marrying Alma didn't seem like a bad idea at all. He was no fortune hunter, but it would be nice to be the owner of his own spread instead of playing court jester at everyone else's. So what if she was a lot older, and a very powerful, headstrong woman? He had had plenty of experience with high-spirited fillies. Nothing he couldn't handle with patience and love.

For two blissful days, the bride secluded her groom in her newly remodeled bedroom with only Katherine, the cook, allowed in to bring food and drink. Then the honeymoon was over, and Alma sent her husband back to Santa Barbara. He handed in his resignation to Jack Mitchell and took up his duties as manager of Samarkand. Thoughtfully, Alma sent along her niece, Ulla, to be his secretary.

Chapter Notes:

1. Florence Rosekrans interview, Dodie Rosekrans tapes.
2. Ulla de Bretteville Awl interview.
3. George Livermore interview.
4. *P.G.&E. Progress,* November, 1935.
5. Walter Piezzi interview, Dodie Rosekrans tapes.
6. *Sonoma Times Index,* August 15, 1968, p. 1.
7. Florence Rosekrans interview, Dodie Rosekrans tapes.
8. Spreckels correspondence, Maryhill Museum.
9. Alma correspondence, Ulla Awl papers.
10. Ibid.
11. Elmer Awl interview, Dodie Rosekrans tapes.
12. Ibid.
13. Dorothy Munn interview.
14. Ulla Awl interview.
15. *Sonoma Times-Index,* February 24, 1939, p. 6.
16. Dr. Charles Albert Shumate interview.

Alma's luncheons at Sobre Vista were festive affairs; her guests were often distinguished or accomplished people. At a party for Latin American consuls in June 1941 she provided musicians in Spanish costumes, to the delight of Dr. Antonio Briceno. (Courtesy Archives, San Francisco Public Library)

CHAPTER THIRTEEN

Marriage by Mail

FOR THE NEXT TWO YEARS, Alma's marriage to Elmer was conducted mainly via the mails. Only occasionally did she send for him or go to him for a weekend. All of her letters to "My dear Honey Boy" were signed, "Love, Mommie," with seven X's to signify kisses. Sometimes, when she was feeling especially affectionate, she wrote, "7 times 7, a real 49'er."

At first the correspondence had to do with the possibility of the Infantile Paralysis Foundation buying the hotel for use as a treatment center. In the days before Jonas Salk and his miraculous vaccine, polio epidemics left thousands of crippled victims in their wake each year.

"Honey, dear," she wrote, "if the I.P. deal goes through I will be so happy. If you and I can do something to help those poor sufferers, won't I be proud? You are so good, you never think of yourself. I am going to do your thinking for *your* care. You are unselfish, my boy. Dr. Berry put up a deposit, so we know it is business."[1]

She learned that Santa Barbara had once been a spa during the 1870s and 1880s, where people flocked to take mineral baths. When Elmer wrote her that there was a surface showing of sulphur water on the banks of a creek just down the hill from Samarkand, she ordered, "Bring in some drilling crews. This is wonderful. If you spent millions you couldn't put sulphur water there. God put it there!" She had them spud in a well in an attempt to tap the source of the sulphur seep. The crews dug down four hundred feet, but they found no sulphur. God put it somewhere else. What they tapped into was plenty of malodorous fumes, making all of Santa Barbara smell like rotten eggs. Her efforts did little to endear her to local residents.

While the Infantile Paralysis deal was pending, Alma's fertile

221

mind raced ahead with alternate ideas for selling the hotel. When a Swedish cruise line, hurt by the war in Europe, announced its policy of sending "neutral ships to neutral ports in neutral waters," she dashed off a note to Elmer directing him to "write to Mr. Lundback. We took a cruise on the *Kungsholm*. He is a friend of mine, and tell him to have the passengers come to Santa Barbara. Tell the Chamber of Commerce to send literature."

With Alex leaning on her to cut expenses, she urged Elmer to fire the concierge "as business is very slack. Hoping to hear from you as soon as possible that you have attended to this."

The same afternoon, by special delivery, Alma shot off another idea to Elmer. "I forgot to tell you that in the past, I talked with an experienced hotel man who recommended this course of procedure: He contacted every oil station owner within a radius of 100 miles and personally invited them to the hotel as a guest. He said that sort of personal contact was worth more than any other kind, as autos always stop for gas..."

After she read one of her French magazines, Alma had another thought. She tore out a page of pictures showing fall fashions displayed together with the latest in automobile designs in a "Concours d'Elegance." Eschewing the fashions, she urged Elmer to get the auto dealers to show their new or vintage cars on the lawns of Samarkand in a grand Concours d'Elegance "here in the good old U.S."

When Alma visited the Spreckels sugar refinery at Manteca ("It was so interesting, no Spreckels has been there for years!"), she wrote, "I left literature as I drove along and also talked to the representatives of the different Chambers of Commerce." When she stopped for the night in Fresno, she also picked up another idea, which she quickly transmitted to her husband. Why not strip Samarkand to the bare essentials and run it as a motel?

"The manager of the El Rancho Motel is a very clever man. He runs his motel with two girls that he only gives $200, and he says that the money is in the transients and the bar. Under separate cover am sending you some literature."

Evidently Elmer didn't think much of his wife's motel idea, but she persisted. Doing some quick arithmetic, she wrote: "Forty three villas we have are supposed to rent for $7, which is $301 per day, and eighteen rooms is $125 per day, which is $427; times that by 30 is $12,810 per month. Then you simply operate a coffee shop...

"I know you are not missing a trick in the management of Samarkand. You have my deepest thanks and admiration for sticking on the job. I am so glad you have Ulla...P.S. When you come here I want you to know I will just live for you...Try to get along with less gardeners. Perhaps just having lawns. That is the way the Fresno motel is. The money is in their bar and transients. Their theory is to keep all the rooms filled continually and not keep such a staff. However, our wish is to get rid of it so I do hope some deal will go through. Please be of good cheer. Give my love to Ulla and all..."

In San Francisco, when Alma's friends gave dinners to honor the newlyweds, the bride attended alone. It was more important that Elmer remain on duty at Samarkand. After one affair, she wrote, "The dinner was very jolly. About 20 people. Everyone asked for you and said such nice things about you. Quite a few said they had never met you but heard such lovely things about you that they would love to know you...Please give the enclosed to Adolph."

While worry over Samarkand dominated her thoughts, she was also worried about her son. Adolph, still in his twenties, was now married to the Baroness Emily Hall von Romberg, twenty-seven, who was the widow of Baron Maximillian von Romberg. The young Baron, whose father had been a German World War I ace pilot, and whose mother was the former Doris Converse, of the New York Banker's Trust family, had been killed the year before in a plane crash.

Alma was shocked when she got word of her son's latest elopement. Ardent Francophile that she was, the idea of her son's marrying a German baroness was devastating. But once she realized how tenuous was her new daughter-in-law's connection to that country, her antagonism subsided. Emily came from one of the prominent families in Montecito, the fancy suburb of Santa Barbara. Besides, she was a pretty, sensible, ambitious girl who edited a society magazine. Alma hoped Emily would be the one who could make her son settle down. They were living in Santa Barbara. It was nice that Elmer could keep on eye on them.

With the approach of the Christmas holidays in 1939, Alma's thoughts returned to the Outdoor Christmas Tree Association, and she urged Elmer to stage another luncheon at Samarkand. "Jean is writing you to get up a Christmas Tree luncheon...Can't you get a movie star to come? It is grand getting Leo [Carillo] here in San Francisco and it will give us grand publicity...I wrote Emily all about the Christmas luncheon and asked her to help you in case you decide to give it."

Jean Frickelton, who had grave doubts about the worthiness of the man who had married her idol, nevertheless wrote to him supporting the idea. She stated that "Your 'Mommie' asked me to write to suggest that it might be a good thing to hold another Outdoor Christmas Tree luncheon at Samarkand. When she first went down she put one on ... was done under great difficulties, but most successfully, as in the case with everything she attempts. Of course you would know much more about organizing such a meeting than I could tell you if I stopped to write a book about it ..."[2]

When Elmer agreed to give the luncheon despite strong opposition from Pearl Chase and her Garden Club ladies, Alma wrote with some asperity that "Mrs. Hall [Emily's mother] said that for seven years she spent a fortune fixing up her garden for the garden tours to please Pearl Chase. Then Pearl took her head gardener away and got him a City job, and when Mrs. Hall wanted to join the Garden Club Pearl told her she was too old and wouldn't let her in. All the family are Christian Scientists."

With the same lack of understanding about why Santa Barbarans thumbed their noses at her just as the San Franciscans had, Alma gave Elmer a detailed list of precisely how good she had been to the unappreciative citizens.

"All and all, I feel I have done everything within my power for Santa Barbara, trying to stimulate them to up-to-date ideas like Cooperative Advertising. I gave two big luncheons at my own expense for the Retail Merchants Association and the Chamber of Commerce. Also gave to the Women's Club, the Junior League, the two Horse Shows as well as the Junior Horse Show, twice I gave trophies and you gave. I gave to the Open Air Bowl, became a member of the Polo Club. I forget all I did. I ran back and forth, thousands of miles, time and time again. The Average Woman would have been dead. I really feel I gave all and the best in me. Well, I got my Awl, so it's worth it ... "

When the Infantile Paralysis Foundation decided it couldn't afford to buy Samarkand, Alma lit upon the idea of selling it to the University of California to use as a dormitory. The fact that the hotel was far from the campus, which was in the town of Goleta, miles away, didn't deter her.

"I have an engagement Wednesday to meet Gov. Earl Warren. Mr. Boyen campaigned for him and he is the speaker on the committee for OCTA and he is going to take me ..." she wrote Elmer. That idea fell through. Next, she tried listing the property with a hotel broker.

"The broker seems to think that he will sell Samarkand for $100,000 in cash by Jan. 5, but I won't believe anything until I see the check. Can't you get Petersen to take some of that furniture now for the bill I owe and call it square?"

When she invited her husband to come up to her OCTA luncheon, held a week before his, she gave him these instructions: "Bring up your swell Ranchero outfit, but for the luncheon please wear that grey business suit and get a new decent hat as you need a new one. I have you at a table with Felix McGinnis and Clarence [Lindner, editor of the *San Francisco Examiner*] and men like that ... If you want to fly up with Leo [Carillo] on Tuesday on Errol's [MacBoyle] plane to Grass Valley you are invited to go. Evelyn Wells is going to write it up ..."

Evidently, Alma's husband made a favorable impression on her friends because after he left she wrote, "Willie Tevis told me that he thought your singing was the best act at the Music Box [a popular night club]. Everybody up here just loves you and all would like you up here ... I am writing a little every day for my Memoirs. I am so grateful, darling, that I thought of that. It must make you a little proud of me. I must have some brains and some ability ..."

She had brains enough to realize that if she couldn't sell the hotel, the next best thing was to give it away and take a tax loss. And why not give it to an organization which could benefit humanity at the same time? Like the Infantile Paralysis Foundation. If they couldn't afford to buy it, she would give it to them. Oh, wouldn't A.B. and her father be proud of her! Loie always said she was a woman of great destiny. She felt destined to help those poor infantile paralysis victims — one way or another.

On December 19, she wrote, "Darling Honey, I am so happy tonight. This is going to be the grandest Christmas I have had in years. I feel so happy I can get out of debt at last and not pay any taxes next year. I have had dozens of conferences on the phone and Alex and McEnnerney and De Fremery are studying everything very carefully. Nothing must be in writing re selling the hotel as you know we have tried for months and months to sell it and have not really had a bona fide offer. So I am justified in taking my loss. You have just been wonderful sticking down there. I want to tell you how much I appreciate your loyalty.

"I think I will leave here on December 23 on the train and be back on the 26th for a meeting. I'll let you know so you can meet me. In fact, you don't need to, as you need your rest and I can take a cab ...

"Honey, I am awfully happy tonight. I had a nice letter from Adolph .... My love to you and Ulla. Lovingly, Mommie." Underneath, she wrote, "7 times 7, a 49'er."

Alma's gift was announced two weeks later at the kickoff luncheon for the annual March of Dimes campaign fund at the Palace Hotel, January 12, 1940. She stood before the microphone and told of her "pleasure and privilege in giving the 32-acre estate which could accommodate 300 patients to the national foundation to aid the fight on the disease." The audience rose to its feet and cheered.[3]

Alma was highly praised by *The Argonaut* magazine. In an editorial titled "That the Lame May Walk," it declared that Alma had "performed a noble and unselfish act which further endeared her to the people of California and brought tears of thanksgiving to the eyes of thousands of sufferers from the scourge of infantile paralysis ... Californians, with pride and gratitude for her outstanding philanthropic and cultural achievements, honor their notable fellow citizen."

The honor was premature. The foundation took the next four months to debate whether or not to accept the gift. The wait was making Alma ill. Early in March, she wrote Elmer: "It was sweet of you to ring me up this morning. I am feeling much better. Yesterday I could not lift my head. I slept most of the day and today I can sit up. I am so glad you are going to the races and the Turf Ball with Ulla. It was lucky I did not plan on going as I would have been unable to move ..."

It never occurred to Alma that, by absenting herself from her husband and generously leaving her young niece in Santa Barbara to substitute for her, she might be encouraging more than a friendship to develop between Ulla and Elmer.

A week later, she wrote to tell him, "I am feeling better. It is a grand day. I know pretty soon something will be settled for us and, after Rancheros, I hope you can come up here and we will go to the ranch. I am on a diet and I want to lose weight. I will. I went to the doctor's yesterday and had a cardiograph made of my heart and had a thorough examination. I don't think there is anything serious the matter with me except too heavy and it takes time to get it off. Yesterday I gave Barbara Hutton a luncheon at the St. Francis. I am very strict re diet. Haven't lost a lot, but I think I have in measurements. All my clothes are too big and am having them altered ...

"I have so much physical and mental energy, I *must* get off this weight. Then, all these years, I have had so much mental worry as well as I worked hard on Sobre Vista, the golf links, remodeling this house, and Samarkand. Love to Ulla."

The following day she wrote, "I fixed it so Harry Williams will be made an Honorary Citizen of San Francisco, and Mayor Rossi will personally go to the preview of the Mildred A. Williams Collection at the California Palace of the Legion of Honor at 5:30 Friday and notify Mr. Williams. I was the one who got them to give their collection and this money, so what I have done for SF is not bad

....The only dumb thing I ever did was Samarkand, and after all, Mr. Awl, I wouldn't be *Mrs.* Awl if I hadn't done it. The Catholics are now saying prayers for us. Miss Copren, my nurse, fixed this. Also the Jews. I ought to get the Protestants next."

She was also proud of what she did for J.D.'s grandson, Jack Spreckels. "Young Jack is coming in to see me at 5. I got Billy Matson to become his lawyer as his lawyer doublecrossed him. He gave him his power of attorney to settle his divorce case and nothing else, and unknown to Jack he took $20,000 and tied him up in a voting trust. That's what becomes of people having children and then the parents getting divorced and putting the children in boarding schools and neglecting them. It is a long story, and I was the only one good to these children. I got their grandfather [J.D.] to put them in his will. Well dear, must run to the office. Love, Mommie."

By the end of March, there still was no word from the Infantile Paralysis Foundation. "I really think it would be better to wait until April 2 for you to come up. I am anxious to get some sort of decision — a final one...I am keeping to my diet — lost five pounds. I really must lose twenty more as I will feel more comfortable...Do you know if Adolph and Emily are getting along and where they are?

"I feel happy I was able to help Jack. I want to feel when I pass on that I have never hurt anybody intentionally and done the best I could for everyone in my power, especially the Spreckels family — those who deserve it."

It finally became apparent that the IPF, after sending architects to study moving the kitchen, the cost of installing elevators and ramps, and other necessary expenses, was not going to accept the gift. It was rumored that the reason was because President Roosevelt wanted nothing to compete with the treatment center at Warm Springs, Georgia. Alma wrote bitterly to Elmer. "I am sorry for all those infantile paralysis sufferers. Since Adolph's passing, I have learned so much of the cruelty and selfishness of man. Mrs. Sullivan told me plenty, but does not wish to be quoted. She and her husband are genuinely interested on account of their daughter [a polio victim]."

By now, Alma was beginning to feel she was practically bankrupt. Alex's constant arguments with her over money, and his dire warnings, caused her to make drastic personal economies. She fired Katherine, the cook ("I still remember how to cook, and she will come in only when I have dinner parties"). She contemplated firing Joe Grasso, the chauffeur. ("I could get along without Joe as all my friends buy taxi books and I can get a chauffeur for five dollars a day to go to the country").

"It's so peaceful and quiet here. I have only Sophie now and it is quite enough. Mr. Swayne, the butler, is delighted with the arrangement as he will have just one side of the house to care for and will not have to cross the hall... The Roths have gone East to attend the Kentucky Derby. I am lucky to have such nice tenants. I never see them, don't know when they are here..."

Trying to balance the scales for the Samarkand fiasco, Alma wrote of her successes: "I rang up Johnny Spreckels last night and asked him how he liked his position. He loves it and said he found the business most interesting. Well, that is one more good thing to my credit — got him an honest lawyer, endorsed his note, got him in the Company and found him an apartment."

Also on the plus side was Harry Williams: "I went out to the Legion of Honor yesterday. It really looks splendid. Mr. Williams is now in New York. He brought us six paintings there and is sending them. Isn't it wonderful? He is not even a San Franciscan, although he signs himself 'Honorary Citizen of San Francisco.' I also did that too..."

Alma's euphoria continued as she looked forward to presiding over the opening of Maryhill Museum, Sam Hill's dream that she had turned into a reality. In anticipation of the trip, Alma bought herself a new traveling suit and a large map of the Northwest. "It shows where we sell sugar," she wrote, "and who our brokers are. I intend to take an active interest in the business. I may go to Tacoma and Seattle while I am up there."

In May, when she was opening Maryhill, Elmer was presiding at a gala equally important to him. He rode with five hundred of the Rancheros Visitaderos, the group he founded, on their three-day ride over the Santa Barbara Hills. As *Time* magazine covered Alma's event, so *Town and Country* was on hand to cover Elmer's. The magazine devoted several pages to a picture spread on the history of the celebrity outings: the leaders of finance, stage, screen and politics who particpated, and "the fine horses and picturesque costumes as everyone joins in the fun of being a kid again." Elmer, the joyous "Uncle Emo," was, as usual, the emcee at the ribald closing campfire.

Just as Alma's museum work in the past had kept her away from her children, so it now intervened to keep her from being with her husband to share in the afterglow of his triumph. But if she had any qualms about it, she took comfort from the fact that Ulla was there.

Alma's happiness over her triumph at Maryhill quickly evaporated when she learned of new marital problems of her children. Dorothy, who had returned to the United States alone shortly before France fell to the Germans, acknowledged she was getting a divorce. Whatever the reason, there was no scandal, no unpleasant publicity. Like all of Dorothy's actions, it was all very quiet, very proper.

It was quite the opposite with Adolph.

Emily was suing him for divorce after one year of marriage. Not only were the papers full of the usual allegations of his brutality, but Emily — dear, sensible Emily — made the sensational charge that Adolph was a Nazi sympathizer. There it was in the papers in September 1940 for all the world to see: Alma's son was being accused of "consorting with, entertaining and choosing as his friends and associates individuals openly sympathetic with or employed by the present Nazi government."[4]

Emily further charged that throughout their brief marriage, and very much against her wishes, "he insisted these persons be entertained in her home and in public places, and he regularly, both in private and in public, proclaimed his admiration for and his espousal of the present Nazi regime." All this caused her to be "shunned and avoided as being un-American."[5]

For the next four months, to Alma's extreme humiliation, the case was argued not only in court but in the press. Adolph countered the Nazi charge by insisting that it was Emily who was pro-Nazi. Her attorney argued that his answer was "a sham, irrelevant and evasive."[6]

Emily told about the night they had gone to eat in Luchow's, a well-known New York restaurant, and Adolph placed a Nazi flag on his table, refusing to remove it at the management's request. While the other diners hissed and booed, the couple was ordered out of the restaurant.

The papers reported that Adolph kept an autographed picture of Hitler on his desk. It read: "From Adolph to Adolph with love." It was all some kind of a horrible joke, thought Alma.

Perhaps it was. Ulla, who had become a good friend of the troubled young man, explained it this way: "Adolph was much more Teutonic than French. He favored the Spreckels side. Aunt Alma's cramming all her French stuff down his throat evidently didn't sit well with him."[7]

Alma responded to this latest act of humiliation and pain by turning her energies to the formation of a permanent maritime exhibition, but we are not ready to sail into that one yet.

Meanwhile, Alma, still unable to sell Samarkand or even give it away, finally swapped it in September 1940 for a dairy farm in Marin County worth $80,000. With all her ideas, she overlooked the most obvious one: the land around the hotel was more valuable than the building. The new owner bought Samarkand not for the hotel but for the unused portion of the thirty-two acres that went with it. He promptly subdivided it and sold the lots off at a nice profit. The hotel itself remained standing through World War II when the military requisitioned all available hotel space in Santa Barbara.

After the sale of Samarkand, Elmer loaded a van with all of Alma's rugs, tapestries, paintings and furnishings; packed his saddles and belongings and those of his devoted secretary, Ulla, and headed north to enter Alma's world.

Alma's friends now had a better opportunity to know her husband. If they thought his exhibitionist behavior strange, he continued to amuse his wife.

Elmer certainly made a strange impression on Jay D. McEvoy, an art dealer whose gallery was adjacent to Paul Verdier's City of Paris department store. He was part of a group of Alma's close friends who met frequently to discuss art over long lunches in Verdier's Wine Cellar in the store.

"I met Elmer at a large reception that Campbell MacGregor gave for him and Alma at his home in Pacific Heights," recalled McEvoy. "There was a doorway between the living room and dining room, and when I was introduced to the guest of honor he was chinning himself on the door!"[8]

Dorothy had an equally vivid impression of her stepfather. "He was a transvestite. Imagine my shock at a dinner party to have him come down in my mother's dress!"[9]

At another party, Elmer walked into the oval dining room wearing a pair of bloomers and sporting a breadbasket worn helmetlike on his head, imitating a football player. The guests watched silently as he tackled the butler. All eyes were focused on Alma to see how she would respond. She laughed uproariously. "Isn't my Honey Boy a card?" she asked the astonished guests. It was the first time English had been spoken all evening; the conversation at the dinner party, in honor of an author from France, was conducted in French. Elmer, unable to speak French, had finally resorted to action.[10]

He was more at ease at Sobre Vista. Millie Robbins, then society editor for the *Chronicle*, remembered his behavior there one afternoon when she was a guest. "We were sitting on the veranda after an elaborate lunch when Elmer came back from washing the horses. He was wet and smelly and the chairs on the veranda were white and elegant. We watched in horror as he plunked himself down in one chair after another shouting, 'Somebody bring me a cold beer.' "[11]

His riding ability impressed the ranch superintendent, Walter Piezzi. "He was very good on horses. He had a horse he brought up from Santa Barbara named Poncho, and that horse pretty near killed him so many times. He finally had to get rid of him."[12]

But not before the palm trees went. "We had about five acres of beautiful lawn," Piezzi continued, "with tall palm trees in there. He told me, 'Walter, I want those palm trees taken out.' We found out later the reason why. Poncho bucked him off one time and he got one of those big spikes up his butt."

"Young Adolph was the only one I couldn't get along with, and he knew it," said Elmer.[13] Alma knew it too, and that could have been the reason for the frequent blow-ups she had with her husband. Adolph, his messy divorce behind him, was a frequent visitor at the ranch. His mother, choosing to believe Emily was the Nazi, had long since forgiven him.

Another cause for friction between Alma and Elmer was her careless disregard for money. He cursed and screamed every time she gave money to her family. He said, "She overdid everything — financially and mentally. She had too much energy. If you said to her, 'I don't think we should do this,' she'd just go ahead and do it...."[14]

After one of their disagreements, Alma wanted to go for a jeep ride around her property. Piezzi recalled what happened next. "He took her up the mountain and he ran off a bridge. She showed me the place later and said, 'You know, Walter, I think he tried to kill me. I'm almost sure!'"

So was her friend Jean Frickelton. "He purposely tipped his car on that narrow road. Gangy fell out but fortunately suffered only a broken rib. Another time I am sure he tried to kill us both as he drove his car in circles on a slippery grass-covered hill. Gangy and I were lucky that the car didn't tip over, and she ordered him to stop. What a vile, evil person he was!"[15]

Vile, evil or not, Elmer quickly became the darling of Sonoma Valley when he began construction of Camp Awl, at the top of the mountain on Sobre Vista. On the spot where Alma had thought of erecting a monument to Queen Marie, Elmer erected a shrine to hedonism. He cleared an area in the midst of the towering redwoods and pines for the horsemen to pitch their tents. He built a giant refreshment center so that scores of thirsty riders could belly up to the bar in comfort. There was refrigeration for an endless supply of ice cubes, a fully equipped outdoor kitchen for catered barbecues, and an open amphitheater to stage the Ranchero shows Elmer loved. Alma was delighted. Her Honey Boy was helping her to put Sonoma County on the map.

Elmer was determined to make the 1941 Fiesta one that the Valley of the Moon would never forget. It didn't. Each June, the town celebrated the Bear Flag Rebellion of 1846, when U.S. citizens led by William B. Ide seized Sonoma and raised the Republic of California flag, with its grizzly bear and star on a field of white cloth, over the town square. The flag raising was followed by the annual Sonoma Rodeo. This year the flag would be raised by a new group, Elmer's "Sonoma Vigilantes."

For weeks preceding the event, the Sonoma paper reported each detail of the happenings at what was now called the Spreckels-Awl ranch. The excitement mounted when the paper reported that Leo Carillo, "Hollywood idol and close friend of Elmer Awl," was flying up to join the Sonoma Vigilantes, along with movie star George O'Brien, heavyweight boxing champion Max Baer, and Jack Mitchell, Elmer's former employer. The Bank of America jumped in to announce it would sponsor a radio broadcast of the "capture of Sonoma" by the Vigilantes.

The ride began on June 18, at Camp Awl, where riders quenched their thirst at the huge bar and consumed such grub as clams with Bordelaise sauce and oysters Rockefeller. Elmer's camp quickly became known as "the little Bohemian Grove." For the next two days, men rode and drank and ate their way from ranch to ranch in the Valley of the Moon, until noon on June 21. Then the Sonoma Vigilantes, one hundred strong, sitting tall in their saddles despite three days of carousing, galloped down and encircled the town square. The radio announcer's voice, describing the scene, was drowned out by the cheering as Elmer Awl, the town's new hero, resplendent in all his silver gear, raised aloft the flag of the California Republic and captured Sonoma for the Americans. Alma, sitting next to Ulla on the reviewing stand, smiled with delight. She was so proud of her Honey Boy.

She was also proud of him the night of the opera opening in San Francisco four months later. Attending the opera was not a favorite pastime of hers. She really disliked music. But opening night of the opera was a San Francisco ritual. It was *the* society event of the year, strictly white-tie and tails for the men and the most elaborate of ball gowns for the women. Everyone went to see and be seen. Alma usually sat as a guest in the box of the Felix McGinnises. But this year she bought her own box. She wanted everyone to see Elmer.

They couldn't miss him. Those who weren't there to see him in person saw his picture in the paper the next day. He stood next to Alma in her white lace gown and ermine wrap. There he was, in white tie and tails nattily accessorized with white boots and a ten-gallon white Stetson hat! Alma's pleased smile was almost as broad as the orchid corsage she was wearing.

"It was Aunt Alma's idea for Elmer to wear the cowboy hat and boots," said Ulla, who was in the "family" box that night.[16] Little Alma and her husband and Dorothy and her new husband, Andrew McCarthy, were also present — although both couples wished they weren't.

"About that orchid corsage," continued Ulla, "Aunt Alma was wearing mine. My date bought it for me, and it was larger than the one Aunt Alma had. She said, 'Oh, that's too big for you to wear.' So I switched with her and she was happy."

Elmer's formal debut into San Francisco high society was also his farewell. Shortly afterwards he was called to active duty in the Navy, where he held the rank of Lt. Commander in the Coast Guard Reserve.

And then the marriage was all over. It was not the war but the telephone company that ended it.

Chapter Notes:

1. Letters from Alma to Elmer, Ulla Awl collection.
2. Jean Frickelton to Elmer Awl, November 17, 1939, Ulla Awl collection.
3. *San Francisco Chronicle,* January 12, 1940, p. 9
4. *San Francisco Chronicle,* September 7, 1940, p. 1.
5. Ibid.
6. Ibid, January 21, 1941, p. 13.
7. Ulla Awl interview.
8. Jay D. McEvoy interview.
9. Dorothy Munn interview.
10. Millie Brown Robbins interview.
11. Ibid.
12. Walter Piezzi interview, Dodie Rosekrans tapes.
13. Elmer Awl interview, Dodie Rosekrans tapes.
14. Ibid.
15. Jean Frickelton interview, Dodie Rosekrans tapes.
16. Ulla Awl interview.

When World War II began, Alma joined the war effort with all the energy she had displayed during World War I. She organized the San Francisco League for Servicemen, converted her garage into a recycling center, supplied musical and medical instruments to military personnel overseas, and collected old costume jewelry for soldiers to use in trade with Pacific Islanders. At a benefit at the Palace Hotel, she receives a check from prizefighter Max Baer for the League for Servicemen. (Courtesy Archives, San Francisco Public Library)

CHAPTER FOURTEEN

Alma Goes to War

SHORTLY AFTER ELMER'S DEPARTURE for the Navy, Alma moved back to 2080 Washington Street and immediately turned the mansion into her own command post where she launched the San Francisco League for Servicemen. Never one to move through organized channels, she bypassed the Red Cross, ignored the American Womens' Voluntary Services, whose local affiliate was run by Mrs. Nion Tucker and "that Burlingame crowd," and set up her own organization. Her cronies Mrs. Prentiss Cobb Hale and Mrs. Felix McGinnis were part of her thirty-woman organization, and her daughters put aside their personal wars with her, and each other, to join in.

Out of the garage for the duration went the rummage and in came mountains of metal cans and paper boxes and newspapers. The Salvage Shop became the Recycling Center where she collected the material "to be turned into shelter and arms for our brave defenders stationed in and around the San Francisco Bay."

While the Red Cross brought servicemen coffee and donuts, and the AWVS invited them home for hot meals, Alma was busy filling more exotic needs. When the commander of a Coast Guard unit doing guard duty at an isolated station complained that his men had to be taken from their posts into town for haircuts, she found him a barber chair. Soon three hundred grateful men were able to get their tonsorial needs attended to right on their base. When she heard that cooks and their helpers at another Navy station were spending valuable time hand-washing their "whites," she had a washing machine delivered to them.[1]

Alma and her League quickly developed a reputation for getting things done, even if it meant fighting City Hall. When traffic accidents occurred with ominous frequency at a busy intersection on the outskirts of the city near an Army encampment, the Army knew where to turn for help. They asked Alma to use her considerable weight downtown. Traffic signals were promptly installed.

She took actress Ina Claire on an inspection of the Cow Palace, the city's livestock pavilion, which had been turned into a staging area for soldiers about to embark for the Pacific. The noted comedienne was now the wife of attorney William Wallace, president of the Legion's board of trustees, and a member of "the Burlingame crowd."

"We went in through doors marked 'Cattle Entrance'," the actress recalled. "There was manure all over the floor. Inside, cots were stacked four high over every inch of floor space in the huge arena. Alma was furious. 'Imagine our brave boys having to live like this! You see why I've got to build a recreation center for them?'

"I realized then why she took me out there. She not only wanted me to entertain the soldiers, she also wanted me to join her League for Servicemen. *That* I declined," said the noted comedienne. "I liked her. She was a great old sport. But she was a character. She talked dirty. I've seen people get up and walk away from her at dinner tables because she was talking dirty.

"I had just moved out here and Alma Spreckels seemed to be a no-no to my husband's friends. I thought, I'm not going to antagonize people by getting involved with her."

Without Ina Claire's help, the woman who was a "no-no" saw that the servicemen got their recreation center. She got all the material and the labor donated. She reinstated the "Drop a Penny, We Need Many" bottles, changed the wording to read "For Our Brave Boys," and collected enough money to buy the basketball and ping-pong equipment, the phonograph records and sound system, and card tables and games to make the center a success.

When the brave defenders were moved overseas, Alma and her League sent them out in style. The League furnished musical instruments for one hundred seventy-six military bands, secured thousands of radios, pianos, toilet articles, typewriters, fishing tackle for lifeboats, athletic equipment of all kinds, fifty-two sunlamps for hospitals in the frozen North, wheelchairs, hospital supplies, and even altar cloths and candlesticks for altars in Africa and the South Pacific.[3]

Her reputation for doing the impossible had reached the ears of Dr. William Lister Rogers, a noted thoracic surgeon who was called to active duty in the Navy as chief of surgery in a special unit to be sent to the South Pacific.

"In a conversation with a friend of the Spreckels girls, I mentioned some things I felt were necessary for an emergency hospital and for the entertainment of three hundred corpsmen," said the tall, handsome doctor who had captained the rugby team that won the championship for the United States in the 1924 Olympic Games. "She told me about Alma. We became good friends. Alma asked me what the corpsmen might need. I said, 'Well, they like music, both to play and to listen to ...' The next thing I knew, she got the equipment for a band and an orchestra. It certainly provided great pleasure everywhere we went.

"When she asked what medical equipment we lacked, I said, 'My anesthetist, Dr. Weiland, could use a portable kit for intratrachial anesthesia. That would make it possible, should the occasion occur west of Pearl Harbor, for me to open and close a chest. No other island facility has it.' No sooner said than done. We sailed with the musical equipment tucked away in the ship, and the precious portable kit locked in Dr. Weiland's gear."[4]

As the war in the Pacific grew worse and casualties mounted, Dr. Rogers was ordered to work with advance units to improve forward medical care for those who couldn't get to hospital ships. He needed an electrical coagulating unit. And he needed it quickly.

"We were scheduled to leave our base in Guadalcanal in a few days and there was no time to contact the mainland to tell them to search the United States for it. I told Captain Cook, the senior medical officer under Admiral Halsey, that I would get a wire through to Mrs. Awl and she would get it for us. " 'Impossible,' he said. 'You don't know Alma Spreckels Awl,' I replied."

Alma went to work immediately. From Dr. Rogers's colleague, Dr. Leo Eloesser, at French Hospital, she found out the firms who made the instrument. Then she got on the phone.

"I need an electrical coagulating unit and I need it fast," she barked. Plants that used to manufacture them had long since switched to producing war materials. Finally after two days of trying, she located one in Cincinnati. "Get it here yesterday," she ordered. "You're holding up the war."

Once she had the unit, Alma went to work on the Navy. She called the headquarters of the 12th Naval District and demanded to speak to the admiral. "Find out where Commander Lefty Rogers is. I have his coagulator thing and I gotta get to him in a hurry."

When she was told that it was impossible to get it to Rogers because he had left his base and was en route to a forward island, she thundered, "Then fly it to that base and send a boat out after him!"

Which is just what the Navy did. The coagulator was dispatched to the South Pacific just as Rogers's ship was steaming out of Guadalcanal on its way to Vella Vella. The package was put on a motor launch with orders to the coxswain to overtake the ship at full speed ahead.

"I was on deck watching this little boat chasing after us and my immediate thought was, 'God bless that woman, she did it again!' " said Rogers. He figured that with the portable anesthesia unit and the electrical coagulator, "we pulled together at least 250 men with bad thoracic injuries who wouldn't have made it otherwise. "After the war," he said, "my wife, Dorothy, and I would be invited to dinner parties frequently at Alma's. She would tell her guests, 'I want the doctor to relate his story.' I would embellish it a little, but not too much. She loved to hear it."

Alma's wartime activities kept her from worrying about Elmer. She knew he was stationed down in Central America, safe from any real danger. Still, she wondered why he wasn't writing. She found out when H.V. McEnnerney, her accountant, brought her a large phone bill for long-distance calls to and from Panama. The bill was charged to Ulla. He watched with alarm as Alma's face turned red with rage and disbelief. Was she thinking, My God, how could that girl do this to me, after all I've done for her? And Elmer, that bastard, sneaking behind my back carrying on with my own flesh and blood!

Shouting at McEnnerney to leave her house, she cried for Sophie, her maid, to bring her a very large pitcher of martinis and a very big box of Kleenex. Then she called her lawyer, Eustace Cullinan, and told him to draw up divorce papers.

Fortunately for Ulla she was not around to feel the full brunt of Alma's humiliation and betrayal. She had left San Francisco for good two weeks before.

"By this time, I was fed up with Aunt Alma running my life for me, and I had moved to Beverly Hills and I didn't leave any forwarding address. Elmer read about my moving in the Sonoma newspapers that were forwarded to him. He wrote to the Mitchells and they gave him my address.

"He wanted me to get his things down from Sobre Vista because he had been served with divorce papers in Panama. So I went up and loaded his car with his saddles and other things and took them back to Santa Barbara. Then he got leave to appear in the divorce proceedings."[5]

Dorothy's divorce in April 1942, after her five-month marriage to Andrew McCarthy, was allotted only a brief paragraph in the newspapers. Alma's divorce, which first appeared in the papers on

October 30, 1943, was a week-long circus. Examples of Elmer's odd behavior made for delicious gossip, like the story of the party for the Latin American consuls and their wives that Alma gave before Elmer had been called to duty. Over one thousand people attended the black-tie affair. Alex testified that Elmer appeared in a cowboy suit and sombrero, and "when called upon to speak, he made himself ridiculous."

She charged that he often refused to attend other parties, and when he did attend, he had "lachrymose jags during social functions at her country estate," that he refused to accept her distinguished friends, that he insulted her guests on their wedding anniversary, and that he "cursed and screamed" whenever she gave gifts to her relatives."

Elmer denied the "extreme cruelty" charges, but he was ready and eager to dissolve the union.

"I told my lawyer, 'Get me out of this. She's too much for me.' And the lawyer went to see her. She offered me $25,000. She couldn't get a divorce because I was in the service, so I gave permission."[8]

In the uncontested divorce, Alma asked for and was granted the right to resume the name of her late husband. Elmer was ordered to Pearl Harbor, where, after the war was over, he married Ulla. They used the $25,000 to buy a home in Santa Barbara where they lived until Elmer died at age 91. Neither one of them ever saw Alma again. Ulla, who had a daughter with Elmer, still lives in the same house.

Immediately after she got her decree, Alma dictated a letter to Cecelia McCue, her secretary, to be sent to Maryhill Museum. It stated, "Will you please have the name of Awl removed from the bronze plaque in the Museum and leave the rest of the name, Mrs. Alma de Bretteville Spreckels, as it now stands. Mrs. Spreckels will be glad to pay for the expense of doing this."[9]

At the Palace of the Legion of Honor, Tommy Howe went into action on his own. "We simply took up a collection among the board to pay for new stationery and had the honorary president's name changed back to what it had been before. We all knew what a sore subject this was — how badly Mrs. A.B. had been hurt — and nobody was going to ask *her* for the money!"[10]

Jean Frickelton, who never liked Elmer and was always suspicious of him, was horrified that he could do such a thing to her idol. Whenever she was asked to supply information about Alma to writers after Alma's death, she always did so with the proviso that they never mention the name of Awl in their account of her. "That impetuous, brief marriage was always a source of great embarrass-

Alma and her elder daughter, Alma Rosekrans, talk with artist Jean de Botton at a reception in June 1944. Alma wears the pearls and diamond clips which Adolph gave her before he died. The small rectangle over her heart is the medal of the French Legion of Honor, which she was awarded almost 25 years earlier. (Courtesy Archives, San Francisco Public Library)

ment and humiliation to Mrs. S. It would really be a pity to bring up such an unfortunate — and really unimportant — incident to cast a tiny cloud on the memory of such a great woman."[11]

Alma had been badly hurt. Blind to human behavior, she had no idea that a relationship had developed between her niece and her husband, a relationship that she herself had done so much to encourage. Florence Rosekrans wasn't a bit surprised. "What can you expect? Alma left him down there alone with that Ulla. He was something..."

It is doubtful that the marriage, even without the complication of another woman, would have lasted much longer after the war. There were too many differences between them. Elmer wasn't big enough for Big Alma's interests. He was bored with her intellectual friends; he cared nothing at all for art, or for French culture. He couldn't understand why she spent so much of her time on museums or spent so much money on sculptures and paintings. "She always wanted to do good — wanted to do something for somebody all the time," said Elmer.[12]

Alma was incapable of maintaining long relationships. The woman of enormous heart, who was big enough to take on the problems of the world, had only one lasting commitment, and that was to her work. She couldn't understand why Elmer turned to Ulla any more than she understood why A.B. had turned to her sister, Anna, or why her children had turned against her.

Her "Danish Hamlet" mood returned after the divorce, plunging Alma into deep depression. When the cloud lifted, she went into action. The first thing she did was to turn Sobre Vista over to the Army for the duration so soldiers and flyers could use it as a rest and recreation center. It had been that ranch that brought her and that louse of a husband together, she reasoned. She had wanted someone she could rely on to run it for her, and Elmer had wanted a ranch he could call his own. Well, that was over now, and she didn't ever want to live up there again.

She held a large reception at Sobre Vista to welcome the military. Standing on the porch of the main house, she shook hands and graciously welcomed the officers. When a tall man in civilian clothes walked up, she boomed, "Who the hell are you? Did I invite you?"

"Yes, ma'am," he replied, too amused to be offended. "I'm General Hap Arnold." They became good friends and she gave Arnold some land on the vast estate on which he later built a home.[13]

The next step she took following the divorce was to check herself into Franklin Hospital for surgery to reduce the size of her stomach. She hated the way she looked. She wanted her Rubenesque figure back again, the figure which had gained for her A.B.'s devotion and attracted Alex Moore and Elwood Rice. Diets would never do it, but with one stroke of the surgeon's knife she could be svelte again and cut out all the unpleasant memories of that worm she had just divorced. The operation, in those days before liposuction, was a radical procedure. Plagued as she had been all her life with a spastic colon, the reduced stomach was later to cause her increased suffering.

"Mrs. Spreckels wanted the operation kept secret. We were told to say she had pneumonia," said Mary Frazer, who ran the elevator at the hospital at that time. Even in the hospital Alma kept up her war work. "She asked me to send her my old costume jewelry," said Mary. "She started this big drive for junk jewelry to send to the men in the Pacific. She said they could use it as barter with the island natives. Imagine *me* giving *my* jewelry to Mrs. Spreckels!"[14]

Like all of Alma's efforts, she overdid the jewelry drive. It resulted in enough rhinestones and fake emeralds, rubies and pearls to bedazzle every native girl in the South Pacific. Only after the Navy refused to ship any more jewelry did she stop collecting.

By the time the war was over, Alma had been decorated by the Navy, by the Army and by the citizens of Caen, France. She was made an honorary citizen of the French city for her aid in the rebuilding of Normandy, a drive she spearheaded with a large donation of her own. She ordered all her decorations sent to the de Bretteville chateau, La Gardette, in Midi, south of Lyons, where a family museum was housed in one wing.

But she was not at peace with herself. Impetuous as always, she changed her mind — briefly — about getting rid of Sobre Vista. When she heard that the William Roth mansion in Pacific Heights had been sold to the Swedish consulate for the sum of $160,000, she decided that, instead of selling the ranch, she ought to sell 2080 Washington. She immediately dashed off a note to McEnnerney, on December 2, 1946.

"I would like you to mail me [the date] when the lease of my tenant Brayton Wilbur expires. As I have decided to keep the ranch, I intend to send my furniture to the ranch. I am in the hopes that the trustees will sell this house as I am tired of being a landlady. You have no idea of what I go through. I can never leave the house. I am never free."[15]

That fleeting idea of selling Washington Street might have been the result of a painful incident Mrs. Wilbur recalls when Alma was her landlady. "We lived in Hillsborough, and my husband had business dealings in the city which sometimes kept him away overnight.

Our son, Brayton Jr., who was a little boy at the time, was very upset over this. He loved to watch his father shave in the morning, and he couldn't do that when his father stayed in town. When we heard that Mrs. Spreckels had an attractive apartment to rent in the city, we decided to lease it as a *pied à terre* so we could all be together. One day, during that time, Mrs. Spreckels invited my husband and me upstairs to dinner. Brayton was very involved in the cultural activities of the city and Mrs. Spreckels evidently thought highly of him.

"For some absolutely inexcusable reason, I forgot the date she gave us and scheduled another engagement for the same night. When I realized what I had done, I phoned Mrs. Spreckels to tell her we couldn't come. She was furious. She said, 'I don't care what you have to do to get out of your other date, you be at my party at eight o'clock!'

"She was so incensed that I didn't dare disobey! All during dinner that night, she just sat there and glared at me with icy blue eyes. I deserved it, I guess, but I never felt so uncomfortable in my life!"[16]

A more pleasant relationship was the one Alma had with Lloyd Howard. The boy who first met her when she attended his parents' dinner party was now a middle-aged attorney, on close terms not only with Alma but with her daughters and son. Howard was in great demand as an extra man at social functions. A talented pianist, well read in both French and English, urbane and cultured, he told amusing stories, adored the ladies and was no threat to their husbands because he wasn't interested in romantic liaisons with women. He also played great bridge, a game which fascinated Alma. Like everything she undertook, she did it to excess. Howard remembered:

> We played every Sunday, and sometimes during the week. Bridge started at 11 a.m. and we'd have lunch at one. Before luncheon was over, Alma would ask how many could stay for dinner so she could have more bridge.
>
> Occasionally, during the week, she'd call my office late in the afternoon and growl, "Whattya doing?" I'd say, "Alma, darling, I'm working." She'd say, "Well, stop. Get in a taxi and come right out here."
>
> Then, of course, they'd be finishing up an afternoon bridge game and I'd take the place of somebody about to depart. We'd stay for dinner and eventually get more people for bridge. She adored to play.
>
> I remember one Sunday game. Dorothy was playing that day.

We went through the usual of all afternoon and dinner and continued playing. About four the following morning, Alma wanted to play yet another rubber. Everyone demurred. She said, 'Oh you damn sissies, you go home. Lloyd, you stay.' So I made her some scrambled eggs at that hour of the morning — plus another drink.

She loved her martinis. She drank well. She had the most extraordinary recuperative powers. I recall one occasion. It was a particularly warm day and Sophie, her maid, was with her. She said, "Sophie, I want a martini." This was a few minutes past eleven in the morning. So Sophie brought in a beaker of martinis. Alma always liked to pour her own, and she'd pour them into a generous-sized glass. Then maybe she'd have another pitcherful. At her table, she always like to direct all conversation and she wanted everyone to listen.

This particular Sunday the conversation was getting a little bit — as the French would say — *brie,* overripe. We were thinking, how are we going to play bridge this afternoon? After the sweets and the coffee, she retired to her room. She came back in about five minutes just as fresh as a daisy. One would think she hadn't touched alcohol for days. And she sat down and played good bridge.

Good bridge to Alma meant playing every hand she was dealt. I recall one time she bid one club. The next bidder doubled. I was her partner and I was sitting with every 2 and 3 in the deck. I passed. On my left the bidder said, "Two hearts," which showed a big hand over a double. Alma bids three clubs. The doubler went to four hearts. I passed. Alma shouts, "Five hearts!" Of course it was doubled and we went down about six tricks. Then she said sweetly, "Lloydie dear, you don't care, do you?"

Of course "Lloydie" didn't care, because he adored her. Her appearance had fascinated him ever since she was a beautiful young matron. Now, although she was in her sixties, she was still attractive.

"She was always well coiffed. She had marvelous hair, and some inquisitive female was always asking, 'Alma dear, do you dye your hair? And she'd say, 'No, I do *not.'* She was always very well dressed, but never to any profusion. She had a jet black costume which had a little coat. It was an evening gown and she wore it with great frequency for many years — to the extent that people used to call it 'Alma's tuxedo.' "

Unlike her daughter Dorothy's magnificent collection of jewels, Alma's jewelry never had any "important" pieces, according to Howard, who had an eye for such things. "She always said you either collect art or you collect jewelry, you can't do both."

But the thing that impressed Lloyd most about Alma was her

great gift as an organizer. "If she wanted something done, it was done," he said, "whether it was organizing a gigantic fund drive or simply arranging a ride home.

"Typical of Alma was the night we were at a bridge game at someone else's home and it was a rainy, stormy night. Her chauffeur was off-duty and she tried phoning for a cab. There wasn't one to be had. So she called up the police department and said, 'This is Alma Spreckels. I want to get home and I can't get any kind of a car.' So the police came in a patrol wagon and drove her to 2080!"[17]

While bridge filled her social life, it certainly wasn't enough for the woman who had a destiny to fulfill, the woman who wanted "to do the best I could for everyone in my power." There was a special urgency about it now. Alma, at sixty-seven, had come face to face with her own mortality with the death of her sister, Anna.

Anna de Bretteville, back in San Francisco after living in Europe for so long, suffered a stroke on the street in June 1948. She was taken to St. Mary's Hospital. Because she couldn't talk, it was some time before anyone could get any information about her to notify relatives.

"She was a very difficult patient," said Anona Dukelow, a large, attractive nurse with a sunny disposition who had a reputation for taking care of difficult patients.

> She was surly and she threw things. A nun asked me to see if I couldn't be of help. We got along fine. The next day, they had located her sister.
>
> "I'm Alma Spreckels," she introduced herself. "My sister likes you very much. I would like to take you home with her to my house. Now."
>
> "Well," I told her, "your sister can't leave until the doctor discharges her."
>
> "Then get him over here to do it," she said.
>
> "I think we'll have to wait until tonight or tomorrow morning, because it's afternoon now, and the doctor is in his office seeing patients," I explained.
>
> "What's his name?" she demanded.
>
> I told her, and she sat down at the phone. In less than an hour, we were packed and on our way to 2080. That was the way Mrs. Spreckels was. She liked everything done yesterday.
>
> The only difficulty we had was getting the patient upstairs in Mrs. Spreckels's home. The ambulance crew couldn't get the stretcher around the bend of the narrow back stairs, so we took her in the elevator. It was small, not wide enough. Anna de Bretteville was a very large woman, like her sister. They had to strap her in tightly and stand the stretcher upright.

Mrs. Spreckels was just wonderful to that sister. When I was there in the afternoons, she'd help me. She would rub her sister's back, and she was very compassionate and loving."[18]

Adolph, with his fifth wife, Kay Williams, was occupying the third-floor apartment at the time. Kay, probably the most beautiful of Adolph's brides, was cool, soignée, a top model who reveled in the Hollywood scene. Before her marriage to Adolph, she had been linked romantically with Clark Gable. When Gable, still recovering from the death of his wife, Carole Lombard, wasn't ready to get married again, Kay accepted Adolph's proposal three weeks after they met.

"Kay was a very strong woman," said Lois Spreckels about her new stepmother. "She had a super sense of humor and a lot of charisma. Right after they got married, Daddy bought her a home in Bel-Air. Daddy hated those big parties — Louella and Hedda and all that. Kay loved it. He was very uncomfortable. They left Bel-Air and moved back to 2080. But that didn't last very long, and they were back in Bel-Air again."[19]

They were gone by the time Anna died, three weeks later. Anona Dukelow recalled:

> We had the same trouble getting the body out. Again she had to be tied to the stretcher and stood upright.
>
> Afterwards, Mrs. Spreckels called down to the Oyster Loaf — she loved oysters — and Little Alma and her husband came over and the doctor who attended Anna and the servants who had been with Mrs. Spreckels for years and they were just like family. We ate the oysters, which were inside toasted garlic French bread, and we washed it down with champagne.
>
> And then, as I was getting ready to leave, and my hand was on the door, Mrs. Spreckels put her hand over mine. Here she was, this six-foot woman — I'm tall, but she hovered over me — with all her height, and healthy as anything, and she said to me, "Mrs. Dukelow, when it comes time to close my eyes, will you come?"
>
> I said, "Oh, Mrs. Spreckels, don't talk like that! You're depressed because your sister died." She said, "I'm asking you, when I call will you come?" Of course I said yes.

Certainly Alma was depressed over her sister's death. How much time, she wondered, did she have left to fulfill her destiny?

"I may live over twenty years more, or I may die today or tomorrow," she wrote in a letter to Clifford Dolph. "No one knows the future. I am grateful to God I had the will, knowledge and heart and love of humanity to help [at Maryhill]."[20]

Chapter Notes:

1. Frickelton papers.
2. Ina Claire interview.
3. Frickelton papers.
4. Dr. William Lister Rogers interview.
5. Ulla Awl interview.)
6. *Sonoma Times-Index,* November 5, 1943.
7. *San Francisco Chronicle,* October 30, 1943.
8. Dodie Rosekrans tapes.
9. Spreckels Correspondence, Maryhill Museum.
10. Thomas Carr Howe interview.
11. Jean Frickelton to Frances Moffet, Frickelton papers.
12. Dodie Rosekrans tapes.
13. John Rosekrans interview.
14. Mary Frazer interview.
15. Spreckels papers, National Archives, Smithsonian, gift of Dorothy Munn, Roll 695-696, December 2, 1946.
16. Mrs. Brayton Wilbur interview.
17. Lloyd Howard interview, Dodie Rosekrans tapes.
18. Anona Dukelow interview.
19. Lois Spreckels Register interview.
20. Spreckels correspondence, Maryhill Museum.

This carefully retouched studio portrait, taken in the 1940s, is inscribed "To Dearest Kay, with much love, Devotedly, Mother Alma." Kay Williams was the fifth wife of Adolph Spreckels Jr., the mother of two of his children. (Courtesy Fine Arts Museums of San Francisco)

The Mother of Maryhill

ALMA HAD MORE THAN "the will, knowledge, heart and love of humanity to help with Maryhill." She also had the energy and a strong writing arm plus an endless supply of purple ink with which to pen a nonstop flow of letters of instruction to Clifford Dolph, a young relative of one of the trustees. Dolph had been brought in to unpack the crates and build showcases and tables. Later, because there were no funds for a director, the title was bestowed on him.

Dolph had no museum training, as little formal education as Alma, but as much commitment to Maryhill as she had. Fortunately, he was also patient. Alma, an insomniac, spent her sleepless nights running the museum from the gold-swan bed at 2080 Washington. For almost three decades she became Maryhill Museum's greatest benefactor and biggest thorn in the side of its trustees.

Once the litigation over Sam's will was completed, Alma had got herself elected, in 1937, to the newly formed board of trustees and had announced her first gift in a letter to Zola Brooks, secretary of the board.

"I am deeply interested in your Museum, and wishing to do something to aid its success, I have decided to loan my fine collection of gold furniture and other objects from the Palace of the Queen of Romania, if you would like to have it.

"The collection includes the Queen's gold throne and other unique pieces of Byzantine furniture; the Queen's cloth of gold robe which she wore at the time of the coronations of the Czar and of the King of England; her gold crown, gold goblets, presents which were among the souvenirs of the Royal family, gifts from the Queen of Serbia, etc, etc."[1]

249

While Alma's desire to aid the success of the museum was genuine, her gift was not entirely prompted by altruism. She had been trying to get rid of the things for a long time. Marie had given the gifts to Alma for the California Palace of the Legion of Honor, but her own board had turned them down. Then she took them home to 2080. But now, as she wrote in a memo to her brother Alex, "The furniture, etc. is only in my way and the moths get under the carpet."[2]

Two years before, in 1935, when the road around Sobre Vista was completed, Alma, in a moment of inspiration, decided to build a monastery and a shrine to Marie on top of the mountain and to move the furniture up there.

In a letter to Marie, dated July 1, 1935, Alma wrote, in part:

> For many years I have hoped and dreamed that America might someday do something to honor Romania and its truly great Queen. Now, with plans being completed for an International Exposition in San Francisco in 1938 to mark the completion of two mammoth bay bridges, the largest in the world, I feel that the time is most opportune to bring my dreams to reality.
>
> It is for this reason, Your Majesty, that I am now making arrangements for the building of a small museum in California, dedicated to you and your country, and filled with marvelous treasures which you so generously presented to us a few years ago and which are too precious to be accorded merely a gallery in a museum.
>
> The site, chosen with extreme care, is one of rare magnificence. It is situated on top of a mountain, on my 3,000 acre estate, and commands a view of seven counties with a radius of nearly 100 miles. Giant redwoods and pines add a grandeur that only nature could create. Within an hour's ride of San Francisco the place is readily accessible and would offer every advantage from an educational standpoint to those unfamiliar with your country.
>
> Since this museum is to be yours, to stand as a monument for all time to your greatness, I thought perhaps Your Majesty would be gracious enough to design the type of building you would want me to erect. I can assure you, it will give me the utmost pleasure to carry out your wishes in every detail. Thus your personality will be reflected in this little museum when it is viewed by thousands of travellers from all parts of the world who come to San Francisco for the Bridge Exposition.[3]

The queen, through her lady in waiting, took too long to reply. Two years later came a note stating, "Her Majesty said she willingly will cooperate with you with all her heart to carry your plans to the most perfect success, making your name immortal."[4] By that time, with the moths in a feeding frenzy and the dust piling up under the carpets, Alma, anxious to get rid of it, decided the collection belonged in the museum Loie and Sam had intended as the monument to Marie.

Zola Brooks wrote back accepting the gift but hinting that what they really needed at the moment was "a large fireplace mantel ...We had hoped that Mr. Hearst could be induced to give one of his many."

The decision to give to Maryhill the queen's furniture, plus a collection of Byzantine icons and other artifacts for which Alma had paid $12,000,[5] did not meet with unanimous approval. One trustee had strong objections to "making the first floor of our museum look like the set from a Balkan light opera."

How historically valuable Alma's gift proved to be was demonstrated in 1986, on Maryhill's sixtieth anniversary, when Queen Marie's grandson, the exiled King Michael, made the journey from Switzerland, where he was born and raised, to the museum in Goldendale, Washington, to get a glimpse of what his life in Romania would have been like.

Because Alma assumed everyone worked at her speed, she expected the museum to be opened very quickly. When it wasn't, she demanded her gifts be returned.

Trustee Brooks wrote: "The furniture and souvenirs of the Queen of Romania are all available at Maryhill, having never been unpacked or set up.

"Their loss to us will be serious, for without them I am afraid we will be unable to open this summer. Owing to construction troubles, we have had to take up the floors, and crews are now laying complete new floors, all oak, throughout the building. It was our plan to start unpacking and checking on display within the next two to three weeks. Their display at Maryhill had seemed so fitting, owing to the Queen's trip there and the fact that Mr. Hill was host...I only trust that if the exhibits are to be taken [back], that it will only be temporary."[6]

Alma relented; the furniture stayed, and she sent an additional vanload containing her Gallé glass collection to the museum. They remained crated for two more years, along with the Rodins and other treasures that Sam Hill had purchased from Loie and the presents Queen Marie had brought with her in 1926. They were finally unpacked and put into place when the museum opened on May 13, 1940.

Alma, slimmed down and dressed in a new blue traveling suit, took Lita Clerfayt with her when she went to preside at the fes-

Maryhill Museum in Washington overlooks the Columbia River about 90 miles from Portland. This photograph was taken shortly after it opened in 1940. (Courtesy Maryhill Museum)

tivities. "Madame Clerfayt was a very intimate friend of Loie Fuller and went to her funeral in Paris, and was also a great friend of Sam Hill and Queen Marie," she explained to Clifford Dolph. Alma's intimate friend, Elmer Awl, her husband of one year, remained behind in Santa Barbara, where he was leading the annual Rancheros ride.

If Alma still harbored any resentment against the women of the Northwest for the way she had been treated on her previous visit fourteen years before, it evaporated in the glow of triumph she experienced now. She was returning as a heroine, the savior of Sam's museum. She, more than anyone there, was responsible for turning the "fake" into a *fait accompli.*

Five hundred guests came to the festivities, including a reporter from *Time* magazine, who described Sam's castle "standing out among the surrounding sage brush as incongruous as a top hat in a jungle."

Before the doors were opened, Alma marched triumphantly to the entrance and unveiled a bronze tablet in honor of Sam. Heading the list of trustees whose names also appeared on the tablet was that of the president of the board, Alma de Bretteville Spreckels Awl. She had no inkling that three years later that "Awl" would have to be chiseled off.

After the unveiling, the doors to a building that had remained uncompleted for a quarter of a century were opened to the public. In the first ninety days, more than thirty thousand visitors trooped through what *Time* magazine called "the world's most isolated art museum."

Alma was pleased by the way young Dolph had displayed the Romanian furniture; she liked the cases he made for her Galle glass collection and the vitrines for the Russian icons. Sam's Rodin sculptures and plaster molds were exhibited effectively, but who in God's name ever heard of rugs in a museum? In the huge rooms they looked like tiny postage stamps. She made a note to see that they were removed immediately. In memo after memo she railed against the rugs for the next ten years until they were finally removed.

The sight of the six hundred head of cattle grazing below, the herd that Sam left to support his museum, brought another thought to Alma's mind: she would demand a periodic financial statement from the treasurer. If she were to remain on the board, then by God, she wanted to know how the money was being spent! Periodically, over the next fifteen years, she would send in her resignation when she failed to get that information. Each time she was persuaded to remain.

Alma was also upset by the fact that there was no tea room in the museum. In a building so isolated, she felt, "it's imperative that people should be able to buy a sandwich and a cup of coffee without going thirty miles to get it." She told Dolph she would send up pots, cups, saucers and other kitchen equipment, plus her collection of posters from her World War fund-raising efforts and, "voila, Pet, you will have the Tombola Tea Room." She sent the things, but it would be nearly a half century later before the museum installed a tea room.

Along with her steady supply of gifts, Alma sent a steady stream of advice. She offered ideas about landscaping Maryhill. "My husband was Park Commissioner for many years and President of the Commission for twelve years. Through our friendship with the Park Superintendent [John McLaren] he sent a landscape gardener to our home who advised us to take out my lawn and plant ivy, which effected a great saving in labor and water costs. I think this would be a practical idea for Maryhill."

When she read in the minutes that the outside of the museum was going to be painted, she wrote that it was "an unnecessary expense. In Europe, the palaces and museums are never painted. The Europeans pride themselves on the ancient color their buildings have acquired by age. I have consulted building experts here in San Francisco and they concur that cement buildings do not need to be painted for preservation ... It is very important to have an elevator and heat *now.*"

On getting board members, she wrote: "It is not necessary for a trustee to be an authority on art. Much more important that he be capable of handling the financial affairs of the museum and properties."

She had definite ideas about the value of women to museums: "I recommend that a Women's Auxiliary be formed. Women are workers, especially Club women. It is not always the rich women who are the most generous. The middle class people give their energy, souls, brains and heart and are willing to learn. I am not even a High School graduate. What I know (I am humble about it and have much to learn) has been acquired by reading and traveling. I have visited Museums all over the world. I think Maryhill has a great future. My idea is to let the public feel that they are a part of it."

She advised against buying from artists directly. "I know artists, they are resentful and ungrateful."

In 1946, after World War II was over and the end of gas rationing made it possible for people to travel to Maryhill again, Alma intensified her gift-giving to the museum. The first thing to be shipped was the Richard Hall portrait of her sitting on Queen Marie's throne. It wasn't so much the fact that she felt the painting belonged in the same gallery as the throne itself. More to the point was the fact that the Legion, to which she had given the Hall painting, hadn't seen fit to display it. She offered it to Maryhill on the condition that it be on permanent display.

Dolph wired back immediately to Tom Howe, the embarrassed Legion of Honor director, "Will you please inform Mrs. Spreckels of our pleasure to know of her decision regarding portrait. We are delighted to accept and agree to the condition involved. Letter confirming this follows."

Alma wanted more than agreement; she wanted evidence. After the picture was sent, Alma's secretary, Cecelia McCue, wrote that "Mrs. Spreckels would like to have a picture taken of the painting and wants you to advise her of the position of the painting in the museum."[7] That portrait, all seven feet of Alma, dominates the main gallery; visitors often assume the regal woman seated on the throne is Queen Marie.

The portrait also provided poor Dolph with a lifetime task. When the museum, at Alma's insistence, had postcard pictures made of its most important treasures, the Hall painting was included. From that time on until her death she constantly ordered him to send postcards to her various friends around the world to publicize Maryhill and — of course — to let people see what Alma looked like at her best.

Typical of the requests was this letter: "I have a friend in Paris who owns the greatest and most beautiful private art collection in the world — costs 25 million," Alma wrote, referring to Mrs. Gulbenkian. "I would so love her to have a photo of my portrait. (Will you write on the back of it that it is my portrait) She is my best friend in Paris. I enclose an envelope..."

Following the donation of her own portrait, Alma was moved to send a whole collection of photographs of her notable friends autographed to her for "a history room, if your trustees will dedicate a room for them." Included in the first batch were signed photos of Alphonso, king of Spain; Marie; Carol, king of Romania; the maharajah of Kapurthala; Albert, king of Belgium; Fridtjor Nansen, the discoverer of the North Pole; the duchess of Vendôme, and Marshal Joffre.

If Dolph liked those, Miss McCue wrote, there were more: "Mrs. Spreckels thinks since Maryhill Museum is a unique museum, different from most museums, that these photos could be appropriately placed there...She has one that Madame Curie, discoverer of radium, sent to her during World War I, signed; one of Flammarion, famous French astronomer; one of General H. H. Arnold signed, and one of Mrs. Arnold."

The same conditions were placed on these as the one on Alma's portrait: "Mrs. Spreckels would wish to know, however, that the photographs would be permanently displayed and not put away where they cannot be seen."

Then Alma decided to do something about Loie. She began collecting things to be installed in a "Hall of the Dance," to be dedicated to her.

In a note to Dolph, which accompanied a bronze bust of Loie, done by Pierre Roche, she told the young man about her friend. "It was Loie Fuller who really inspired Sam Hill to make the museum at Maryhill, and for that reason I feel it is particularly fitting that this bronze be installed there as a memorial to this great woman. It was Loie Fuller who introduced Sam Hill to the Queen of Romania, and she also helped him get a great many things for your museum."

Alma had also promised to acknowledge publicly all Loie had done to help her with the Legion of Honor museum. "I would not be worth the name of de Bretteville if I did not give justice where justice is due." If she didn't give Loie the justice due her in that place, Alma was going to do it here. The gallery at Maryhill remains the only permanent memorial to the *"Fée Lumineuse,"* where sculpture, drawings, posters and photographs attempt to evoke her magic.

To add to the dance collection, Alma leaned on her friends to contribute. She persuaded Paul Verdier to give a bronze of Loie that he owned, and she pressed May Slessinger Buchman, now a wealthy widow, to part with her bronze sculpture of Loie.

Then she went to work on Malvina Hoffman. In a letter of instruction to Dolph, Alma wrote:

"Please send to Malvina Hoffman (she was a pupil of Rodin and is the most famous woman sculptress in the world). She did *Races of Man* for the Field Museum in Chicago. She showed this collection in Paris, in miniature at the Ethnographical Museum (she is a great friend of mine) and then I paid to have the collection shown in San Diego and San Francisco. "Please send her just postals of your Rodin Collection, Maryhill, my portrait and not a lot of mediocre Art. I don't say that the Art is not worth while, but I have reason for wanting to interest her in Maryhill. Do you have any galleries available in case Malvina would send the miniature collection?"

When Malvina wasn't interested in donating anything to Maryhill and the trustees weren't interested in buying any of her work, Alma spent $5,500 for three small bronze figures of Hoffman's pertaining to the dance.

Alma felt money spent for sculpture was money well spent. "Loie always said Sculpture lasts forever," she wrote to Dolph. "I saw wonderful museums of Sculpture in Naples and, of course, the Louvre."

Underscoring her belief in the importance of sculpture, Alma decided to move her Riviere collection, including *The Roghi,* from the Legion of Honor to Maryhill. She gave a written lecture on *The Roghi* to the ever-patient Dolph.

> Mr. Samuel Harding Church, chairman of the Carnegie Foundation, saw it and wrote me for a photograph, and we became acquainted, and he gave me a magnificent dinner in Pittsburgh.
>
> It depicts the Pretender to the Throne of Morocco in a cage. It is a true incident and Mr. Church saw the cage in Africa and it is now at V-I-N-C-E-N-N-E-S (France). His followers are in chains and the mob is threatening him.
>
> Riviere was the first sculptor since the time of Phidias to work with ivory and jewels and his *Salome* is in Luxembourg.
>
> In your last letter you spelt B-A-R-T-H-O-L-M-E wrong. I think there is an accent on the last E. Good luck, now, and cheer up. Maryhill is valuable as a Tourist Attraction. It should be publicized by Portland Chamber of Commerce, Tourist Bureau, etc., but let us get those collections set up and get the Bank of America on our side.

Despite her generosity, Alma could also be tight with money. At the same time that she was spending thousands on gifts for Maryhill, she was conducting a war with the trustees over $400. That was the amount of money she laid out to have eight chairs reupholstered on a dining room set donated by her friend Campbell McGregor ("It is worth in excess of $15,000," Alma wrote to Dolph.) To the struggling museum, which never asked for and had no need of the banquet-size table and eight chairs for a board room they didn't have, the expenditure seemed unwarranted. Alma had no intention of asking McGregor for the money. Not after he had given the gift and paid to have it shipped up to Washington. And she emphatically did not think, in view of all the things she had given to the museum, that she should have to pay it. In a note to her secretary she instructed:

"Ask the Board of Trustees why they did not vote to repay me the $400 ... Confidentially, they voted to buy a sword for $200 from a relative of the Trustees, so can you ask them to send a full report of expenditures voted at this meeting — I don't want to get Mr. Dolph, who told me this, in trouble."

Eventually she was repaid, but the need to be fully informed about expenditures was a recurring theme in Alma's correspondence. "My respect for Sam Hill makes me very anxious for the welfare of the museum. I want to do all I can to help, but I do not care to lend my name to any institution about whose affairs I am not fully informed... With the understanding that I be kept fully informed, I consented to be Honorary President."

In the fall of 1948, Alma decided to visit the museum. She wrote to Dolph: "Is there any place in the Museum that could be fixed up for sleeping quarters? I would like to fix up one or 2 bedrooms and maybe a dining room. I would send the furniture up. I would rather stay in the Museum and also any friend that I bring. I would send dishes, cooking utensils, linen, silver, etc. I am not fussy. All I like is my own bathroom. It is too much trouble to be running away to the Inn. I am a good cook and love to wash dishes.[8]

The friend she decided to bring up was Jean Frickelton. "Miss Frickelton is a Stanford graduate and owns her own advertising business and is a very brilliant person. She does the publicity for the Legion of Honor Museum and she knows campaigning, etc...."

With Jean coming, Alma's basic requirements for the visit changed. "We would need two bedrooms and 2 baths. We are not fussy, but would each want our own bathrooms, [and a] sitting room and we would want to hire a driver."[9]

Since the only item on the list Dolph was able to provide was a driver, Alma stayed at the inn. On her return after the brief visit, she flooded the mails with her list of suggestions.

> According to your minutes, Mr. Brooks will receive $6000. I cannot understand why he is retained as Secretary and Manager at $100 a month [The museum is open six months of the year, because of the weather, from April to November.] when the museum has so little money. Mr. Dolph works for a nominal salary... I see no reason why a stenographer cannot be hired to take the minutes of the meetings and write them up afterwards.
>
> There is conclusive evidence that Brooks mismanaged the Ranch. He is a lawyer and he may know the law but he knows nothing about agriculture. Mr. Berry [treasurer of the board of trustees] had written me before he died that he intended to have a friend of his who is in the cattle business come out to Maryhill and make a survey of the ranch. I hope he contacted him before he died. He might be able to gave us some valuable advice about the Ranch...
>
> I don't think it at all undignified to solicit outside financial help. The other Museums do it. This has brought wonderful results to the California Palace of the Legion of Honor.

Alma backed up her "suggestions" with some concrete help. She used an acquaintanceship with Henry Ford's son, Benson, who had been a guest at Sobre Vista during the war, to get a tractor and other ranch equipment at wholesale prices.

She told Dolph the three-story museum should have a freight elevator. When she got home she wrote, "I am returning the estimate of the Otis Elevator Company showing the approximate cost of $7,200." The next day, after she went out to inspect the elevator at the Legion of Honor, she penned another note, telling him that she found "it is a hydraulic elevator, much less expensive to operate and install than an electric one."

While the trustees balked at a freight elevator — electric or hydraulic — they did act on her suggestions about heating and about the ranch equipment. By spring, Dolph was writing to thank her: "I can also tell you that the oil burner is completely installed and works fine... As you are largely responsible for these accomplishments, it is a pleasure to acknowledge and thank you for your help."

Alma was more concerned with what she was not able to accomplish — such as securing a collection of Indian paintings by Theodore Wores, a well-known San Francisco artist.

"I have been trying to secure the 52 paintings for Maryhill," she wrote. "It is a magnificent collection. Mr. Verdier, Mr. Howe and I went to see them...

Mrs. Wores, the widow of the artist, is a very rich woman. Recently she inherited three estates. However, she is a very difficult woman to deal with. At one time she asked $100,000 for them. I have tried to tell her that the U.S. Government would get most of the money if she sold the collection, and to persuade her to send the collection to Maryhill as it belongs in the great Northwest." Mrs. Wores took Alma's advice about donating them, but despite Alma's persistent pleading — or maybe because of it — she gave the collection to the Museum of Natural History in Los Angeles.

"It was a bad decision," said Dr. A. Jess Shenson. He and his brother, Dr. Ben Shenson, also a San Francisco physician, have been avid Wores fans ever since they inherited a collection of his paintings from their mother, who was a friend of Wores's widow. "The Museum of Natural History rarely lends and seldom displays those pictures."[10]

If Maryhill couldn't open its 1949 season with a headliner like the Wores paintings, Alma was determined to substitute it with something equally compelling. She decided to buy back Whistler's *Gold Scab* and send it up there.

The man whose name is most associated with his *Composition in Black and Gray,* better known as *Whistler's Mother,* proved he

Maryhill Museum by 1988 has acquired no neighbors, but trees now frame the handsome building Sam Hill never lived in. (Photo by Steve Terrill, Courtesy Maryhill Museum)

could also dip his brush in vinegar when he painted the *Gold Scab*. In it, he poured out all his festering ire for his British sponsor, Fredrick Richards Leyland, a Liverpool shipping magnate, whom he believed had cheated him out of money owed him. The painting, a vicious caricature of one of England's wealthiest and most cultured gentleman of the nineteenth century, was done in response to a quarrel Whistler had with his patron over the painting of the Peacock Room in the Leyland mansion in London.

Alma's connection to the painting is almost as bizarre as Whistler's. She had purchased *The Gold Scab* originally for $25,000 from Gump's in 1915. After A.B.'s death, she decided to get rid of it. It was too ugly, she thought. She sold it to French & Company for $20,000. In December 1948, she wanted it back. She made a deal with Mitchell Samuels, her friend at French's ever since the Paris trip when she met Rodin. The terms of the sale were "$3,500 cash and an allowance of $16,500 for two important pieces of French furniture."[11]

From the beginning, *The Gold Scab* proved an outstanding feature attraction for the museum. "It has made a name for Maryhill, with people coming here from many parts of the country to see it. You were so right when you said it would be an extremely valuable exhibit for us," wrote Dolph in 1956, when Alma requested that Dolph send the painting back so it could go on exhibition at the Carnegie Museum and the Corcoran Gallery. "In expressing the hope that it is not leaving here permanently, I am very sincere..."

Alma had hoped that the painting, while it was on tour, would attract a buyer. But it was returned to Maryhill three years later when, despite the exposure and attention it had attracted, nobody wanted to buy it. *The Gold Scab* remained at Maryhill until Alma's involvement with another project, the Patrons of Art and Music, an auxiliary of the Legion of Honor, about which we will have more to say later. She donated half an interest at a time to that group so that she could claim income tax deductions over a two-year period, 1960 and 1961. Today, with the combining of the Legion and the de Young into one association, the painting has been moved to the de Young, where it glowers from a wall in a gallery of American painters.

Alma was responsible for another of Maryhill's famous exhibits, the French Mannequins of the Théâtre de la Mode. The fashion exhibit was born in 1945, right after World War II, when the French fashion industry was eager to show the world that the German occupation had not robbed it of its imagination. Since fabric for the first postwar collection was not available, they used scraps and small pieces of prewar fabrics to dress the two hundred little dolls — *poupées* — made in correct proportions of one-third human size.

The mannequins were dressed by leading French couturiers including Schiaparelli, Maggie Rouf, Lanvin and Balenciaga. Jewelers like Cartier created real jewelry to scale. Coiffeurs designed hair, bootmakers created shoes, and lingerie designers created exquisitely made lingerie not even visible to the viewing public. The mannequins were placed in tableaux painted by leading French artists, with special music written by French composers, and sent out on a twofold mission: to proclaim that Paris was once again the inspiration for *haute couture,* and to raise money for French war relief. For nearly five years, everywhere the dolls went they drew overflow crowds. The exhibit toured the United States and eventually reached San Francisco, where Paul Verdier used it in a display to celebrate the one-hundredth anniversary of his City of Paris department store in 1950.

When the mannequins, their mission completed, were to be returned to France, Alma pounced on Verdier to save them. What a wonderful gift the little *poupées* would make for Maryhill, she pleaded. What a fitting gift for him to make to the museum they both loved so much! Verdier finally agreed, and the Théatre de la Môde — minus the Cartier jewelry, which was returned to France — found its new home in Goldendale, Washington, when the museum opened its 1952 season.

In exchange for all she had done for Maryhill, Alma felt she deserved some recognition. She hoped she might get it at the annual banquet of the National Institute of Social Sciences in New York. She urged Dolph to write a letter to its president, the father of Adolph's first wife, the irresponsible Lois.

"Mr. Lewis Latham Clarke, 299 Park Avenue, New York City, wants detailed information and photographs of what I have done for Maryhill. He knows nothing re same.

"I have belonged for over 20 years to the NISS and no one can belong unless he has done something worth while. An annual dinner is given every year in New York City and medals are awarded. Men such as John D. Rockefeller, Herbert Hoover, Barney Baruch, Mr. Tom Watson, etc. have been so honored. The Directors of the organization have to meet and vote as to who will be recipients."

She didn't make it.

By this time, Alma was also working hard on another project, her dream of a maritime museum. She expanded the concept into what she envisioned as a Museum of Science and Industry. Perhaps she could earn an NISS award for that.

Chapter Notes:

1. Spreckels correspondence, Maryhill Museum.
2. Alma to Alex, undated, John Rosekrans papers.
3. Alma to Queen Marie, July 1, 1935, John Rosekrans papers.
4. Ainsoara Stan to Alma, March 11, 1937, John Rosekrans papers.
5. Letter from Attorney Walter Slack to Alex de Bretteveille, March 9, 1937, John Rosekrans papers.
6. Spreckels correspondence, Maryhill Museum.
7. McCue to Dolph, December 16, 1946, Spreckels correspondence, Maryhill Museum.
8. Alma to Dolph, August 29, 1948, Spreckels correspondence, Maryhill Museum.
9. Ibid, September 15, 1948.
10. Dr. A. Jess Shenson interview.
11. Letter from M. Samuels to H. McEnnerney, December 10, 1948, John Rosekrans papers.

In July 1948, Alma and actress Ina Claire look pleased about the newest prize at the Legion of Honor Museum, Rembrandt's Portrait of a Rabbi. *Museum director Thomas Howe explains its merits. (Courtesy Archives, San Francisco Public Library)*

CHAPTER SIXTEEN

Alma Heaves To on the Maritime Museum

 IF THE PALACE OF THE LEGION OF HONOR was conceived in reponse to "the call of French blood in my veins," Alma was equally responsive to "the Viking in me." She felt that deserved a monument, too.

"Mrs. S. conceived the idea of the Maritime Museum for San Francisco following the Exposition of 1939," recalled Jean Frickelton, "where they had a magnificent collection of ship models owned by various people like Mayor Roger Lapham, etc. She thought, what a shame to let it die when everybody loved it so."[1]

The only way to keep the exhibit intact was to buy it. That would cost money, which Alma didn't have at the moment. She was still mired in the Samarkand fiasco. But just as she had made up her mind to buy the Rodins for her French museum, so she was determined to buy those ships for the start of her newest museum.

The collection had been assembled by Edward S. Clark, a founder of the Pacific Model Society, whose aim was to encourage the preservation of Pacific Coast maritime lore. Alma found space for it in the Merchants Exchange Building, where the figurehead of the *Davy Crockett,* which A.B. had donated many years before, was a permanent fixture. After Alma agreed to pay all transportation costs, most of the pieces were kept together in the new location.

Next, Alma incorporated the project into a nonprofit corporation, under the rubric "San Francisco Museum of Science and Industry." Loie had always taught her to think big, and she decided to expand the maritime concept to cover much more than ships.

An announcement of the new organization appeared — Frickelton was right on the job — in *The American Neptune,* a quarterly journal of maritime history. It read in part, "In addition to sea transportation, the trustees hope eventually to include exhibits of land and air transportation, mining and agriculture." Edward Clark was named as director of the new museum, and Alma designated herself as "President of the Board of Trustees."

When the collection expanded and got too big for the Merchants Exchange Building, Alma secured space early in 1941 in a building then called the Aquatic Park Casino. The building had been constructed in the shape of a ship, during the early 1930s, as a WPA project. It was largely empty except when it was rented for weddings or other such occasions. Aquatic Park Casino was a perfect home for the models, but it proved to be a very temporary one. World War II put a halt to the project. The Army needed the building.

With the cessation of hostilities, Alma was ready to go full steam ahead again. She didn't know she would be embroiled in a Guadalcanal of her own against a young man named Karl Kortum.

Mere mention of Alma's name still makes Kortum bristle with anger more than twenty years after her death. The director of what is now the National Maritime Museum in San Francisco is still defending his right to sole credit for founding the highly acclaimed museum. He still keeps on hand cabinets full of memos, letters, board meeting minutes and other minutiae — all to document his place in San Francisco history, which he still fears Alma threatens to take away from him.

If Kortum bristles with anger, the papers left behind by Alma show that she was consumed with fury over him.

"Kortum was so nasty and mean to her," said Frickelton. "He had no appreciation whatever of what she had done for him. I really boil when I see something about his being the founder. Why, he came to her for a job! Kortum was just off a ship with a friend of his. They were interested in forming a maritime museum and they came to her because they heard she was interested in this. She gave them a place to live in the basement of 2080, she paid their salary herself and she did everything in the world for them.

"Then, which makes me so mad, one year when she went to Europe, Kortum and some others decided that they were the ones who founded the museum and they gave her no credit whatsoever. It was terribly mean, because she had done so much for them."[2]

Frickelton's version, although biased in favor of her idol, is basically correct. Kortum scornfully dismisses her as "Mrs. Spreckels's paid companion and publicist." Paid publicist she was. Despite Jean's claims that she never took a cent from Alma for all the work she did for her, Alma frequently picked up Jean's salary for publicity done for the Legion of Honor and later for the Maritime Museum by earmarking contributions to those museums specifically for Jean. But as for her being a "paid companion" — never! Her devotion to Alma was something no amount of money could buy.

When Kortum rang Alma's bell, in 1948, accompanied by a shipmate, Jim Walpole, he didn't want her to give him a job. He wanted her to give him her maritime collection, which, by this time, she owned. A lanky farm boy with a shock of bushy hair, a self-described "hayseed from Petaluma," he needed her collection as the nucleus for his own museum. Ushered into her drawing room, Kortum, awed by all the splendor, approached Alma with some timidity.

His idea, he explained, was not to create just another maritime museum. Sure, start there, with her collection, but go beyond that. The young man, who had been interested in model ships since he was a kid, talked enthusiastically about his plan, which he called Project X. He explained the dream he nurtured all during his long months at sea in the Merchant Marines.

"I want to use live ships — historic ships — floating in a lagoon near the museum that would show the world San Francisco's great history as a maritime center. Ship preservation, that's the key to my plan. Like they did in Mystic, Connecticut, where people flock to see the restored whalers.

"We have more exciting ships than that available for restoration here," he told her. "I want to begin with the *Star of Alaska*. It was originally known as the *Balclutha,* a full-rigged sailing ship which had made many trips around Cape Horn, and it epitomizes the era before the opening of the Panama Canal.

"The ideal spot for all this is Aquatic Park," he said confidently. "That WPA casino is even shaped like a ship, and right next to it is the lagoon. Perfect!"[3]

Kortum was disappointed when Alma didn't respond to his enthusiasm. He was unaware that Alma had opened her museum at Aquatic Park in 1941; that she had used the WPA building until the Army sent her packing. He didn't know that, all during the war, Alma had clung to her precious models, storing as many as she could at the Legion of Honor and keeping the rest under her golden swan bed. He didn't know that the models were now on Treasure Island only until she could return them to Aquatic Park. As she wrote to Clifford Dolph:

"I am working to get Aquatic Park Center back... Our models are temporarily at Treasure Island (belongs to the Navy) and the Navy kindly gave us a temporary home. Pass required to get in. We are fortunate to be allowed to put them there — no maintenance. Janitor service, guards, etc. are gratis. But we are never able to

*Adolph Jr. took time out from his marriage and his many scrapes to inspect
a tapestry with his mother. His glum expression suggests she had to use
persuasion. (Courtesy Archives, San Francisco Public Library)*

grow due to passes being required ... Hope to move to San Francisco *soon.*"⁴

Living ships didn't interest Alma as much as living railroad trains
and airplane models. For her transportation section of the Museum
of Science and Industry she had already been promised a half-section
model of a Pan American plane, from Thomas Wolfe, vice president
of Pan Am, and she was working on Gilbert Kneiss, president of
the California Historical Railroad and Locomotive Society, to get his
organization's collection of rolling stock and cable cars. If Kortum
wanted to expand on her original concept, that was the way to do
it — not by pouring money into old, broken-down ships. The young
seaman struck her as being a one-idea man. She felt her vision was
much broader.

But Kortum, whose drive and determination equaled Alma's,
came back again to Washington Street a year later. This time he had
the support of the city's four newspapers and Mayor Elmer Robin-
son. This time he was accompanied by David Nelson, the amiable
young waterfront reporter from the *San Francisco Chronicle.* Nelson's
boss, editor Scott Newhall, an enthusiastic seaman himself, had
spearheaded the drive for acceptance among the newspapers and
City Hall after being approached by Kortum. Newhall gave Nelson
six months' leave to work on making Kortum's concept a reality.
With political skills gained from studies at the Coro Foundation,
Nelson was a natural tactician, likable and confident, with none of
Kortum's dogmatism.

"In a seaport town like San Francisco, Kortum's idea caught
fire," said Nelson. "Everyone we talked to, from Harry Bridges of
the Longshoremen's Union to the heads of the steamship companies, who could never agree together on anything before, was excited
about his Project X. It was like selling ten-dollar bills for seven dollars. But the nucleus of the new museum had to be Alma's collection.
So I was sent to woo it from her."⁵

Nelson, who was an observant reporter, remembers precisely his
first meeting with Alma in the fall of 1949. "She received me in the
Italian Room. It had a huge fireplace. Nubian slave figures, with little
loincloths, holding spears, were chained to each side of it by their
rhinestone collars. Mrs. Spreckels was seated in a very tall chair with
knobbed arms and a red velvet cushion. Like a throne. Her hair was
beautifully coiffed. She wore a black robe with a large, black boa
draped around her. A huge diamond pin, as big as your fist, sat on
one shoulder. On her feet were electric blue slippers such as you'd
find at Gallenkamp's. In front of her was a card table. On it were
a telephone, pill bottles, note pad and pencil, address book and a

round Steuben pitcher of martinis from which she drank. She drank too much, and she would smack her lips in a way that was not very pretty."[6]

After the meeting, Nelson wrote a succinct report for his editor:

> This woman is the 'grande dame' of San Francisco. She is lonely. She is 68. And she's afraid of dying. Mrs. Spreckels, on one drink, promised us her entire maritime collection. Two days after we visited her, she called and offered to underwrite the whole project. A day later she offered 'a check for $500.'
>
> Her part in the Aquatic Park program is not predictable. In one week's time, Mrs. Spreckels ran the gamut from benefactress, to bemused dowager, to positive threat to the Aquatic Park program ...
>
> Mrs. Spreckels has been plugging a Maritime Museum for San Francisco for nearly ten years. She has gathered a collection of models and figureheads that is two thirds good. And she has the money to put into this thing.
>
> She keeps repeating that all of her friends were dying and you can't take your money with you to the grave. When Kortum presented his plan to her last year, she could not grasp it. She showed no interest in a full-rigged ship. This time, with the *Chronicle* interested, her outlook changed ... She combines senility and energy in a dangerous way.[7]

The woman who "combined senility and energy in a dangerous way" was very sincere in her desire to do good before she died. Her father had endowed her with *noblesse oblige;* her mother, with energy; and her husband, with money. She knew she had a destiny to fulfill. That's why God saw that she got all those gifts. If people didn't give her the respect she deserved then it must be because she wasn't doing enough. Now she felt she was racing against time. Her body was beginning to fail her.

First it was her teeth. Years of painful dentistry couldn't save them. Oh, how she hated wearing dentures! What did she care about the way people stared when she took them out and dropped them in her crystal water goblet during her fancy luncheons and dinner parties? What did they expect her to do when those damn things hurt so much?

Then it was her bowels. Because of them, she spent more and more time conducting meetings in her bedroom, which had once been the front part of the Louis XVI ballroom. It was close to the bathroom with the fireplace.

Jim Rambo, the decorative arts curator at the Legion of Honor, remembered one painful meeting in her bedroom. "The doctor came to examine her. He wanted to do some rectal procedure where he had to insert a lighted tube into her colon, a sigmoidoscopy, he called it. I got up to leave, but Alma ordered me to stay."

Rambo, discreetly as possible, turned his eyes away. When it was over, and the doctor had left, Alma pulled her robe around her indignantly and bellowed, "See what they did to me, a rich woman? Imagine what they do to *poor* women!"[8]

Relieved that the examination revealed she had no tumors or polyps, Alma rekindled her interest in the maritime project. Nelson's initial impression of her quickly changed. "We got to be good friends. I was invited to dinners and other social gatherings she'd give in connection with promoting the museum, and I'd have to rent a tuxedo," he said. "The newspaper got tired of paying for them. I finally refused her invitations and told her why."

The next day, Nelson got a call from Paul Verdier's secretary at the City of Paris, asking him to come in and be fitted for a tuxedo.

"Is Mrs. Spreckels at the bottom of this?" Nelson asked.

"Well, yes, and we are to send the bill to her," was the reply.

"I phoned Mrs. Spreckels and told her, 'No woman is going to buy my clothes.' She roared with laughter. After that, we'd meet for lunch, either at her house or her other favorite spots, Jack's or Verdier's Wine Cellar.

"She loved the press," continued Nelson. "I remember one night we had to go to the St. Francis Hotel and she asked if she could ride in my tiny Austin because it had a press card on the window.

"When we drove up, I got a curt reception from the doorman until she rolled down her window and glared at him. Once he recognized Mrs. Spreckels, we got the royal treatment."

In the beginning, she won over Kortum with her generosity. With no job and no place to live, he accepted Alma's invitation for free housing, first with his shipmate, Jim Walpole, in 1949, and then with his wife, Jean, a museum volunteer, whom he married in 1951. They continued to live on Washington Street until the birth of their first child in June 1953. Alma also gave him money from time to time until he went on the city's payroll in 1952.

"We would remember Mrs. Spreckels with much fondness," Jean Kortum wrote, " for having provided our picturesque honeymoon quarters ... for the lovely gift of a bassinet for our first child, and a scarf which I wear to this day... if she would allow us. But it is difficult to be charitable when she is busy writing Karl's trustees that he is a rascal. I recall one evening at a reception at the Society of Pioneers when we went up to her to pay our respects and she boomed out, 'Kortum, you're a liar.' Karl tried to smooth it over...

*This 1951 aerial view of 2080 Washington Street looks south; the enormous lawn
stretching down to Jackson Street dwarfs a gardener wielding a hose in the spot
where Alma will later build a swimming pool. The islands in the middle of Octavia
Street (right) were Alma's way of slowing down traffic when noise disturbed
Adolph during his final illness. At left the arched doorway in the retaining wall
is the entrance to the huge garage where Alma ran her salvage shop for
decades. The house's enormous scale dwarfs its neighbors to the west.
(Photo by Tom Moulin, courtesy Kjeld Storm)*

I deserted both of them, so humiliated was I by this public attack.'"9

In Alma's opinion, Kortum certainly was a liar. Look what he did while she was in Europe showing Frickelton around Paris in May 1951. *He* took all the credit for the Aquatic Park Maritime Museum!

When the museum opened, Alma read the San Francisco papers sent to her in Paris. They were full of the wonderful new attraction with its "reminders of the past." The newspapers lauded seaman Karl Kortum for his plan for a museum to make San Francisco more aware of their city's maritime history. *His* plan for a museum! In all the stories there was no mention of how *she* had started it all. Where in hell did Kortum think those "reminders of the past" came from? From her collection, that's where.

The only time her name was mentioned was for the fact that she paid longshoreman Eric Swanson $5,000 to build the twelve-foot model of a five-masted schooner, the *Preussen,* which she donated to the museum.

The *Preussen.* It had cost her a hell of a lot more than the money. It almost cost her her life. When she commissioned Swanson to make his model in 1945, the war wasn't over yet. She began to get threatening letters telling her to stop "while others are fighting and starving." She remembered the chills that ran through her when she read, "I am giving you fair warning. We CIO men are damn sore and don't mean maybe. You and your toy ships will get what we want to give the Japs. Blow them up."10 She remembered the sinister phone calls telling her the gates to her house would be blown off. She fled town. When she returned, she found the gates had been blasted off their hinges.

She was furious at Kortum's account of how *he* founded the museum at Aquatic Park. Bitterly, she recalled that she had invited him to live in her house under the mistaken impression that the two of them could work together. In an effort to be as helpful as possible, Alma even called in Dorothy's friend, architect George Livermore, to remodel the inside of the Aquatic Park Casino. In a letter composed, as usual, in the middle of the night, shortly after Kortum moved in, Alma wrote to George Livermore:

> There is one more thing also you could look at. Perhaps the porch [on the building] could be enclosed — not all glass. Then exhibits could be put there. Who is going to steal iron? I also got a rowboat which the Norwegians gave me. Two Norwegian boys escaped from Norway during World War II and rowed across the English channel and escaped to England. I don't know where Mr. Kortum put it. I also got a model of a tanker fourteen feet long from Bechtel . . .
> That building really needs to be studied . . . the second floor is

really very well arranged, but if the Park Commission will, at their own expense, take out those two lavatories, Mr. Kortum can use them. I don't want either of those rooms for membership rooms. Let him fix up those two lavatory rooms for whatever he wishes. I want to work with him and help him.

As I have worked since 1936 on maritime museums and have visited over 20 foreign countries besides the U.S. and seen their museums, I am a little qualified. I don't know everything, I am willing to learn.[11]

But she couldn't learn from Kortum, nor he from her. "Kortum was dogmatic, Alma was dictatorial, and they became adversaries," said Nelson. "Kortum was a whiz at designing displays. His idea was to get those models out of the glass cases and create large displays — actual chunks of vessels and well-written captions. Scott Newhall once said Karl was probably the best natural-born designer that he'd ever seen."

Annoyed as she was at Kortum for claiming sole credit for the idea of the Maritime Museum, Alma, when she came home, continued to let him live in her house and continued to give him money periodically. She also remained active in the Maritime Museum. The woman who had the money to pour into the project continued to do just that. She gave a large party to kick off a membership drive, for which she paid Frickelton, via a contribution, to do the publicity. She reactivated her salvage shop, renaming it the San Francisco Maritime Museum Salvage Shop, and until 1955 it brought in $500 every month. She personally contributed $65,000 in cash during the same period, as well as adding to the collection of model ships.

Her generosity didn't impress Kortum. "She boasted that when she contributed $20,000 it only cost her $2,000 of real money because of her tax situation. She never really 'sprang' for the museum; she played a cat-and-mouse game and got attention in the process."

To Kortum, Alma was "a mild eccentric sitting solidly on frugal peasant underpinnings...We could have gotten along famously if it weren't for the broken-down set of sycophants, dentists masquerading as commanders [a reference to Dr. Howard McKinley, a commander in the Naval Reserve], paid flacks, and so on, who gathered at the martini pitcher at five o'clock in the Italian Room and poormouthed our sailorly efforts to get a museum going."

If Kortum thought he was the sole subject discussed at the five o'clock gatherings at the martini pitcher, he was mistaken. The woman who wanted to do the best she could for everyone in her power had much more on her mind, such as playing Cupid. She wanted to find a husband for her devoted secretary, Cecelia McCue.

Cecelia, according to Dave Nelson, was a "tall, thin, tough, go-to-hell woman, every inch a lady."

Alma had experience as a matchmaker. She once designed another marriage with the help of a spiritualist named Mother Becker, who headed a church in Pacific Heights. "I'll arrange to get my friend down here so you can say, 'I hear voices and they are saying you should marry Sam,' she instructed the spiritualist. It worked.[12] But such a tactic wouldn't work with Cecelia. She was too smart for that. Besides, she was Catholic.

Then Alma remembered Marc Cremer. He was Catholic, too. Cremer had been head of the Marine Exchange for years. It was in his building that her maritime exhibit had found a home after the Treasure Island fair in 1939. He was now a member of the board of the Maritime Museum.

"Cremer was a solid, plodding man who always wore three-piece suits. He did his business in a very nice 1932 style, caught in a time warp," recalled Nelson.

When Alma heard that Cremer's wife had died, she launched an intensive campaign. "Your dear wife is gone, you need someone to take care of you... You mean you go home to dinner every night *alone?* Who sends your shirts out and takes care of your cleaning? You need to get married, and I have just the person for you."[13]

Cremer, unable to stand up against Alma's ceaseless prodding, dutifully presented himself at one of the five o'clock gatherings. Soon after, Alma wrote to Dolph at Maryhill. "Remember that lovely Philippine lace I sent to you? If you are not using it at the museum, would you send it back? My secretary is getting married — at my house — and it would make a lovely present. Write a little note that it is from you. Her name is Cecelia McCue, soon Mrs. Marc Cremer."[14]

After a brief honeymoon, the bride resumed her duties as Alma's secretary, and the groom had his laundry, his cleaning and all his other needs taken care of.

Joe Paget-Fredricks was also on Alma's mind. The boy who had once danced in Loie's troupe as a child was now a middle-aged Peter Pan, artistic and impractical, possessed of a fine collection of paintings, sculpture and artifacts relating to the dance. Joe, who claimed he was a descendant of Russian nobility, owned costumes belonging to Anna Pavlova, who had once been his uncle's mistress. Alma wanted them — as well as the costumes of her beloved Loie and of Isadora Duncan, which Joe also possessed — for her latest idea, a Museum of the Dance.

Paget-Fredricks, who liked to use the title Baron, lived in Berkeley with his mother, whom he adored to the point of reverence. When she died in his arms in December 1951, he was devastated. Alma quickly stepped in to fill the void. She offered him a place for himself and his collection at Washington Street.

"Dear Paget," she wrote, "Mr. Kortum, who is occupying the garage, sent me a wire. He married at Reno, so I am hoping he will vacate the garage. It is nice and warm there and with a little alter- ation and color it could be made very attractive. I have some very attractive furniture belonging to Dorothy which I am sure she will lend or give, and if I were you, I would send things here belonging only to the Dance and not all those old paintings and Chinese things which would not belong there.

"I could put in a piano and, when famous dancers arrive, you could have small parties and as there is a kitchen, serve tea, etc. You could still keep your apartment at Berkeley if you wish, but what worries me is that someone might steal those works of art.

"I think this will be an excellent start for Dance museum. I went to see May Bachman. She is very ill. She has two wonderful bronzes of Loie Fuller. She might be persuaded to give them to a Museum. Happy new year!"[15]

But Kortum and his wife remained for another year, and while Alma kept up her friendship with Paget-Fredricks she could not fill his mother's place in his life. When he died ten years later, he left his entire collection to the Bancroft Library at the University of California, Berkeley.

Alma's next blow-up with Kortum came in 1955, after he had finally got the Maritime Museum's board to agree to purchase the old *Balclutha*. Once it was restored and opened to the public, he planned to charge admission. The money thus derived, he felt, would make the museum self-supporting. Alma was adamantly against it.

"If you buy that vessel, I'll no longer have anything to do with the Maritime Museum," she threatened. "It's going to cost too much to rehabilitate, and we're going to have to spend too damn much money to maintain it."

Kortum attributed her reluctance to stinginess, "or maybe she didn't think the *Balclutha's* decks were suitable for her social shin- digs." Nelson was more intuitive. "She was against it because she felt if they charged admission, they would soon have enough money so that they wouldn't need her. I don't think Mrs. Spreckels had a very high opinion of herself.

"We had a meeting at her home, and the people there were heads of steamship companies — Matson, Bethlehem, the American Presidents Line, Grace Line, etc. They said, 'Hey, we came into this thing because we expected it was going to walk by itself and not be dependent on Mrs. Spreckels's money.' And they added, quite ruthlessly, 'If she wants to walk away, let her walk.' "

Alma sent in her resignation from the board, but she couldn't cut herself off completely from the project. When the Longshoremen's Union donated their time to restoring the ship, and the shipowners donated the materials, Alma wrote a check for a party to celebrate its completion. She continued to purchase models, sometimes at Kortum's request, and she sent a check for $20,000 to buy an old warehouse near the museum to be used as a roundhouse for Kneiss's railroad trains and cable cars. She promised an additional $20,000 the following year when the project got under way. It never did, and she never got an answer as to where the initial $20,000 went.

She was slightly mollified when Louis Ets-Hokin, then president of the Maritime Museum board, sent her a letter in 1956 informing her that the board had "unanimously elected you Honorary President of the organization." She immediately had the resolution photostatted, and the copy was sent to the de Bretteville "family museum" in the chateau in France.

Alma closed the books on the Maritime Salvage Shop, turned over a final check of $900 and reopened the shop for the support of her newest project, an auxiliary to the Legion of Honor museum, the Patrons of Art and Music. But that was not the end of her involvement with Kortum. He was to cause her even more pain in the future.

In August 1959, war broke out between the two adversaries after an eleven-page spread — complete with pictures — about the Maritime Museum was published in the U.S. Navy's publication, *Proceedings*. Not one line nor one picture mentioned Alma's part in the museum.

Kortum was proud of what he had accomplished. His Project X, with "living ships" floating in the lagoon, was a reality. And there was more. Thanks to an allocation of tidelands oil revenues for park use, for which Dave Nelson had lobbied successfully, he also had his Victorian Park with the cable car turnaround depositing visitors right at the doorstep of Aquatic Center. Now, with William Matson Roth, a member of Kortum's board, restoring the old red-brick Ghirardelli chocolate factory into a beautiful shopping and eating complex (an idea for which Kortum took credit), the whole area was to become a prime tourist attraction and a great asset to the city.

Poor Alma! Reading the story, she felt as rejected as she did when Queen Elizabeth refused to pin a medal on her. Fuming with anger, she took the same course of action she had then. She began a letter-writing campaign in support of her claim that the Maritime Museum was "merely the outgrowth of the San Francisco Museum of Science and Industry," which pre-dated Kortum's efforts by ten years. Unfortunately, most of the people who could substantiate her claim were dead. In a letter to William Wallace, husband of Ina Claire and president of the Legion of Honor board, Alma wrote:

> Walter Walsh was an attorney. His office was in the Monadnock Building and our Board used to meet there. He secured the papers from Sacramento, making it a non-profit organization.
>
> The last time I saw Walter Walsh was at my home when we had a Museum meeting . . . He had an attack the next day and was unconscious for years and died at the Veterans' Hospital.
>
> My secretary met her husband here in 1949 and later married him. Her name is Mrs. Marc Cremer. He had a heart attack and died suddenly . . . The model of the *Queen Mary* (see enclosed) is a magnificent model which I purchased for $5,000, intending to give it to the Maritime Museum in memory of Mr. Cremer. But years ago, I found out that they changed the by-laws, saying they could sell any gift they wished. The California Palace of the Legion of Honor cannot sell anything without permission of the city. Because of their by-laws I presented it to the Legion instead, then they loaned it to the Maritime Museum where it is now on exhibition.
>
> Mr. Thomas Carr Howe is writing me a letter recounting a motor trip I made with him in 1941 from Washington, D.C. to the Maritime Museum at Annapolis.
>
> I would like to tell you the inside story regarding the occupancy of the Aquatic Park Center. If you will note, we first started with the Marine and Aviation Section over twenty years ago.
>
> General H.H. Arnold wanted to give us his magnificent private collection of airplane models . . . Kortum, who was a sailor, was not interested in airplane models. Therefore we lost the collection and it is now [at the Air Force Academy] in Colorado.
>
> When you have time and have examined these papers, I would like to confer with you. I am not well at present, and again I say to you I do not want any credit. Mr. Kortum owes his position to me and also to the men who used to serve on the Board for years. These men contributed money regularly for years. Most of them are dead and I do not think it is right that an employee should continually write that he founded it.[16]

Wallace read the letters, and all the enclosures, and asked Alma what she wanted to do about Kortum. She replied: "A letter might be directed to the president, officers and trustees of the Museum, demanding that they stop the director, Karl Kortum, from giving out to editors, publishers and publicity media of all kinds, the false information that he and he alone is *individually and solely* responsible for the founding of the San Francisco Maritime Museum.

"I do believe that most of the officers and trustees would be fair about this matter if they were apprised of the true facts, as they are busy men and do not necessarily know what the director has been doing in this regard."[17]

At their November board meeting, the Maritime Museum trustees passed a unanimous resolution praising Alma for her devotion and generosity. "Mrs. Spreckels' maritime collection and transportation museum constituted a nucleus around which the present institution was formed. We wish to acknowledge that without Mrs. Spreckels's unstinting gifts of time, talent, energy and substance, this dream of a great San Francisco Maritime Museum would never have become a reality."[18]

"Anything to shut her up," was Kortum's comment on the resolution.

Chapter Notes:

1. Frickelton interview, Dodie Rosekrans tapes.
2. Ibid.
3. Karl Kortum interview.
4. Spreckels papers, Maryhill Museum.
5. David Nelson interview.
6. Ibid.
7. Karl Kortum papers.
8. Kjeld Storm interview, as told to him by Jim Rambo.
9. Jean Kortum letter, never mailed, Karl Kortum papers.
10. *San Francisco Chronicle,* March 4, 1945, p. 7.
11. George Livermore papers.
12. David Nelson interview, as related to him by Alma.
13. Ibid.
14. Spreckels correspondence, Maryhill Museum.
15. Page-Fredricks papers, Bancroft Library, U.C. Berkeley.
16. Alma Spreckels to William Wallace, October 27, 1961, John Rosekrans papers.
17. Ibid.
18. *San Francisco Chronicle,* November 8, 1961, p.7.

*Alma conspires with one of her closest friends, Paul Verdier, owner
of the fabled City of Paris department store, in August 1949. Verdier
was a* bon vivant *and a scamp, and Alma knew all his secrets.
(Courtesy Archives, San Francisco Public Library)*

CHAPTER SEVENTEEN

The Patrons
of Art and Music

 ALMA'S IDEA OF A SUPPORT GROUP for her Legion of Honor Museum grew out of her anger at a 1953 exhibit she found very inappropriate. It was called *Arms and Armor.* The trustees evidently were of the same opinion, since only three out of sixteen members saw fit to attend the preview. And fewer than that supported it financially. When Howe sent her a letter stating, "We would be deeply grateful if you should feel disposed to make a contribution to the limited fund used to offset the expenses we incurred," she shot off a steamy reply about why she refused to contribute. But she would send money for something else:

"For years I have tried to arouse interest in the formation of a group which might be called Friends of the California Palace of the Legion of Honor... but I have been unsuccessful. At this time I again urge that such an organization be started, and I personally will pay any expenses incurred in getting it started. It is a well-known fact that it is women who have the time and are looking for such a worthy project to work for, and I can guarantee a large number who would be happy to join and work."[1]

She followed with a check for $2,000, and a promise that she would add to it the following year if necessary.

Alma was happy to make cash contributions. She was tired of the constant battles with the IRS over the appraisals of her art gifts on which she claimed tax deductions. She had her secretary, now Cecelia Cremer, write a letter to her brother Alex de Bretteville, keeper of Alma's funds, explaining her actions:

"As you know, Mrs. Spreckels has made large gifts to the Museum in the past in the form of gifts of painting, sculpture, etc. that were on loan at the Museum. As the Federal Government has consistently reduced the value of those gifts, we have decided not to make those gifts until her returns are brought up to date, and therefore she is free to make a donation of cash, about which there can be no question later. Also she has already given almost everything that was on loan out there."

Then, in an effort to appease Alex, who kept a careful watch on Alma's funds, Mrs. Cremer added: "You understand that these gifts of cash will cost her only 10 or 15 percent of the actual gift."[2]

Alma made another contribution to the fund the following year, 1954, and in 1955 she summoned Howe to her home. "When I got there, she said, 'Here's a check for $10,000. I want you to go out and start that auxiliary,' " Howe related.[3]

> I said, "Mrs. Spreckels, I'll have to think hard, because I don't want to make ours a copy of the others." There was already a de Young membership organization. It was used exclusively for purchases, and the Museum of Modern Art had one that helped maintain the museum along with city funds they received.
>
> She said, "Oh, you'll think of something. Take the check along and let me know how it goes."
>
> I talked to my wife and said what about making it a combination of music and art because we have the beautiful Little Theater — what Alfred Frankenstein, then music critic for the *Chronicle,* called "the finest small opera and concert hall in northern California."
>
> My wife said, "You've got to get help from the girls." I said, "You're darn right." We got Grace Kelham, J.D.'s daughter, and Mrs. Peter Folger. Mrs. Folger was later killed in the Sharon Tate murders. And we got Whitney Warren. Our first meeting was at the Buena Vista Cafe. First move was to make up a list of names to have on the board. At the next meeting, at Mr. Warren's magnificent house on Telegraph Hill, we decided we needed a distinguished name to head it, and that we would incorporate music with the organization. We decided to call it the Patrons of Art and Music.
>
> For chairman, I suggested my oldest and nicest friend in the community, a man who would interest the old, deeply entrenched Jewish element, Joe Bransten, of the MJB Coffee family. I called him up and told him we were organizing and he was the unanimous choice to be the first chairman. I asked him to accept as a favor to me. Joe said yes, but ever afterwards he said, " 'I didn't know what I was doing, but you talked so damn fast!' "
>
> Mrs. Alexander Albert agreed to be chairman of music. We couldn't have had a more distinguished person. Agnes was active on the symphony and opera boards; she was a wonderful pianist

and all the musicians adored her.

We also had to have a chairman for art. Joe said, 'You have no choice. If you want to raise money you had better ask Jean Magnin [Mrs. Grover Magnin, whose husband was then president of I. Magnin]. She was a trustee of the de Young. I had been working on them a long time — they were going to leave everything to the de Young. As it turned out later, we got half and the de Young got half. Well, Jean accepted, and of course she let me do all her work. Jean cared about nothing but Mr. Christian Dior and his clothes. She even had an agreement with him so that she could send them back to Paris to be cleaned when they needed cleaning. Right to Mr. Dior!

We set our membership goal at sixteen hundred. We arrived at that number because our Little Theater seats four hundred. We couldn't have a membership that is overwhelmingly large because if we had a famous soloist and everybody wanted to come, it would be disastrous. I consulted with theatrical people and they said if you can accomodate four hundred then confine your membership to sixteen hundred, because, as a rule, never more than a fourth show up.

We got our sixteen hundred members easily. Then we had a waiting list. People considered it like being asked to join the Junior League.

The opening event of the PAM in January 1956 was, in Howe's words, "a very glossy affair. We had thirty-eight musicians from the symphony in a program of the works of Mozart. But the best part of all was the guest soloist."

When the group was having a difficult time getting someone well-known, Agnes Albert turned to her mother, Mrs. Tobin Clark, for help. She called Howe and asked if he thought Elizabeth Schwartzkopf would do.

"I gasped, 'The cost!' 'Who said anything about cost?' replied Mrs. Clark. This is a lady who invited the entire Budapest String Quartet to play at her house whenever they were in town on a Sunday afternoon. She was a great patron of music, and her daughter, Agnes, followed in her footsteps. And they had the money to do it."

Alma received a Benefactor Life Membership in a beautifully worded letter by Joe Bransten in which he spoke about her "neverending generosity to the California Palace of the Legion of Honor." He expressed the hope that she would be gratified in the years to come with the knowledge that the "infant society, planned and made possible by your magnanimous gift, has grown into one of the most important and valued cultural organizations in the Nation."[4]

The PAM had certainly attained that lofty peak by the time David Pleydell-Bouverie decided to give his dinner party at the museum prior to a PAM gala preview of a Boldini-Sargent exhibit in October 1959.

Pleydell-Bouverie, a tall, aristocratic English squire, has a country estate in Sonoma, where he met Alma in her Sobre Vista days. "I was in a bar at the Swiss Hotel up there in about 1940. The bartender, an Italian man named Mr. Mateoni, knew only one English phrase, which he used as a one-word greeting. I was sitting drinking my beer when in walked a large woman in a nightgown over which she wore a rather ratty mink coat. He gave her his customary greeting, 'Hi, somabitch.' Then he brought out a pitcher into which he put ice and gin and a dash of vermouth. That was my introduction to Alma Spreckels."[5]

The two became fast friends, and soon Pleydell-Bouverie found himself serving on the Legion's board of trustees. Not long after that, he was responsible — with Alma's help — for securing for the museum one of its greatest treasures.

> I was in New York and I heard from my lawyer that his uncle, Edwin Vogel, was moving into the Sherry Netherland and was going to sell some of his great impressionists. I phoned Tommy Howe and said, "Which of Edwin Vogel's collection, if you could get it, would you like to have?" I don't believe he thought we could have anything out of the Edwin Vogel collection, but he said, "It would be very nice if you could get Manet's *At The Milliner's.*"
>
> By great good fortune, Mr. Vogel knew my name. My slightly disreputable cousin by marriage, the Hon. Mrs. Peter Pleydell-Bouverie, was known to him because she collected impressionists — the finest ones — while she was married to a man who had a store in Chicago, called Marshall Field. Mr. Vogel gave me a two-week option to buy the Manet for $120,000, which was a steal, even then.
>
> I came back to San Francisco and called a meeting of the trustees to tell them about my great coup. I knew the museum had the money to buy it. Alex de Bretteville said, "I don't think any picture is worth more than $50,000." Whereupon Whitney Warren said, "Well, I have to agree with that."
>
> Well, I was almost stumped. Two people backed me to the hilt: Jack Rosekrans and Harold Zellerbach. But the rest of them stayed on the fence. So I rushed downstairs and dictated a letter from Mrs. Spreckels to the board. Then I phoned Mrs. Spreckels and told her I had to see her, that it was urgent.
>
> I went over to her and explained the situation and waited for what she was going to say. And what she said was, *"Of course*

we should get it. Let's stop piddling around." Those were her exact words. Then she said, "What do you want me to do?" I said, "I want you to sign this letter." I took it out of my pocket. She signed it, and the next day the purchase was approved. And that's the story of the Manet, the only good Manet on the West Coast, which is now worth millions and millions and millions.

When Pleydell-Bouverie gave the 1959 dinner party he did it to try to get people to increase the endowment fund, which was very low at the time. "I purposely made it very difficult to get an invitation. People struggled to come. We limited it to eighty people, and I insisted that they all be seated at one table."

For weeks before the event, the society pages were full of details about the elegant affair. Guests were asked to come in Edwardian clothes reminiscent of the Boldini and Sargent portraits. Mrs. Claude Lazard, a San Franciscan married to a member of the French banking firm, sent to Paris for a diamond dog collar in the vault there. The Princess Rainieri di San Faustino borrowed back the tiara and other emerald jewelry her mother had given to the Legion.

Adding even more excitement to the event was the Alice Roosevelt Longworth story. Pleydell-Bouverie recalled:

> Alice came to my house shortly before the party. I said, "I wish we could get the portrait of your father, Theodore Roosevelt, by Sargent, for the exhibit, but of course we can't." She asked, "Why can't you?" And I said, "Because the White House never lends things."
>
> "Where's your telephone?" She went to the telephone, looked in her little book for a number and dialed. "This is Mrs. Nicholas Longworth. I want to speak to the president of the United States." The voice apparently told her the president wasn't available at the moment.
>
> "Then give him this message word for word: Mrs. Longworth would appreciate his approval of sending Theodore Roosevelt's portrait by Sargent to San Francisco for one month for a show there. Signed, Mrs. Nicholas Longworth."
>
> A week later, Tommy Howe got a telegram approving the loan, which was unheard of!

Millie Robbins, society editor for the *Chronicle,* wrote excitedly about the table at which the eighty invited guests were to be seated. The long table would be covered with 135 yards of rose-colored satin. All the appointments on it would be gold... huge gold epergnes filled with pink carnations... gold cupids to hold the placecards ...enormous gold candlebras holding hundreds of candles would furnish the only light to be used that night.

Millie was also a stringer for *Life* magazine, and she called for one of the magazine's photographers to cover the event. "When we got there, people were having cocktails in the room across the hall from where the dinner was to be held," she recalled. "Everybody was waiting for Alma. Someone went to phone her home. She had left. Nobody seemed to know where she was. My cameraman was impatient. He had to fly to Alaska that night. He said, 'Oh, to hell with it. I can't stay here any longer.'

"I said, 'Well, as long as you're here, it's worth taking a picture of that table.' So he lugged in a ladder and brought in his cameras. It was dark. We lit a light. And there, at the head of this gorgeous table, was Alma Spreckels, her head resting on the pink satin cloth. I said, 'Mrs. Spreckels, they're all waiting for you.' Without raising her head, she growled, in that raspy voice of hers. 'Let 'em wait.' "[6]

What was Alma thinking of, all alone in the dark? What sent her spirits plummeting in the midst of all the splendor in her beautiful museum? Perhaps she was still brooding over the hurts inflicted upon her by Kortum ... that eleven-page article that never mentioned her. Was it worth it to work so hard and to be ignored so completely? All she ever wanted was to do the best she could for everyone. Where had it gotten her?

Her mood changed quickly as people started drifting in. The candles were lighted, and in the soft glow that flooded the room, Alma brightened perceptibly. She lifted her head and assumed a regal pose at the head of the beautiful table.

She wasn't receptive to a letter Pleydell-Bouverie wrote her shortly after his dinner party. In it he told her that the merger of the Legion with the de Young Museum was inevitable and "since it will happen after we are dead, wouldn't it be wonderful if you instituted it now?" He told her that "just as Napoleon described the Piazza San Marco as the finest drawing room in Europe, so the Legion of Honor museum could be the finest reception room in America."

When he got no response after two weeks, he phoned. " 'David,' she said, 'do you know Herbert Fleishhacker?' And she proceeded to give me her opinion of him. Then she said, 'Do you know Mike de Young and his daughters?' Well, there was no love lost there, either.

" 'Only over my dead body will there be a merger,' she said with finality."

The PAM continued to be a leading social and cultural force in the life of the city until 1972. That year, over the dead bodies of both Alma and Helen de Young Cameron, the two museums were merged, and with the merger went the dissolution of the Patrons of Art and Music.

Chapter Notes:

1. Alma Spreckels to Thomas Carr Howe, April 27, 1953.
2. Cecelia Cremer to Alex de Bretteville, October 12, 1953, Spreckels papers, California Palace of the Legion of Honor.
3. Thomas Carr Howe interview.
4. Joseph Bransten to Alma Spreckels, October 20, 1955, John Rosekrans papers.
5. David Pleydell-Bouverie interview.
6. Millie Brown Robbins interview.

Alma receives Dr. Francis Redewill and supervisor (later mayor) George Christopher, at the opening of a special exhibit of works on loan from the Rheims Museum in France, in March 1952. For sixty years, Alma knew all the mayors of San Francisco, and they often called on her for help or advice. (Courtesy Archives, San Francisco Public Library)

CHAPTER EIGHTEEN

A Museum for Loie

ALMA'S LAST PROJECT, the one she called her "swan song," was her effort to form a Museum of the Dance as a memorial to Loie Fuller.

She wrote of her progress in a letter to Lloyd Howard, her longtime admirer who was vacationing in Antibes at the home of their mutual friend, Florence Gould. Florence was the widow of the fabulously wealthy Frank Jay Gould and owner of a great art collection. Alma had had her eye on it for a long time. She scrawled a letter to Lloyd in her purple ink:

> Please keep following confidential until it is accomplished. We have had several meetings here of very prominent men and women and are now forming a Museum of the Dance and Theater. We may — keep your fingers crossed, Lloydie — get a fireproof building belonging to the City for the museum and I am giving my collection of the Dance. I have the showcases earmarked for all my bronzes. They will be painted white. Paget-Fredricks is giving his Children's Collection. I saw it exhibited in the City library and it is superb. He's giving it in memory of his mother.
>
> As you know, in 1937 I saw the Museum of the Dance in one building, in Paris, and in a small white stone building in back of the museum, there was a collection of Pavlova — her costumes, medals, portraits, slippers, etc. Paget was left by Pavlova a collection which he will lend.
>
> It takes time and we will start small. I remember when the Rodins, now in the Legion of Honor, were here in my ballroom, then the beautiful furniture, souvenirs, etc., of Queen Marie of Romania were here, now in Maryhill Museum, Washington. Then fourteen ship models, which are now in the San Francisco Maritime Museum. Now my Dance Collection is here, and then it will be the Dance Museum. It has been my dream to do it for years,

my Swan Song.

I know you love the theater and will be happy to know our beloved San Francisco will be the only city in the world to have a Dance Museum.[1]

"Lloydie" presumably uncrossed his fingers about the fireproof building belonging to the city after the supervisors voted it down because of the high costs of maintaining security. Then Alma explored the idea of adding a wing onto the Legion of Honor. She called in George Livermore, the architect who was a friend of her three children. His studies proved that wasn't feasible.

Because of Livermore's interest in ballet, especially the Diaghilev period, Alma appointed him the director of the nascent museum. "We worked quite hard on this Museum of Dance. I designed big, black display cases, and we had pedestals made and the little statues were all put on them."[2]

Livermore remembers a luncheon Alma gave at her house during that time. "It was a great big sit-down luncheon for twenty-four people — exactly twenty-four and she didn't want more than twenty-four. She discovered during the cocktail period that there was an extra person. So I went up and whispered in her ear that I don't have to stay, I'm just like a member of the family. She said, in her very loud voice, 'No, you stay here.'

"Then she shouted across the room, 'Hey, you, over there! You go out and get yourself a good lunch!'

"That man happened to be a consul from one of the countries who was stationed here. But that was typical of Alma, God bless her. She just didn't want us to put another chair at the table."

Since the statues were kept at 2080 while the search for a building went on, Alma decided, in the interim, to display her collection there, in one of the vacant first-floor apartments, before a select group. She wanted to get more public support. Millie Robbins arranged to view the exhibit the day before the big event:

Mrs. Spreckels was in her bathrobe. When I tell people that, they say, "Oh, you mean she was in a negligee?" And I say, "O.K., if that's what you want to call an apricot chenille bathrobe."

She had on those gorgeous pearls. I said to her, "Oh, my, those pearls are gorgeous. And I don't have to chew on them to know they're real."

"Whattaya mean, you don't have to chew on them?"

"Well," I said, "you know, if they are real you can run them over your teeth and they are scratchy." That fascinated her, and we started talking. Soon she was telling me, "You know, I was a working girl myself!"

After she took me on a tour of the exhibit, which was quite lovely, she ushered me into her bedroom, where she wanted to show me something by Malvina Hoffman which had arrived too late to be displayed. I said, "Malvina Hoffman was a protegee of Rodin's, wasn't she?" Mrs. S. gave me a broad wink and said, "Yes, among other things!"

We got into this magnificently appointed room with all this elegant furniture and the huge gold bed and there beside the bed sat an orange crate. A plain old orange crate filled with books. She saw my shocked expression. "It's convenient," she said.

Then she wanted to show me a picture of her daughter, Dorothy. "When I got it," she told me, "I phoned her and said it's nice, but who's the old man with you? Go in and take a look at it." I did. The old man was the duke of Windsor.[3]

Dorothy was now married to Charles Munn, the quintessential socialite. A former widower many years her senior, Munn not only had inherited wealth, but he had added greatly to it by inventing the totalizer used to figure betting odds at racetracks. A man of exquisite taste and manners, he maintained residences in Paris and New York as well as Palm Beach, where he was known as "Mr. Palm Beach." It was at his estate there, Amador, that the picture Alma showed Millie was taken.

The private showing of the dance collection the next day was a success, and Alma immediately dispatched Tom Howe to Europe to do some more buying for her. "When you're in Paris, I want you to look up my Romanian friend, Tepee Lionadu. He knows a lot of ballet people. Get his advice on what to buy for the museum,' " Alma instructed him.

"When I met this horrid little creature — he was a gigolo who was kept by various women who wanted an escort or something — he was terribly disappointed that I wasn't of his emotional persuasion," said Howe. "But he did have a lot of contacts, and I told him I had this money and Mrs. Spreckels told me to buy through him — presumably she wanted him to get his cut.

"I was bedevilled to death by him. He took me to meet all these figures from the Diaghilev days. He was so excited about them. I couldn't have cared less. I had lots of other things to do in Paris. But I bought a number of things and they pleased Mrs. Spreckels, and they are in the collection."[4]

With Howe's purchases, Alma now had a dance collection which reflected a generation of artists who revolutionized the art of ballet decor throughout Europe. It contained about two hundred items, both graphic works and sculpture. Studies by Alex Benois and Leon Bakst comprised one of the strongest areas. Most of the paintings involved the Diaghilev Ballets Russes during the period 1909-29, and some of the works were specifically designed for the Diaghilev ballets.[5]

By now, Alma considered herself something of an expert on Diaghilev. She displayed her knowledge shortly after Howe's return, when she staged a luncheon honoring Alexandra Danilova, the greatest ballerina of the time. Danilova was in town for an engagement at the Opera House. Present also was impresario Sol Hurok, who had arranged for Danilova's performance. During a lull in the conversation, Alma turned to Hurok, and her booming voice rang out over the room.

"Mr. Hurok, do you know why they wouldn't let Diaghilev dance in Russia?"

Hurok, bemused, knew the answer. Diaghilev was not a performer. He was an impresario, like himself. But he let Alma answer her own question.

"I'll tell you why," she replied. "Because he wouldn't wear a jockstrap!"[6]

Despite all of Alma's efforts and the expense to which she went to obtain a collection, the Museum of the Dance never became a reality. Alma knew why. She explained it to Ellen Magnin Newman, who was invited to 2080 with her father, Cyril, head of the Joseph Magnin chain of women's clothing stores. Ellen, then a young matron of twenty-two, was already taking an active part in both the company and volunteer work.

"Mrs. Spreckels told me that private individuals can give and support a cause only so long. If the public doesn't pick it up, then it must die of its own. The idea of perpetuating your desires through your personal funds or foundations is wrong. I quote her often not only in private circles but business ones. You give the start-up funds and give for a long enough period so the developers are not looking over their shoulders, and then if it doesn't take off, let it go. It was a valuable lesson in how to give."[7]

Alma's dance collection is stored in the Palace of the Legion of Honor and makes periodic appearances in dance retrospectives on performers such as Pavlova and Nijinsky, waiting for the time when the public is ready to pick up the idea of a Museum of the Dance.

Chapter Notes:

1. John Rosekrans papers.
2. George Livermore interview.
3. Millie Brown Robbins interview.
4. Thomas Carr Howe interview.
5. Nancy Van Norman Baer, guest curator, Pavlova Commemorative Exhibition, Legion of Honor Museum, January 31 - April 26, 1981.
6. John Rosekrans interview.
7. Ellen Magnin Newman interview.)

In her late 70s, Alma wore her usual "tuxedo" gown, with the pearls and clips Adolph had given her and a curious pin in the form of an Asian dancer. Although the pitchers of martinis and the all-night bridge games have taken their toll, plenty of power remains in the expression. (Courtesy Anona Dukelow)

CHAPTER NINETEEN

Gangy

WHILE ALMA CONSTANTLY embarrassed her children, she never shocked her grandchildren. She was much closer to them than she had been to her daughters and son, particularly to Johnny Rosekrans, the oldest son of Little Alma. Unlike his mother, who never rose before afternoon, was notoriously late to every invitation and had little ambition for anything but bridge, Johnny inherited his grandmother's ferocious energy and determination to succeed. To Johnny, Alma was "Gangy," someone he intuitively understood and loved. Nothing she did embarrassed him, not even what happened at his first wedding.

Johnny was still a Stanford student when he married his college sweetheart, Rose Marie Rousseau, at an elaborate June wedding in 1949. It was held in the gardens of his Aunt Dorothy's Hillsborough estate, La Dolphine. Never did the grounds of the residence, built as a replica of the Petit Trianon, look lovelier. Special boxed orange trees, blue hydrangeas and a multitude of other flowering potted plants were placed on the terrace to make a charming setting for the buffet table. An aisle for the bridal party to emerge from the house was marked by bamboo containers filled with regal lilies. The path wound around the pool in the sunken garden. There, before an antique urn, which had been filled with white stock and topped with a golden cross, the couple were to take their vows. Hundreds of beautifully dressed guests were seated in rows of delicate, gilded ballroom chairs on the lawn.

Johnny stood before the antique urn, waiting for his bride. His mother and his aunt were seated in the front row, and an usher brought Gangy down to her place of honor. As she lowered her considerable weight onto the little chair, it was like a hammer pounding down on nails. The chair's legs were driven into the ground, dumping Alma on the grass. She swore in Danish and in French, and uttered a few choice Anglo-Saxon expressions as a swarm of ushers pulled her up and extricated the chair. While his mother and aunt watched with horror, Johnny thought the whole episode was quite funny.[1]

Several years later, when the marriage ended in divorce and the settlement left the young man financially depleted, Gangy came to his aid by renting him one of the apartments at Washington Street at a bargain rate. Johnny had only two complaints. One was that he never knew what the apartment was going to look like from day to day.

"The way some people play tennis, Gangy moved furniture! Stringers sent a truck with four men out there daily. Every time I'd come home there would be new furniture in my apartment. Fortunately, all my clothes were in built-in closets so she couldn't move that," he said.[2]

The other thing that bothered Johnny was the way Alma would pop in on him unannounced. "It was kind of unnerving. I'd bring a young lady home to spend the night. The next morning, as the gal emerged from her tub, this tall, stout, elderly woman in bedroom slippers and a robe would charge in and demand, 'My God, who the hell are you?' "

When Lois Spreckels, Adolph Jr.'s daughter with his first wife, announced her engagement in 1956 to Sam Register, a fellow student at Stanford, Gangy announced that she would host the wedding reception. Having been cheated out of all of her son's nuptials, she wasn't going to be left out of his daughter's. First thing she did was call in the painters.

"I want everything white for the wedding," she instructed them. The order included the splendid murals that decorated the round ceiling in the Pompeiian Room.

"We wanted a small wedding, just family," recalled Lois. "Gangy wanted a big one."[3]

To make sure it would be small, the bride-to-be accompanied her grandmother to the printer's when she ordered the invitations. "Gangy ordered the amount I specified, but what I didn't find out until later was that she ordered double the amount of envelopes. Then she went around collecting back the invitations from the family after they received them and remailed them to her friends! Everybody in San Francisco was there!"

Everyone except the bride's father. While the reception was going on in the Italian Room, Adolph lay in a drunken stupor in a first floor bedroom. His cousin, Claude Spreckels, gave the bride away.

"Uncle Adolph was getting drunk and passing out at Gangy's on the bathroom floor a lot in those days," recalls Charles Rosekrans, Little Alma's youngest son. "Gangy would phone my mother and say, 'Please, Alma, can Charles and Johnny come over and pick him up?' My mother was furious."[4]

Big Alma didn't have a starring role in the marriage of her grandson Adolph Rosekrans, but it was a memorable one.

"There was this dinner planned for us at the St. Francis," recalls Adolph, "and Gangy invited the whole party to cocktails first at 2080. After about an hour of drinks and hors d'oeuvres, she said, 'You have to go now. I'm tired.' "[5]

The group left. Only later did they find out why the party ended so abruptly.

"One of my friends arrived at Gangy's late," said Adolph. "He told us that when he got there, he found a party going on, but it was the wrong party. He didn't know anyone there. Gangy wanted us out because she had another party of her friends coming in!"

"There never was a time when I didn't find Gangy enormously intimidating," said Charles Rosekrans. "She was like a Wagnerian soprano in her great velvet gowns and diamond clips — this huge woman in the gigantic house."

He still remembers how intimidated he felt when he was ten years old and sat next to his grandmother at a family funeral. "Gangy turned to me, and in a very loud whisper she said, in that way she had of dragging out her vowels, 'Baaby, your breath is baad. You need an eenemaa!' "

Realizing later that this was just an indication of her concern for people, he loved her for what he saw as her very human qualities. "Gangy had this tiny Filipino chauffeur, and he would drive her down to Woodside to visit us. It was about an hour's ride. I remember hearing her say, 'O.K., Tony, time to go wee wee now before we drive back.' And he very dutifully said, 'Yes, Mrs. Spreckels,' and he did as he was told.

"She screamed at people — she was always at odds with my mother — but she didn't bear grudges. She wanted to be a peacemaker." Charles remembers the time he was in New York studying music and his grandmother visited him. Knowing how much he loved opera and that he couldn't afford a season ticket to the Metropolitan, she offered to get it for him — with a condition attached.

"I was on the outs with my mother. Gangy pointed to the phone and said, 'Give your mother a call.' I didn't get the ticket until I made the call."

When Charles accepted the position as conductor of Houston's

A family dinner in the oval dining room on Washington Street in 1960, clockwise: Alma at the far end, Alma II (Mrs. James Coleman), John Rosekrans, Virginia Rosekrans, Kjeld Storm, Jean de Bretteville, James

Coleman, Alex and Gus de Bretteville (Alma's brothers),
Lois Spreckels Register (granddaughter), Adolph
Rosekrans, Bernice Ker (cousin), Sam Register and
Maud Galvin (cousin). (Courtesy Kjeld Storm)

Little Symphony Orchestra after his studies were completed, Alma was delighted.

"Do you have a car? You don't? Well, you're gonna need one. Texas is awfully big. Here, take these," she said, throwing him the keys to her sedan.

"Gangy had bought the car, a big black Buick, in Paris in the mid-fifties. On the back was a big F, because it was purchased in France. When I got to Houston, I wrote Gangy, I was immediately known as the guy in the F-ing Buick!"

Kjeld Storm, a Copenhagen relative whose de Bretteville grandfather was Alma's cousin, was also the object of her generosity. The young man asked her to sign immigration papers as a sponsor so that he could come to the United States. Alma did more than that. She immediately began planning his future. Did he say he was interested in studying law? She spoke to every lawyer she knew to find out which were the best schools.

'Harvard law school near Boston is the best — very expensive," she wrote. "This friend of mine has relatives in New York, one of the biggest law firms, and his cousin is on the Harvard Board of Trustees. He is writing to his cousin today."[6]

In another letter, she asked him to "write me all about yourself as it is no good to come over here and not know anything." One of the things Alma wanted to know was, "How much per month are your parents going to give you as an allowance?"

To reassure him that there was nothing wrong in working his way through school, she wrote that "my grandsons worked on their vacations as my daughter did not want to spoil them and wanted them to know the value of money... Pres. Herbert Hoover studied to be a mining engineer at Stanford and worked as a waiter there as he had no money. He became wealthy and built the Hoover Library at Stanford as a gift."

All of Alma's attempts to find the right law school for Kjeld puzzled him because he had already finished law school in Denmark. "I realized later that Aunt Alma didn't listen to others very closely. She heard the words "law student" and immediately took off in that direction in an effort to be helpful."[7]

Alma invited Kjeld to live at 2080 when he arrived in November 1953. He lived there, with a friend from Denmark, for just three days. Then she found them a nice boarding house. Next, she found them a Chinese laundry. "Wing Chun, this is his name and address. They do things very reasonably. Here is $20 for you," she wrote.

Alma put him to work in her Salvage Shop. With the holidays approaching, she needed all the help she could get.

"Dear Kjeld," she wrote, "Please keep key and try to be at shop by ten o'clock on Friday. Also use your judgment and sell the goods for what you can get. Do you mind sweeping the sidewalk? Please get metal chairs out of bathroom after lunch and clean and set up for meeting."

She invited him to Christmas dinner, but she canceled it. She had received an invitation so rare, so important to her, that she couldn't turn it down. Cecelia Cremer wrote Kjeld a note of explanation: "Mrs. Spreckels wishes to tell you that her daughter, Alma, has invited her on Christmas Eve and therefore she will not be at home. I believe she has asked you in that evening. As a Christmas present to you and your friend, Mrs. Spreckels is sending a check to your landlord for another months' room and board for you and your friend. She thought this would be a more practical gift than something you might not find useful."

When she did invite him back, some time later, Kjeld found himself the target of a verbal joust at Alma's dinner table.

" 'Your grandfather is a stinker!' Aunt Alma boomed at me. 'He wouldn't even buy his wife a new dress even though it was her money.'

"My grandfather, Louis de Bretteville, Aunt Alma's cousin, was a lawyer who had married a girl from a well-to-do family," said Kjeld. "From what I have heard, it was quite possible that what Aunt Alma said was true. What bothered me was that she said it in the presence of complete strangers.

" 'You are probably correct, Aunt Alma,' I responded, 'since you knew him better than I. He died when I was only ten. However, the de Bretteville family has produced a goodly number of characters!'

"Everyone present was holding his breath, not knowing whether this would be allowed to pass. Aunt Alma said nothing. She just gave me a hint of a smile and a big wink! I don't know if she was pleased because I had stood up to her or if she felt being called a character was a compliment."

A warm relationship continued between the two, and when Kjeld sent her flowers on Mother's Day, 1958, she wrote, "Many thanks for thinking of me on Mother's Day...I was very ill on Sunday and in great pain. May 11, I was married 50 years. I hope you will go on Thursday to the preview at the Legion and would appreciate your writing me about it. I don't want anyone to know where I am. I need a rest. You don't know how people pester me. If I did not have an unlisted number, I would be in the cemetery."

The pain Alma was experiencing grew worse. In addition to colitis and arthritis, she was also suffering from gout. It was ten years since she had made Anona Dukelow promise to "close my eyes for me when my time comes." Alma called to tell her the time was now.

As Mrs. Dukelow recalled:

> She was in a lot of pain when I saw her; she was acting very badly. I don't know how many doctors had come and gone and how many nurses. She'd fire them and tell them not to come back. She wanted me to take the night shift.
>
> She said to me, "Mrs. Dukelow, I'm dying."
>
> 'Yes, you are, Mrs. Spreckels, but you have nobody to blame but yourself," I had the gall to tell her. "You have all these good doctors and you're not doing a thing they're telling you."
>
> The poor thing was so neglected. Her hair was plastered down. I don't know when it had been shampooed last. She was a terrible patient. She'd throw things like her sister did. She felt she'd been mistreated at the hospital with high enemas and all.
>
> 'What do I have to do?" she asked me.
>
> 'Well, you have to change your lifestyle. Cut out martinis. You've got gout. You won't be able to drink that good, strong coffee in the morning either. Just decaf. You've got to take some weight off and you have to get up out of that bed."
>
> Obediently, like a little child, she crawled out of bed and into a chair and lit a cigarette. Then, I went into the kitchen and got a large piece of wrapping paper, the one they wrapped the turkey in which had been delivered that day. I brought it back to Mrs. Spreckels's room and I got on the floor and drew her a picture of the alimentary canal and the liver and the heart and explained what alcohol was doing. She was fascinated. I felt I had really gotten through to her. We didn't have any more fuss about medicines after that.[8]

During her mother's illness, Dorothy and her husband, Charles Munn, who came to spend the fall opera season in San Francisco each year, were in residence in the top-floor apartment. They came downstairs frequently to see her. It pleased Dorothy that her elegant husband was so fond of her eccentric mother. Munn, described as "a multimillionaire social tribal chief," was often beset by social climbers who clamored to be included in his annual who's-who lists. He was quick to recognize phonies and pretentious people. They got nowhere with him. But he appreciated Alma for what she was — a straightforward, civic-minded, big-hearted woman who didn't give a damn what people thought. His genuine fondness for his mother-in-law did much to alleviate Dorothy's constant embarrassment about her. When Dorothy proposed that they rent the third floor from her mother and do it over, Charles readily agreed. Although her father had left the house to his three children, it was with the proviso that it was her mother's as long as she lived. "My mother, the landlord," Dorothy said.

Dorothy called in George Livermore, who promptly remodeled it into a luxurious apartment. With the help of her interior designer friend, Archibald Taylor, Dorothy's quarters quickly became a showplace. Even her mother was impressed with the museum quality of her collection of antique French lacquer tables and the casual elegance of the leopard rug in her formal living room. But Alma was decidedly not impressed with the oil portrait of Dorothy which decorated one wall. It was done by surrealist Salvador Dali, a painter far too modern for Alma's tastes. Using symbolic references to Dorothy's love of water, he painted her as Venus, astride a dolphin, with sea creatures cavorting in the background. This Venus, being the very proper Dorothy, was fully clothed in an evening gown.

Dorothy's love of water also impelled her to order Livermore to construct a swimming pool in the area of the gardens that had once been tented off for her debut. The outdoor pool was built into the hillside by means of thirty-foot concrete caissons sunk into the slope. It was enclosed by a ten-foot-high fence. In the short interval between the completion of the pool in 1958 and the time she took ill, Alma, braving the San Francisco fog, used it more than Dorothy did.

During the time Anona Dukelow was nursing Alma back to health, Jean Frickelton, who lived only a block away, came every night at five and had dinner, served on a tray, with Alma in her room. Then the two would play cards, and by seven she was gone. Adolph, now a bachelor, was living temporarily in one of the two first-floor apartments. His marriage to Kay Williams had ended after eight years. At first, it had seemed like a good marriage.

"Daddy adored the son they had, Adolph III, nicknamed Bunker," said his daughter Lois. "Kay even got him to stop drinking for a while. They were part of the Hollywood scene, and Dad, to get away from that, bought a ranch at Ojai, but Kay never went there with him. Clark Gable was in and out of the picture all during their marriage. Kay left Dad after Bunker was born, but they went back together again. Then they had a second child, a daughter, Joan. They were divorced in 1957, after eight years. Happy years mostly. Daddy tried so hard to pull his life together. When Kay left him, it was the beginning of the end."[9]

While Kay went on to marry Clark Gable, taking Bunker and Joan with her, Adolph tried his sixth marital fling a few months later with an eighteen-year-old schoolmate of Lois's, Judy Powell. "She was sort of wacko," said Lois of her most recent stepmother. "They were married at Twentieth Century-Fox Studios. It lasted six weeks.

*A dinner in the Porcelain Gallery at the Legion of Honor Museum
circa 1960, finds Alma at the head table with Cyril Magnin and
Anona Dukelow on her right, and to her left William Goetz, Alma*

Spreckels Coleman, and at far left Adolph Rosekrans, who later
remodeled the museum's sculpture gallery in memory of his
grandmother. (Courtesy Fine Arts Museums of San Francisco)

I didn't speak to my father for a year after that."

Little Alma was now married to Jimmy Coleman, scion of one of San Francisco's pioneer families. Her twenty-four-year marriage to Jack Rosekrans ended in divorce when she discovered a love letter indicating he was having an affair with one of her friends. It was rumored that Jack, a gentleman always, had deliberately left the letter in a suit pocket knowing Little Alma would find it before sending the suit out to the cleaners. It was his way of allowing her to divorce him.[10]

Big Alma was heartbroken. She loved Jack, and when Little Alma resigned from the Legion of Honor board because getting up before noon was an impossibility for her, Big Alma insisted that Jack be appointed in her daughter's place. "He may be your ex-husband, but he's still the father of my grandsons," she told her irate daughter.[11]

"During the long nights when her visitors were gone and Mrs. Spreckels couldn't sleep, I'd entertain her with stories of the trip to Europe my husband and I made to celebrate our twenty-fifth anniversary," said Mrs. Dukelow. "I would act out about Marie Antoinette and how she was in that prison they take the tourists to, and I would repeat what they told us. Mrs. Spreckels was fascinated. She said, 'I've been to Paris. I know it better than I do San Francisco, but I never saw that place.' Then she said, 'Tell you what I'm going to do, Pet. You get me better and next summer I'll take you on a trip to the Europe that I know and you've never seen.' I told her she had a deal."

Meanwhile, as Alma's strength returned and she was anxious to get out again, she coaxed Mrs. Dukelow to switch to daytime duty, take off her uniform and become her companion. Paul Verdier had a live-in companion. He highly recommended it. Why shouldn't she have one?

"I agreed to do it, but not to live in. I went home to my husband every night," said Mrs. Dukelow.

"Do you like to wear black?" Alma asked her. "I'd like you to wear black. It's such a ladylike color."

"So I wore black, and my God, she was so active and she had so many things to do and places to go that I had to be dressed for everything," said Mrs. Dukelow.

Her solution was to turn the backseat of her little Volkswagen into a clothes closet. "I had a cousin who worked at Saks Fifth Avenue, and she found me a box they use to deliver wedding gowns. It was the length and width of the backseat. In it I kept a black suit, a dress and a full-length dinner gown, a couple of hats and several pairs of white gloves. Every day, as I rang the bell at 2080,

I would say to myself, I wonder what today will bring."

One morning when Mrs. Dukelow came to work she found Alma seated at the bridge table in her bedroom, fully dressed, ready to leave.

"Have you had your breakfast yet?" Alma asked her companion, who nodded her head. "Good, because we're going to a funeral."

Alma, without a car of her own since she gave Charles the Buick, climbed in the tiny Volkswagen next to the nurse. On the way, she explained that it was the funeral of Eric Swanson, her seaman friend, the one who had built the *Preussen* for her. Mrs. Dukelow had met him when he came to visit Alma while she was ill. Later, when Alma was well enough to take rides, she'd have Mrs. Dukelow drive by the waterfront hotel where he lived above a bar.

"We'd stop and she wouldn't get out to see him, but she'd leave him a note and a nice bottle of bourbon," recalled the nurse.

"The funeral was out on Valencia Street, and we were the only women there. Mrs. S. in her mink stole and her little flowered hat sat there with her hands crossed and listened intently.

'She whispered to me, 'You better go out and find out how much this funeral is going to cost. Don't use my name, but find out.' And she reached into her purse and pulled out a roll of money and gave me the whole roll. I found out it was going to cost $700. She said, 'Pay it, but don't let him know my name.'

'Then we went right out to the grave with all those seamen, and afterwards she told me to drive to that bar on the waterfront. We got there the same time as the rest of the sailors.

"'Close the door, and pull down the blinds,' Mrs. S. ordered the bartender. 'The drinks and sandwiches are on me.' When they quieted down, she started to speak. She told them what a great man Eric was. How kind he was, and what a great artist and craftsman he was. She did a better job than any minister could because she knew him. The sailors just loved her. I knew she was just dying to drink with them, but I gave her a look and all she had was a couple of beers."

Alma soon tired of the tiny Volkswagen. Not only was she cramped in it, but even worse, she couldn't talk in the car. Mrs. Dukelow told her that as long as she was driving, she couldn't "visit" with her. Alma wasn't used to keeping her mouth shut.

"She said to me one day, 'Let's go down to Van Ness Avenue and pick out a car. I like a Buick. Let's go to the Buick place.' We did. There was this car on the floor. She opened the door. She got in easily. 'Now you get in, Dukelow. Let's see how you fit on the other side.' I did. It had a nice armrest in the middle you could put down. She looked for the cigarette lighter. There was one close by. She said, 'How do you like it?' I said it's very nice. She said, 'Do you think I can afford it?' I said, why don't you ask Mrs. Cremer? She said, 'If I want it, I'm gonna have it. Tell them we'll take it. Tell them to get it off the floor and bring it to my house tomorrow.' I found a salesman and told him. He looked bewildered. He made a sale without opening his mouth!"

Since the car was a limousine meant for a chauffeur, Alma reluctantly hired one. "Dukelow doesn't talk when she drives," she sniffed.

When the Patrons of Art and Music had an important gala coming up, Alma decided she felt well enough to go.

"Mrs. Spreckels, who never wore any jewelry beyond her diamond clips and pearls, suddenly felt the need for an important ring," recalled Mrs. Dukelow. "She had given Frickelton a diamond some time before which had come out of Mr. Spreckels's ring. She had this man come from Magnin's and design a ring. She looked at the design and said, 'It should have a good-sized diamond in the center.' She called up Jean and said, 'When you come to dinner tonight, would you bring that diamond I gave you? I need it.' Well, Jean nearly died over that. She wept for months."

Alma made good on her promise to show Mrs. Dukelow Europe, in the summer of 1959. She also took Jim Rambo, the decorative arts curator who had suffered through her sigmoidoscopy with her. They sailed on the new Swedish-American ship, the *Gripsholm*. Alma was the subject of an extensive newspaper interview when the ship landed in Copenhagen, where she was hailed as the "dazzling great-grandmother."

In Paris they stayed at the Ritz, and Alma took Mrs. Dukelow shopping. "She would walk in very noncommittal and look things over. She had a great eye for beautiful things, and she knew their value. One day, after she looked around, and we were back in the car, she said, 'You know those three clocks sitting on the desk with the ormulu on them? Go back and buy them. I want one for me and one for Alma's new home and one for Dorothy's apartment. If they knew I wanted them, they'd raise the price. Offer them what I have written down here. That's what they're worth.' "

On another shopping trip, a merchant offered Alma an exquisite chocolate set that Napoleon had bought for Josephine. It was still in its original presentation case. Alma turned it down.

'My God, that was beautiful," Mrs. Dukelow remarked after they were back in the car. "How could you pass it up? That belonged to Bonaparte!"

"Pet," laughed Alma, "the original chocolate set that Napoleon bought Josephine is in the Legion of Honor. I bought it years ago!"

Alma loved to walk the streets along the Left Bank and talk to the artists. "I saw her get down on the curb, which isn't so easy to do when you have arthritis, and sit there happily talking to these men just like she did with the sailors in the waterfront saloon after the funeral."

When they returned home to 2080, Dorothy asked her mother one day over lunch what she enjoyed most about the trip. "I loved swimming in the nude on the *Gripsholm*. You know, if you put a roof on the pool, I could swim that way every day," replied Alma.

By dinner that night, George Livermore had been summoned and the three of them were busily planning a roof which would retract automatically with the push of a button. The following morning, lumber and other necessary supplies were delivered to 2080, and in record time the huge outdoor pool was turned into a showplace pavilion.

Alma, now in her eighties, was still outrageous. "Come on, you sissies," she would say, after a long bridge session, "anybody want to come skinny dipping with me?"

Chapter Notes:

1. John Rosekrans interview.
2. Ibid.
3. Lois Register interview.
4. Charles Rosekrans interview.
5. Adolph Rosekrans interview.
6. Kjeld Storm papers.
7. Ibid.
8. Anona Dukelow interview.
9. Lois Register interview.
10. Charles Rosekrans interview.
11. Thomas Carr Howe interview.

September 1960 found Alma still able to visit her museum, and to convey an opinion with a look. (Courtesy Archives, San Francisco Public Library)

CHAPTER TWENTY

Alma Becomes a Recluse

 THE DAILY SWIMS, the cheerful companionship of Nurse Dukelow, who kept a close watch on Alma's eating and drinking habits, and the partial return of her enormous vitality brought a sense of well-being to Alma. It didn't last very long. She was soon immersed in grief so overwhelming that it sent her into seclusion from which she never emerged.

Three days before his fiftieth birthday, on the night of October 28, 1961, Adolph died in a bar in Phoenix. The bar was in a sleazy motel where Adolph, unwilling to wed a seventh time, was living with a woman named Loretta. His daughter Lois got the news of his death from Dorothy Munn.

"Daddy was supposed to come and see me ride in a show in Atherton. Instead, he went off to Phoenix to help Loretta. She was not a nice woman. When I got word of his death, I took my two daughters to the Munn's. Aunt Dorothy said he died of a heart attack. That's not what I found out when I flew to Phoenix.

"The doctor there told me Loretta tried to get Daddy to marry her. He wouldn't. They had a fight. He went down to the bar, coming out alone. There were adobe pillars in the lobby outside the bar. The man at the desk claimed Daddy fell against the pillars and suffered a brain hemorrhage and died.

"They held a coronor's inquest. No one knew what happened. I had to identify the body. When I saw him, he had an indentation on his head, like a blackjack hit him. There were police around. I sent them out. I called Dr. Nelson, Daddy's doctor in Ojai. We decided we wanted to spare Gangy the publicity, so we got Loretta out of town. She was to be the key witness at the inquest.

"They ruled it accidental death. I think she set him up. She inherited the Ojai property, and Daddy left money for the education of her son."[1]

While Lois flew to Phoenix, back at home Alma's daughters were wondering how to break the news of the tragedy to their mother.

"Dorothy called me at 3 a.m.," said Anona Dukelow, who went home to her husband every night. "They thought I should be there when they told their mother. So I got dressed and went.

'When I got there, Little Alma had just arrived. We all went into the bedroom. Mrs. Spreckels saw the look on Little Alma's face and said, 'What's the matter? Is Jimmie drinking again?'

" 'No, Mother, it's not my husband. I wish that's all it was. It's Adolph. He had an accident. He's dead.'

"I watched her carefully," Mrs. Dukelow continued. "She was in shock. She didn't even make an outcry. She threw back the covers, got out of bed, flung on her robe and went to her chair. She grabbed the arm, and just sat there staring into space."

Adolph's body was shipped home after the inquest. The next day, Alma, her face heavily veiled, went to the cemetery where Adolph was laid to rest beside his father.

"After the funeral she came right off the elevator and went into her room," said Mrs. Dukelow. "I followed. She said, 'Close the door, we're not going out there.'

"I had ordered food from Herman's delicatessen, but she wouldn't come out of her room to see people. She was grieving, and I knew it would take time. She loved that boy so!"[2]

Did she grieve because she felt she had failed her son? She had tried so hard to get him to do something with his life. A.B. left him the Napa ranch so he could breed horses. When that burned down, she bought Sobre Vista and fixed it up so that he could be a gentleman farmer. But he wasn't interested. He was so good with his hands. He built a room for Lois at his Ojai ranch. He could have been an architect. He loved to paint. Everyone knew he had talent. He could have been an artist. Nothing she suggested interested him. She loved him so much, she only wanted to please him. She gave him everything he ever wanted. She accepted readily each of his wives, entertained for them and opened her house to them. She tried to keep his marriages together with gifts of money and jewelry. Why did he always fight with her and scream at her? What had she done wrong?

"Daddy realized he never led a productive life," said Lois. "He wanted me to be different. He made me work for everything I got. He never indulged me. I wanted a horse very badly. In Los Angeles, he had horses and he showed them. Then I rode, but he never bought me a horse. He didn't want to spoil me. I had to work for everything I got. He didn't want me to be frivolous. He cared about me. He was very proud of me. He knew he muddled his own life."

For two years, Alma tried to fight against the overwhelming depression that engulfed her. One of her first acts was to give a gift to the Maritime Museum in memory of Adolph. It was the large and very valuable Charles Rollo Peters painting of A.B.'s *Lurline,* the first of the Oceanic Steamship liners. That painting had meant so much to A.B. Before she gave it, she laid down two conditions: "That the painting become part of the permanent collection of said Museum and that it be on permanent display," otherwise "said picture shall be and become the property of the California Palace of the Legion of Honor."[3]

Alma tried to see people, tried to revive her interest in bridge games and in museum affairs, but it was only a flagging attempt. Her enthusiasm, her zest for life was gone. Even when the San Francisco Sponsors, a group who raised funds for struggling artists, actors and musicians, honored her in 1963 as the person who had contributed most to San Francisco art and culture, she sent Johnny to pick up her award at the Bohemian Club dinner. When Johnny brought her the special casting done by C. B. Johnson in sandstone, ordered for her by Sponsors president Norman Coliver, she gave it a brief glance and, with some of her old asperity, rasped, "I hate that modern stuff."

The *Examiner* honored her with the Phoebe Hearst Medal in December as one of their Ten Distinguished Women of 1963. She was called "San Francisco's Truly Grande Dame." In the last interview Alma ever gave, the reporter observed, "Despite all of her achievements, there appears in the makeup of Alma de Bretteville Spreckels a wistful desire to be certain that she has done everything she can for her loved ones, her beloved city and the thousands who have benefitted from her gifts . . ."[4]

She made her last visit to the Legion shortly after that interview. Tommy Howe planned a Rodin exhibit featuring all of her ninety-nine gifts of the Master's works, plus other works from the Louvre.

"I really wanted her to attend," said Howe. "I sent a special messenger to her with the catalog, which mentioned that she was the first great patron of Rodin outside of France."[5]

Alma didn't go to the preview. She had Mrs. Dukelow take her the night before, when no one was around to see her.

"She went in her nightgown, with her big mink coat thrown around her and her feet in slippers," said Mrs. Dukelow.

"I had no idea she had seen the exhibit," said Howe, "until the

Alma was photographed in her living room on Washington Street in April 1961, for a national magazine. No more martinis; tea is the drink of the day. (Courtesy Archives, San Francisco Public Library)

next day, when her chauffeur came to the house with a box from Shreve's. In it was a handsome clock. It was her way of telling me she liked the show."

Then even the bridge games with her intimate friends stopped. "One day," said her next-door neighbor, Mrs. Felix McGinnis, "she said she had a headache, and I never saw her again."[6]

It was all too much effort. She just didn't care to see people anymore. Or to write to them. The purple ink that flowed from her pen had dried up, along with the overpowering vitality she once possessed.

Now each day was the same. "In the morning, she swam in the pool," said Mrs. Dukelow. "Then, after lunch, we'd go for a drive.

First, we'd stop at the grocery market at Fillmore and Washington, where the owner was Mrs. Spreckels's distant cousin. She'd send me in to get some cash, and he charged the amount to her grocery account. Then she'd put the cash into envelopes. She had me mark them, one for Gus, her brother, and one for Adolph Rosekrans, her grandson. Sometimes we'd take an envelope to Lois, who lived down the peninsula. Johnny, her favorite, was living in one of the downstairs apartments with his new bride, Dodie Naify Topham, so she didn't have to drive to see him."

Except for the occasional trip to see Lois, the blue Buick followed the same route every day. The car would cross the Golden Gate Bridge to Tiburon, and Alma would deliver silently the envelope to Gus. Then it would go over the Bay Bridge to Berkeley, where young Adolph, just starting his career as an architect, lived.

"She'd give me the envelope, sit back in her seat and press a button and the window would roll up. That was her way of saying goodbye, and you had to get your arm out very quickly, or else..." laughed Adolph. "The money came in very handy in those days. My wife took it to buy groceries."[7]

"When we got back to the city, she'd have the car drive around Union Square, where she loved to look at her statue," continued Mrs. Dukelow. "Next, we'd go to Paul Elder's bookshop on Sutter Street and I'd pick up an Erle Stanley Gardner mystery book. Mrs. Spreckels loved Perry Mason stories. She read one a night. When we ran out of titles, I just started all over again."

Then the Buick would stop at the home of Alma's friend Mrs. Frederick Doyle, widow of a Pacific Gas and Electric executive. Each day Alma would bring her the book she had finished the night before, wordlessly hand it to her, and drive on.

Last stop would be at Jean Frickelton's apartment, a block from 2080. "Every day of her life, until she was almost gone, Gangy wrote me a note and left it by my door," said Frickelton. "Her writing wasn't good."[8]

Part of Alma's withdrawal from the world was due to her physical condition. In addition to the arthritis that crippled her feet, and the problems with her bowels, she was also incontinent. A proud woman, she felt betrayed by her body.

'When she had accidents in the car, they had to be ignored," said Dukelow. "Sometimes I would see her take one end of the enormous mink stole she had on and she'd tuck it under herself. We never discussed it. When we got home and she undressed, I'd quietly remove her things, send them to the cleaners and they would be back hanging in her closet ready for the next time she wanted to wear them."

Then Alma broke her hip. "It was on a weekend," said Dukelow, "and I was away with Ken, my husband. A nurse was with her when she fell in the bathroom. They took her to the hospital and she had a pin put in. It was very successful. She was in the hospital two weeks. When we went home, she couldn't wait to get into that pool. So she had a contraption with a chair on it sent out and then she could be lowered into the water. She hated the idea of being an invalid. Once in the water, she was fine. She could stand up; she could swim."

She wasn't fine for long. She caught pneumonia. Her lungs, weakened from long years of incessant smoking, did not respond to treatment. On the seventh of August 1968, Mrs. Dukelow was summoned at 2 a.m.

"The night nurse who had been with her called me and I went immediately," said Mrs. Dukelow. "By the time I got there, Mrs. Spreckels was dead.

"I really did have to close her eyes. They were staring straight ahead. I called Mrs. Munn and she came right down. We phoned Little Alma. She came at two the next afternoon. Then we went to N. Gray & Company, the undertaking establishment, to select a casket. Little Alma picked it out. It was platinum-plated and cost $10,000!"

The two daughters, who were always at odds with each other, now had something new to squabble about. Where would the wake be held? Little Alma wanted it at her new Broadway home, which had finally been completed. It had taken almost six years. Construction was halted constantly because of her inability to make decisions. Dorothy wanted the wake held in her apartment at 2080, the mansion where her mother had reigned for over half a century.

Then Dukelow reminded them about Anna de Bretteville's undignified exit, with her body strapped to a stretcher standing straight up, sans coffin, inside the tiny elevator, the only way possible to get her out of the house. They looked at the huge casket and Dorothy lost the argument. They would hold the wake, by invitation only, on Sunday at Little Alma's house.

But Dorothy wanted more than that for her mother. She wanted a funeral fit for a queen. Her mother ought to lie in state, in the Palace of the Legion of Honor, for all who wanted to pay homage to her.

The same thought occurred to Johnny. His Gangy belonged not only to her family, but to the people of the city. He made arrangements with Ian White, the successor to Tommy Howe, who had retired, to clear the main gallery on Monday so that people could pay their respects to the museum's founder.

On Sunday, at the wake at Little Alma's, the body in the open coffin was placed in a corner of the large living room that overlooked San Francisco Bay.

"Mrs. Spreckels looked beautiful," said Mrs. Dukelow. "She had on a white lace dress, with her clips and her lovely pearls. She looked just as she did ten years before when I first met her. It seemed impossible that this woman, who had always seemed so indestructible, was gone. I guess it was hard for her daughters to believe, too. The day before, I was having lunch with the Munns when Little Alma phoned. She couldn't decide what color lipstick her mother should have on. I thought that was odd because the undertakers, who had three days to work on Mrs. Spreckels, had delivered her all fixed up."

Little Alma was still nervously fidgeting with the body of her mother when the Howes arrived for the wake.

"We had gotten there early," recalled Howe. "Little Alma directed us where to go. 'How do you think she looks, Francesca?' she asked my wife. Francesca thought she looked wonderful, but Alma persisted. 'I think she looks awfully pretty, but I think she could do with a little more color, don't you?' So she fished out a lipstick and worked on her mother's face."

"Little Alma had attended a wake for one of the de Young sisters who had died the week before," said Mrs. Dukelow. "She was determined that her mother's wake would be equally impressive. She only had four days to plan it, so it must have been difficult for her."

Did Little Alma's extraordinary efforts after her mother's death stem from feelings of guilt over the love she withheld from her during her mother's life?

"The private services were beautifully done," recalled Howe "Every dignitary in the city was there, even Archbishop Quinn, which was nice, because if ever there was an ungodly family it was Alma's! Even the remaining de Young sisters came. Johnny asked me to recite the Kipling poem *L' Envoi,* and the whole thing was very dignified."

The new director of the Palace of the Legion of Honor had set the scene well for what the newspapers later called "the most opulent funeral in the city's history." The main gallery was cleared of all paintings except one, a portrait of Alma by John Lavery, done some six years after she sat for Richard Hall. The painting was hung against a wide, black velvet drape that covered the center wall from ceiling to floor. The open coffin, with its blanket of cymbidium

*Possibly the last picture taken of Alma de Bretteville Spreckels, this enlarged
snapshot shows her shortly before the time she became a recluse. Someone who
knew her during the last thirty years of her life told us, "You must include
this picture; it shows Alma as she really was, raspy voice and all.
She was a magnificent old ruin. We'll never see her like again."
(Courtesy Anona Dukelow)*

orchids, was placed beneath it. On each side of the coffin were tall candelabra flanked by masses of floral tributes. Surrounding her were many of those first Rodin sculptures she purchased, *The Iron Age, St. John the Baptist, The Call to Arms.* On a side wall, under one of the *Joan of Arc* tapestries which the French government had given her as a gift so long ago, was a portrait of A.B.

From 10 a.m., when the museum opened, until the funeral services began at 3 p.m., a steady stream of people came to pay their respects to the controversial lady who wanted to feel that "when I pass on that I have never hurt anybody intentionally and did the best I could for everyone in my power."

Even in death, Alma could be outrageous. As she lay there in state, a group of tourists looked over at the supine figure that filled the massive platinum-plated casket. Their guide informed them that they were gazing at a wax effigy of the museum's founder. Immediately, Elvin Howard, the museum's senior guard, stepped over to hiss, "That is *not* an effigy. That is Alma de Bretteville Spreckels!"[9]

They were all there, from the Burlingame crowd, who withheld from her their stamp of approval while she lived, to the little old lady in a green coat, carrying a paper bag full of flowers, who came because "she made it possible for people like me to enjoy seeing good things."

At 2:30, the guards cleared the room so that chairs for four hundred people could be set up for the funeral services. Tommy Howe opened the rites by reading a letter of tribute from Claude Batault, the consul general of France in San Francisco. Then he recited again the Kipling poem, the poem she loved all her life, a copy of which she ordered placed in the cornerstone of the museum after young Adolph dug the hole with his gold shovel. "When earth's last picture is painted..."

Dean C. Julian Bartlett, of Grace Cathedral, walked down the aisle between the mourners in his vestments of black, white and purple, and conducted the simple Episcopal services. Just before it ended, Dorothy turned to Mrs. Dukelow and whispered in her ear. "Put this letter to my mother in the coffin before they close it," she said between sobs. One of her children could finally express the love none of them had found the words for when she was alive.

Then the coffin was closed, and the lid came down on the woman who had such an extraordinary sense of her own destiny, who put all of her enormous strength into pursuing that destiny. What had it cost her?

She never had a satisfying personal relationship — not even with A.B., whom she adored. When he couldn't gratify her sexually, he tried to compensate by giving her money so that she could throw herself further into her work. Her Rodins became her "children."

She felt closer to them than to her daughters and son. She thought by her accomplishments she would make them proud of her. Instead, she drove them away. She felt she had to buy affection. She turned to Jean Frickelton for love and companionship. In her loneliness, she asked people to live with her, first Edith de Bretteville, then Ulla and finally Mrs. Dukelow. She alienated the people she most wanted to please. "She had too much mental and physical energy," complained Elmer Awl.

The funeral procession started from the columned courtyard graced by a single Rodin, *The Thinker.* A light mist was falling and fog horns mourned.

The long line of limousines wound their way through the park where her husband had served as Park Commissioner for so many years, past Spreckels Lake, named in his honor, and slowly made its way to the Spreckels family mausoleum at Cypress Lawn Cemetery in Colma.

The Woman of Destiny, the little girl who had come in through the back doors of the rich and wound up as the city's Queen of Culture, who went to her grave wondering if she had done everything she could for her loved ones and her beloved city, was laid to rest.

Chapter Notes:

1. Lois Register interview.
2. Anona Dukelow interview.
3. Deed of Gift, February 1962, Rosekrans papers.
4. Joan Woods, *San Francisco Examiner,* January 13, 1964.
5. Thomas Carr Howe interview.
6. Frances Moffet, *New York Times,* October 9, 1966, p. 90.
7. Adolph Rosekrans interview.
8. Jean Frickelton interview, Dodie Rosekrans tapes.
9. Barbara Roberts interview with Elvin Howard, July 1976, Pat Sanders papers.

Epilogue

BY THE TIME SHE DIED, Alma, who was once the richest woman in the West, was down to her last million. Most of the other $14 million she had given away. In her will, she left the bulk of the remainder to her six grandchildren. To Adolph's daughter Lois she left her pearls and diamond clips and what little other personal jewelry she had.[1]

Dorothy and Little Alma were left in joint possession of 2080 Washington Street, and Alma bequeathed all the furnishings to Dorothy. No additional provision was made for Little Alma, because, Big Alma wrote, "she has already received substantial gifts from me."[2]

When the French government began a restoration of the Palace of Versailles, Dorothy donated her mother's bed, the one kings had made love in, to the project. It was immediately placed in the Madame Pompadour Suite.[3]

Always the provider for her family, Alma left $50,000 each to her impoverished brother Gus and his wife. Ten thousand dollars was left to a relative most people weren't aware that Alma had, her cousin Ove de Bretteville. Ove was Ulla's brother. Alma brought the boy, who was mentally retarded, over from Europe shortly after Ulla's arrival and got him work at Sobre Vista. Despite the pain that his sister caused Alma, she continued to provide for him the rest of her life.

Not so forgiving was Jean Frickelton. Shortly before her death, in 1977, when it became apparent that she could never write Alma's biography (she had lost sight in one eye, and her hands and feet were crippled with arthritis), Johnny asked her for the material his grandmother had collected for that purpose. She dictated a letter stating, "I would be grieved if anything derogatory or embarrassing

321

The audience at Alma's funeral at the California Palace of the Legion of Honor was limited to 400, the capacity of the main gallery; thousands had come earlier to pay their respects to the woman who had given so much to her beloved San Francisco. (Courtesy San Francisco Chronicle)

to Gangy or the Spreckels family would be used to denigrate the memory of this truly great woman. In going over papers and her confidential letters to me, I am destroying all such material so it will never get into the wrong hands, and many confidential things she told me will go with me in silence to the grave."[4]

On the first anniversary of Alma's death, her grandson, architect Adolph Rosekrans, then the chairman of the board of the Patrons of Art and Music, announced that the PAM had established a fund for a memorial to Alma. The money would be used to redesign, under his professional supervision, the main sculpture gallery beyond the rotunda at the museum's entrance. In it would be regrouped the entire Spreckels collection of one hundred Rodins, so that "every visitor to the Legion of Honor can feel the impact of the richness and magnitude of this collection as soon as he steps into the building." In 1972, when the project was completed, the Spreckels name appeared for the first time in the California Palace of the Legion of Honor. Over the gallery's entrance are the words "The Adolph B. Spreckels and Alma de Bretteville Spreckels Sculpture Gallery."[5]

On the sixtieth anniversary of the dedication of Maryhill Museum, November 3, 1986, the honored guest was Queen Marie's daughter, the former Princess Ileana of Romania. The princess, who was seventeen when Maryhill was dedicated, is now Mother Alexandra, the abbess of the Eastern Orthodox Monastery of the Transfiguration, in Pennsylvania. She was driven from her country in 1947 when the communists forced the family's abdication. Mother Alexandra praised her mother's foresight in preserving cultural and historic artifacts.[6] Today, Maryhill is the only place in the world where the royal heritage of Marie's Romania can be seen. To this isolated museum Marie's grandson, King Michael, born and raised in Switzerland, made a pilgrimage in the spring of 1986, so that he could learn about his grandmother and the country that he has never been allowed to enter.

At the National Maritime Museum, Karl Kortum, who is now a federal employee with a high rating, is still fighting to preserve the integrity of the museum he claims sole credit for founding.

The spirit of Alma lives on in her grandson Johnny. He and his wife, Dodie, an international figure in the art world, are vitally interested in the preservation of the city's culture. Spearheading a fund-drive for the Palace of the Legion of Honor, Johnny, as outspoken as his grandmother, recently told members of the board that "trustees have to do more than sit on their asses. They have to provide for the financial well-being of this organization or get off the board."[8] The current board has apparently heeded his advice.

Thanks to the success of recent fundraising efforts, when the museum is closed in the near future for extensive repairs, plans also call for expansion of the gallery facilities. And John pursued the trustees of the Florence Gould estate with all the vigor his grandmother had used in chasing her friend Florence Gould when she was alive. He had better results. When it became apparent the museum could get none of the Gould art collection (Mrs. Gould's will stipulated that her paintings be put up for auction, with the proceeds going to the Gould Foundation), he concentrated on the small print. The will provided that the foundation could issue grants to qualified museums which furthered French culture. Johnny secured a grant for the much-needed renovation of the museum's Little Theater. Reopened in 1988, it is now known as the Florence Gould Auditorium.

In Palm Beach, Dorothy Munn, whose collection of jewelry is as fine as her mother's art collection was, treasures one piece of jewelry above all others, and wears it daily. It is the Phoebe Hearst Medal, the last award given to her mother.

Adolph's son, Adolph Spreckels III, used his inheritance to no better end than his father had. He died in 1977 at the age of twenty-seven, of an overdose of drugs. Ironically, the last of A.B.'s family to bear his name died in the place where the first Spreckels made so much of the family fortune, in Hawaii.[9]

Adolph's daughters did much better with their lives. Lois, who earned a master's degree in psychology at Stanford, counseled alcoholics at the Veterans' Hospital in Palo Alto and is currently racing horses under her grandfather's colors: red, white and blue. Joan, whose mother was Kay Williams, is an art restorer working for museums in Los Angeles. She has thus far, in her mid-thirties, shied away from marriage.

In 1989, Dorothy Munn, realizing she would never make another visit to 2080 Washington from her Florida estate, finally agreed to put the mansion up for sale. The asking price was $13.5 million. The most interested buyers for the house were author Danielle Steel and her husband, John Traina. As of this writing, the property has not yet been sold. Prospective buyers were waiting for a decision by the San Francisco Board of Supervisors on the status of the mansion.

Like everything else connected to Alma, controversy swirls around the sale of the house. The uproar she created in Pacific Heights during her lifetime has erupted again two decades after her death. On one side of the dispute were the Pacific Heights Residents Association and neighbors who want landmark status for the mansion and for its vast, sloping rear lawns, the largest privately held single-home backyard in San Francisco. On the other side were the heirs, their realtors and potential buyers, who feared the landmark designation would be used to keep the Jackson Street side of the estate from being developed. After two years of public hearings and votes by various subcommittees, the Board, in April 1990, finally decided to grant landmark status only to the mansion, exempting the grounds.

When the mansion, which withstood the October 1989 earthquake, is finally sold, Dorothy will receive half the money. The other half will be divided among Johnny and his brothers and the two children of Kay Williams — Joan Spreckels and John Clark Gable. The late movie actor's son inherited his share from his half-brother, Adolph Spreckels III. Lois Spreckels Register's share was sold to her aunt, Little Alma, many years before when Lois needed money.

In France, at the family museum at La Gardette, the de Bretteville descendant whose awards and citations equal those of the patriarch himself, Le General, is the family member who was born not in France, or even in Denmark, but in the sand dunes of San Francisco. She is the little girl who came in through the back doors of great houses in San Francisco, and lived to become its Queen of Culture.

Chapter Notes:

1. *San Francisco Chronicle,* November 14, 1968, p. 9.
2. Ibid.
3. Dorothy Munn interview.
4. John Rosekrans papers.
5. *San Francisco Chronicle,* August 14, 1969, p. 52.
6. *Maryhill Quarterly,* Winter, 1986.
7. *San Francisco Chronicle,* April 12, 1986.
8. *Connaisseur* magazine, April 1986.
9. Lois Register interview.

The le Normand de Bretteville Family Tree

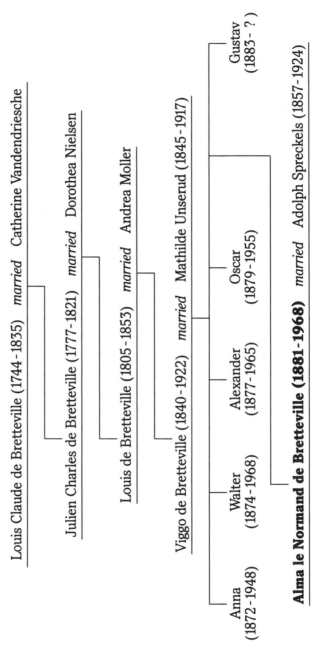

The Spreckels Family Tree

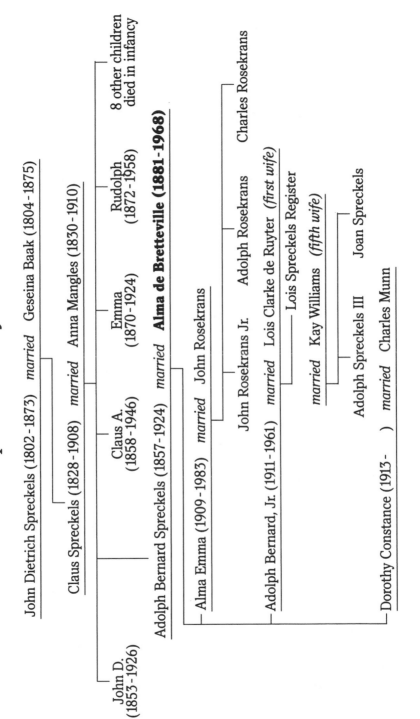

John Dietrich Spreckels (1802 - 1873) *married* Geseina Baak (1804 - 1875)

Claus Spreckels (1828 - 1908) *married* Anna Mangles (1830 - 1910)

John D. (1853 - 1926)

Claus A. (1858 - 1946)

Emma (1870 - 1924)

Rudolph (1872 - 1958)

8 other children died in infancy

Adolph Bernard Spreckels (1857 - 1924) *married* **Alma de Bretteville (1881 - 1968)**

Alma Emma (1909 - 1983) *married* John Rosekrans

John Rosekrans Jr.   Adolph Rosekrans   Charles Rosekrans

Adolph Bernard, Jr. (1911 - 1961) *married* Lois Clarke de Ruyter *(first wife)*

Lois Spreckels Register

married Kay Williams *(fifth wife)*

Adolph Spreckels III   Joan Spreckels

Dorothy Constance (1913 -   ) *married* Charles Munn

Selected Bibliography

SAN FRANCISCO:

Altrocchi, Julia C.: *Spectacular San Franciscans,* New York: Dutton, 1949

Dickson, Sam: *Streets of San Francisco,* Stanford, California: Stanford Press, 1955

Gentry, Curt: *The Madams of San Francisco,* Garden City, New York: Doubleday & Co., 1964

Heyneman, Julia, *Arthur Putnam, Sculptor,* San Francisco: Johnck & Seeger, 1932

Lewis, Oscar: *This Was San Francisco,* New York: David McKay, 1962

Lewis, Oscar: *Bay Window Bohemia,* Garden City, New York: Doubleday & Co., 1956

Levy, Harriet Lane: *920 O'Farrell Street,* New York: Doubleday & Co., 1947

Moffit, Frances: *Dancing on the Brink of the World,* New York: G.P. Putnam's Sons, 1977

Neville, Amelia: *The Fantastic City,* New York: Houghton Mifflin, 1932

O'Brien, Robert: *This is San Francisco,* New York: McGraw Hill, 1948

Todd, Frank Morton: *Story of the Exposition,* New York: Putnam, 1921

Wilson, Carol Green: *Gump's Treasure Trade,* New York: Thomas Crowell Co., 1965

LOIE FULLER:

de Morinni, Clara: *Chronicles of American Dance,* New York, 1948

Flanner, Janet: *Paris was Yesterday,* New York: Viking, 1972

Fuller, Loie: *Fifteen Years of a Dancer's Life,* Boston: Small & Maynard Co., 1913

QUEEN MARIE:

Bolitho, Hector: *A Biographer's Notebook,* New York: MacMillan Co., 1950

Elsberry, Terence: *Marie of Romania,* New York: St. Martin's Press, 1972

Pakula, Hannah: *The Last Romantic,* New York: Simon & Schuster, 1984

Tuhy, John E.: *Sam Hill, Prince of Castle Nowhere,* Portland, Oregon: Timber Press, 1983

INDEX

About the Author

Bernice Scharlach, a journalist-historian, has progressed through the ranks of newspaper work from reporter to editor, and finally has arrived at what she likes best, writing about San Francisco history. Born in New York, she was raised in San Francisco. She attended Galileo High School and the University of California at Berkeley, where she received a degree in journalism. She has written for newspapers in San Francisco and Contra Costa County, as well as for national and regional magazines. As public relations director for the Jewish Welfare Federation of the Greater East Bay, she edited the Jewish Observer. *Big Alma* is her second book. Her first, published in 1983, was *House of Harmony,* a history of one of San Francisco's oldest clubs, the Concordia-Argonaut, founded in 1854.

Previously published by Scottwall Associates

Hometown San Francisco
Sunny Jim, Phat Willie and Dave
by Jerry Flamm

Pioneers of California
True Stories of Early Settlers in the Golden State
by Donovan Lewis

Irish Californians: Historic, Benevolent, Romantic
by Patrick Dowling

Lincoln Beachey: The Man Who Owned the Sky
by Frank Marrero

Alaska Gold: Life on the New Frontier, 1898-1906
Edited by Jeff Kunkel

The Farallon Islands: Sentinels of the Golden Gate
By Peter White

California Heartland
A Pictorial History of Eight Northern California Counties
by Sandra Shepherd

San Mateo: A Centennial History
by Mitchell P. Postel

History of Palo Alto: The Early Years
by Pamela Gullard & Nancy Lund

Mount Tamalpais: A History
by Lincoln Fairley

Scottwall Associates, Publishers
95 Scott Street, San Francisco, CA 94117
Telephone (415) 861-1956   Fax (415) 626-6844
e-mail: scottwall@hooked.net